WARD S. MILLER

WORD
WEALTH
JUNIOR

ILLUSTRATIONS BY JOHN MOMENT

NEW YORK
HOLT, RINEHART AND WINSTON

To JAMES M. SPINNING

His quick sympathy, keen sense of humor, creative vocabulary, and zestful originality are just a few of the qualities that make Rochester proud to acclaim him.

TO THE TEACHER

"The difficulty of literature is not to write, but to write what you mean; not to affect your reader, but to affect him precisely as you wish."

ROBERT LOUIS STEVENSON

Control-group experiments have demonstrated that improving a pupil's vocabulary — systematically — raises his standing slowly in all of his studies.[1] Outside of school, according to Johnson O'Connor, "An extensive knowledge of the exact meanings of English words accompanies outstanding success in this country more often than any other single characteristic which the Human Engineering Laboratory has been able to isolate and measure."[2] Vocabulary tests are now used almost universally in personnel selection and in many kinds of aptitude tests.

Such statements are but an indirect reminder that virtually all kinds of human achievement depend abjectly on communication in one way or another. Obviously, one cannot understand what another has said or written unless he knows the meaning intended by each word. This is true whether the words have so many meanings that they become semantic problems or are specific in reference but relatively unfamiliar in meaning.

While it is certainly possible to think without words, it is

[1] A. C. Eurich at the University of Minnesota was one of the first to discover the values of systematic vocabulary training. His experiment is described in "Enlarging the Vocabularies of College Freshmen," *English Journal* (Coll. Ed.), XXI, 135. Johnson O'Connor tells of a similar experiment which first attracted wide attention as described in his article, "Vocabulary and Success," *Atlantic Monthly*, February, 1934, pp. 160–166.

[2] Quoted in *Time*, January 3, 1938, page 32. Johnson O'Connor is director of the Human Engineering Laboratory, Stevens Institute of Technology, Hoboken, New Jersey.

not possible to transmit carefully qualified ideas; and it is difficult to see how one could even formulate carefully qualified ideas apart from a cultivated command of words and the ability to adapt them skillfully to one's purposes. What Robert Louis Stevenson said with regard to literature applies equally in the practical world of today to advertising, selling, and personal relationships in a hundred different ways. Anyone who has studied words carefully knows that learning new words and relating them to familiar ones helps him to understand the familiar ones better and to use both the new and the old more intelligently. Moreover, a vocabulary of adequate dimensions is a remedy for the semantic difficulties surrounding dozens of overworked words which one will use if he has few others and little flexibility of diction in clarifying his meanings.

The growing conviction among educators that vocabulary needs to be taught — systematically, persistently, and with some sort of long-range plan, beginning in junior high school — is not surprising in the light of these considerations. Word work is certainly as necessary as any other technical phase of English, and it is not difficult to demonstrate that it is more necessary because its life ramifications are more vital and more varied than those of grammar, punctuation, spelling, letter writing, and other skills. This is especially true now that the vocabulary-building values of Latin are lost for the great majority of pupils.

It was in the light of these considerations and in response to a widely felt need for a junior high school vocabulary builder embodying the merits which have made *Word Wealth* so popular, that this book was prepared — at the request of the publisher. It provides, in conjunction with *Word Wealth,* a six-year plan that does not make exorbitant demands on class time. It can be covered in two years, however, by accelerating the pace or omitting the special units; and it has attractive possibilities for general or retarded classes in senior high schools.

Although it began merely as a downward extension of *Word Wealth* technique, *Word Wealth Junior* has become considerably more — a vocabulary builder and a speller with several innovations of its own to offer in scope and technique. A rather detailed explanation is therefore necessary if the book is to serve with full effectiveness the varied purposes for which it is designed.

The basic conviction with which this book began is that a junior high school vocabulary builder should meet as well as possible the following requirements:

1. It should be attractive and well motivated.
2. It should be easy to use, for both pupil and teacher.
3. It should be efficient and practical.
4. It should adapt itself readily to individual differences within a class.
5. It should foster flexibility in the use of words as well as a larger recognition and a more precise working vocabulary. It should encourage the study of groups of synonyms and words with related meanings.
6. It should provide, for teachers who desire it, a treatment of spelling at least equivalent to that obtainable in separate spelling books.
7. It should provide adequate practice and testing material.
8. It should encourage use of the dictionary without depending on it to such an extent that pupils become bewildered and discouraged by its complexities.
9. It should encourage creativeness.

The Regular Units

Two-thirds of the 75 units in this book are regular vocabulary-building units much like the ones in *Word Wealth* except that they are shorter, less difficult, and more spelling-conscious. Part One has 12 words per unit, Parts Two and Three have 15, whereas each unit in *Word Wealth* has 25.

The teasers which have been an attractive feature of *Word Wealth* at the beginning of each unit are intended to serve also as a rough pretest in *Word Wealth Junior*. Questions following the study guide are a new feature designed not only to provide fun and to encourage independent work, but also to offer a measure of spelling insurance by directing a pupil's attention to words and parts of words which may cause difficulty.

The study guide is constructed, as in *Word Wealth*, to provide for individual differences. Mastery of the base words for recognition alone may be all that a retarded pupil or class can achieve. An accelerated pupil or class, on the other hand, may be familiar to some degree with most of the base words at the outset but needs experience using them and should be expected to master the variant forms and supplementary words, do what the questions suggest, and perhaps write a creative paragraph or verse, even though none is suggested in the unit.

An efficient teacher may well divide a class into ability groups and scale the requirements accordingly, or the grouping may be informal. Pupils will benefit by collecting clippings and quotations containing the words they learn and by stalking new words not found in the book. Individual notebooks will be needed for spelling, but the clippings and new words may be handled as group activity.

The objective of the first practice set in each regular unit is meaningful recognition of each of the base words. The pupil is directed to copy the words because copying them helps to fix the spellings in mind, but the set may be done orally by pupils who do not need this assistance or have had sufficient spelling practice through writing illustrative sentences of their own. The second practice set is intended to offer an experience in using each of the base words intelligently, and it goes a step farther as to spelling by requiring a pupil to recall the words. The set may be done orally if spelling does not need further attention, or the first practice set may be done orally and the second one in writing.

In the second practice set, there will often be animated arguments about which word goes in one of the blanks. There are places where more than one word is acceptable, but usually subtleties of context indicate why two or three words are usually not interchangeable. It would be unfortunate, however, to kill the spontaneity of a class by being too arbitrary where plain clues do not appear.

The final tests at the end of each part provide a check on mastery of the base words of each unit, and the *division tests* offer a way to measure progress (on the regular units) at the end of the year or half year. A division test may be sectioned, with only minor adjustments for semester or quarterly use, and adaptation may be made if one of the units which it covers has been omitted for any reason. The division test on supplementary words will serve as a convenient check on the marginal progress of average and superior pupils.

It should be noted that the division tests may be used for pretests as well as terminal examinations on each of the three parts of the book. Used as pretests, they will help a teacher to decide whether to use Part One or Part Two with a particular eighth grade, for example.

Space did not permit inclusion of objective-type division tests, but these may be constructed quite readily for either pretesting or final testing. Simply write down groups of 10–15 base words in a column and arrange their definitions in corresponding groups but irregular order (within each group) opposite. Insert two or three plausible misleads in each group of definitions.

One unit a week is a normal rate of progress. It is ordinarily better to spend a few minutes each day rather than to complete an entire unit in one or two class sessions. On a weekly basis, the procedure may well be as follows:

First Day: The list of base words is read two or three times. The teaser-pretest is taken up briefly — to the point of arousing interest and gauging the range of familiarity without too many wrong answers. The study guide is read silently or orally.

Second Day: The study guide is read again. Pupils compose sentences using several of the words. A brief discussion of related words and supplementary words ensues. Questions following the study guide are taken up or assigned outside.

Third Day: First practice set is written and scored. A creative paragraph using some of the words in the unit may be undertaken or a pupil dictation using some of the supplementary words done orally.

Fourth Day: The second practice set is administered and scored.

Fifth Day: The final test at the end of the division is given.

On a three-day plan, the study guide may be covered the first day, the practice sets the second, and the final test the third.

Selection of Words

The winnowing process by which nearly six hundred base words were selected for the regular units began with a survey of junior high school literature and the reading of a collegiate dictionary. The list of several thousand words thus achieved was then subjected to analysis in terms of such lists as the Buckingham-Dolch Free Association Study, Horne's Adult Writing Vocabulary, the Payne-Garrison Speller, Jones's *A Concrete Investigation of the Material of English Spelling,* the Johnson O'Connor list of 1118 words arranged in the order of difficulty, and Thorndike's *30,000 Words.*

After careful analysis, the base words were selected largely though not rigidly according to the following criteria:

1. Frequency. Most of the base words are within the first 20,000 on Thorndike's list, and a majority in Parts One and Two are found within the first 10,000.

2. Difficulty. The words range from short ones which are not too familiar as to meaning (few are below 7th–8th grade level in the Buckingham-Dolch lists) to words more difficult in form and meaning, including introductory groups of foreign terms in Part Three. The Horne lists helped to determine the practical value of many words for purposes of usage.

3. Usefulness and suitability. While a few are included primarily for their currency in literature, usefulness with relation to normal experiences was the dominant consideration. The percentage of Anglo-Saxon words is much higher than in *Word Wealth.*

4. Root or prefix values. Words derived from a familiar Latin or Greek root were quite largely segregated as material for the units on roots and prefixes instead of being presented as separate base words.

5. Correlation with *Word Wealth.* Overlapping between the two books is confined to the units on roots and prefixes. This material belongs normally to the ninth grade, where the two books meet. It is given as an appendix in *Word Wealth,* but is a vital and an integral part of *Word Wealth Junior.*

The words deemed most suitable in terms of frequency, difficulty, general usefulness, and other considerations were then organized into units. Words very simple in form and concept were assigned to Part One, and those more complicated were included in Part Two and Part Three. The process was much like the one for the original *Word Wealth.* Relatively simple words will be found to some extent in Part Three, but words difficult in form or concept were carefully excluded from Part One.

Consciousness of word origins was made a feature of Part Three by building several units according to sources. This device should create some interest in the English language as a language. The units which present words or phrases from French, Spanish, and Italian of necessity disregard the selection principles somewhat but compensate, it is hoped, by the introduction they give to the spelling, pronunciation, and nature of words imported from those languages.

The "foreign" units merge into a series of topical units, for variety and attractiveness. Though these also depart considerably from the Thorndike "gold standard," they will no doubt be forgiven and remembered by a majority of the pupils who study them. Meanwhile, the units presenting roots and prefixes will, by their versatility, extend a pupil's vocabulary insight at a rate not achieved by any of the others and to some degree will make practical amends for the Latin he usually does not take. Part Three is incidentally an introduction to general language without pretending to be a substitute for such a book as Lilly Lindquist's *General Language.*

In effect, the six hundred base words of the regular units (counting each prefix and root as a base word) represent only about one-third of the words actually presented in the regular units, if supplementary words, variant forms, and applications of roots and prefixes are counted. The base words are simply a minimum essential, a psychological device, a point of departure, and a basis for organization of the book rather than the total vocabulary growth that may be expected.

Words on the original list which offer difficulty in spelling rather than meaningful familiarity were set aside for the special units in spelling. Familiar words which belong to important and typical word families were assigned to units in word building. Hundreds more were added later from standard spelling lists and other sources to round out the special units and make them as serviceable as possible.

The Special Units

Three different kinds of special units are inserted among the regular units. The first or *word-building* kind offers pupils experience filling in verb, noun, adjective, or adverbial forms of a key word. Such activities foster flexibility and directness in expression. They can hardly fail to improve (*1*) a pupil's working vocabulary, (*2*) his meaningful recognition of the less familiar forms of a word through their juxtaposition with familiar forms, and (*3*) his spelling.

While spelling is not the primary objective of the word-building units, it is an important phase for pupils who need it. Writing the words that go in the blanks gives guided practice in correct spelling and encourages helpful generalization and systematization. Errors should not be tolerated, as a rule, or the cause (if other than carelessness) should be carefully sought. The question sets are intended primarily as spelling practice and should be omitted with classes or groups of pupils who do not need them. The dictations may well be used as a pretest to determine how much of the unit needs to be written, and pupils or classes who score very high should omit the question sets and do part of the blank-filling orally. Those who spell poorly need to write the entire unit and take a dictation test covering it more completely than does the one furnished.

The second type of special unit approaches spelling partly through pronunciation or enunciation (avoiding the latter term because it is unfamiliar). In many cases exaggeration is encouraged because it will provide helpful ear associations that are not likely to affect a pupil's normal pronunciation.

The third kind of special unit is simply, frankly, and wholly a spelling lesson. Words are grouped around specific types of spelling difficulty to a large degree and in many cases repeated in more than one group if more than one type of difficulty is involved. A special effort has been made to handle spelling scientifically as far as reliable principles have emerged in the study of spelling.

Word Wealth Junior as a Speller

Taking the special units as a whole and to some extent the regular units also, *Word Wealth Junior* undertakes to provide a coverage of spelling equal or superior to that of any conventional spelling series for junior high school. All of the units in the book have been subjected to a careful correlation with the *Spelling Vocabulary Study* of Prof. Emmett Albert Betts,[1] which gives the grade placement of some 9000 words in seventeen different spellers. As it now stands, *Word Wealth Junior* covers *most of the junior high school words in most of these spellers* [2] — together with scores of others that are worth including as spelling words. A word is considered to be covered if the pupil must write it, as instructions are worded, in doing one of the special units, or, if it is one of the base words in a regular unit. The words most frequently misspelled are nearly all presented in the special units.

In using spelling dictations, a deduction should be made for any error that is made, whether the word is in the unit or not. Severe penalties are suggested, 10 points or more for each word on the basis of 100. Additional dictations, when needed, may be made up by the teacher or by outstanding pupils and administered to the entire class or to a low-scoring group within the class.

Each pupil should keep a Never Again list of the words

[1] American Book Company, 1940.

[2] At least 75–80% of the words with a median grade placement of 6–8 which appear in five or more of the seventeen spellers, plus many which do not appear in five of the seventeen spellers or have a median grade placement of 5.

missed, whether he accumulates clippings, quotations, and new words, as suggested above, or not. This list is of value to the teacher for diagnostic and remedial purposes as well as to the pupil for individual and deficient-group efforts. Penalties should be more severe the second time a word or group of words is dictated on a test.

The assumptions on which the spelling aspect of *Word Wealth Junior* is based, many of which enjoy almost the status of generally accepted principles, may be summarized as follows:

1. Spelling is more readily learned if words are grouped to some extent around specific type(s) of spelling difficulties.

2. Rules are of doubtful value but are most likely to be helpful if worked out to some extent by the pupils inductively.

3. Word-building activities foster correct spelling by showing how words are constructed, by providing practice, and by encouraging the kind of sound generalization that accounts for the incidental learning by which a large part of any student's knowledge of spelling is acquired.

4. The teaching of similar pairs like *hoard* and *horde* has been found to be slightly more efficient if the pairs are taught together and in contrast rather than separately.

5. Careful enunciation is an important and effective means of teaching spelling and overcoming errors.

6. Exaggerated pronunciation of words difficult to spell establishes ear associations which foster correct spelling responses and is not likely to affect the pupil's normal pronunciation of the words.

7. Syllabication provides a natural, logical, and helpfully analytic approach to spelling.

8. The correct spelling of a difficult part of a word may well be emphasized by some device such as underlining or colored chalk. (Gates disagrees, and studies show that the majority of missed words often display quite a variety of misspellings.)

9. Derivation data sometimes help a pupil to spell a word correctly.

10. The habit of checking a word in the dictionary when a pupil is in doubt should be encouraged.

11. Individual Never Again lists are an essential part of any spelling improvement program.

12. Indirect, incidental teaching of spelling (as in the regular units and the word-building type) tends to reduce the self-consciousness which often afflicts pupils when confronted by the challenge of direct teaching and testing.

13. Spelling dictations are more satisfactory when words are presented in context rather than separately.

14. Spelling material should be confined to a few thousand common words which pupils are most likely to use in their writing.

In Conclusion

Word Wealth Junior is designed to be useful under a variety of circumstances and adaptable to many different situations. It is constructed so as to be self-educative to a very high degree. *Only in the hands of a skillful teacher can it achieve its full value, however.* It is in no sense intended to make teaching unnecessary or to make an automaton of the teacher. Exercise material is none too plentiful, even in the regular units, creative topics had to be largely omitted, and space did not permit the inclusion of a tenth of the supplementary material with which the study of the words may be enlivened.

Collecting sentences from newspapers, magazines, or books containing words which are being studied is just one of the activities which teachers have sponsored in vocabulary work. Dictionary training is necessary, and dictionary games are valuable if time permits. An article of mine in the *English Journal* for January, 1948, contains several detailed suggestions, most of which are adaptable to junior high school. The only limitation is the one imposed by the steel hands of an impatient, impartial, insensitive clock face on the wall of the classroom.

Ward S. Miller

Rochester, New York
August 15, 1949

ACKNOWLEDGMENTS

Although *Word Wealth Junior* for the most part employs methods which were tested thoroughly in connection with *Word Wealth,* sample units of the present material were tried out in Rochester and elsewhere. The writer is indebted to the English Council of the Rochester high schools for undertaking to use several of the units in their original form before they were re-worked, and particularly to Harold E. Cowles, East High School; Charles H. Carver and Mrs. Jennie Stolbrand, Monroe High School; Miss Blanche Thompson (since retired) and Lester Parker at Benjamin Franklin.

The writer wishes also to thank the following who aided in testing Part One units in elementary buildings at sixth or seventh grade level: Miss Margaret C. Kenny and Miss Mary Helen McBride (then) in Lake View School; Mrs. Walter G. Fotch and Miss Alice Baker in No. 21 School. Mrs. Lillian M. Brooks and Miss Mary E. Foley made suggestions that proved helpful.

Mr. W. E. Wenner, superintendent, and Miss Ruth L. Wisman of Harbor High School, Ashtabula, Ohio, tested several units in a very fine school where the author once taught. Mrs. Mary D. Greenfield, Northside High School, Corning, New York, and Mrs. Harford I. Weld (as Miss Carolyn VanAlstyne) in Keego Harbor, Michigan, also participated in the testing.

Miss Ruth M. Stauffer, head of the Department of English, Divisions 1–9, in the Public Schools of the District of Columbia, gave the author useful material and valuable suggestions when he was laying the groundwork for this book in 1946; and Miss Clyde Roberts of McKinley High School, Washington, D. C., also aided materially with advice and experience.

The pupils who participated, several hundred of them, deserve credit, even though they must remain nameless; also, a dozen or more persons who did clerical or secretarial work. The author's wife, Phyllis Trayhern Miller, was one of the latter.

CONTENTS

Part Two

CONTENTS

Part Three

CONTENTS

WORD WEALTH JUNIOR

PART ONE

WORDS HAVE FAMILIES

Words come in families just like people. Take *kind,* for instance. Your mother is *kind.* You like her *kindness.* She treats you *kindly.* She is never *unkind.* Sometimes one word fits best into what you want to say, sometimes another. If you need a gentle word for a person who looks and no doubt is kind, you could use *kindly:* Granddad has a *kindly* manner. His *kindliness* makes you feel good. Thus you know six words from the Kind family, and there are at least two more — *unkindly* and *unkindness.*

When you meet members of the Fierce family — *fierce, fierceness, fiercely* — it is nice to know that all contain the same six letters, f-i-e-r-c-e, in that order, with the *i* first as in *fire.* In fact *fierce* is like *fiery* in spelling as well as in meaning.

Meeting words in families helps us to understand them and also to spell them. You would know what a *kindless* villain is without looking in the dictionary, and *superfierceness,* if there were such a word, would mean fierceness beyond anything you ever saw before.

How well do you know the families of everyday words? Can you fill each of the blanks in Group I, page 4? Copy the guide words and go to work. Make sure you copy each word correctly. When you finish, all the nouns should end in *–ness* and all the adverbs in *–ly.*

GROUP 1

Adjective	*Noun*	*Adverb*
Example: glad	gladness	gladly
1. apt	aptness	aptly / aptly
2. aware	awareness	
3. cautious	cautiousness	cautiously
4. curt	curtness	curtly
5. exact	exactness	exactly
6. fierce	fierceness	fiercely
7. happy	happiness	happily
8. holy	holiness	
9. pert	pertness	pertly
10. pleasant	pleasantness	pleasantly

(Handwritten answers appear in some cells.)

Questions

1. Which words require a slight change in spelling to get the noun form? What is the change? Can you think of other words, such as *weary,* which make the same spelling change?
2. Write the opposite of the adjective in lines 2, 3, 7, 8, and 10 by placing *in–* or *un–* in front of it.
3. Write the noun and adverb forms of *awkward, bad, clever, mad, prompt, strange,* and *sad.*
4. Are these words new to you?
    apt — skillful, quick to learn
    curt — sharp, brief to the point of rudeness
    pert — clever (almost boldly so), frank (almost saucy)
Use them in sentences: The letter was curt. She smiled pertly.
His aptness for schoolwork is amazing.

Can you fill the blanks in the following table? Each noun will end in *–ment* and each adjective in *–able*.

Verb	Noun	Adjective
1. agree	agreement	agreeable
2. amend	*amend ment*	*amendable*
3. *argue*	argument	
4. *employ*	*employment*	employable
5. *encourage*	encouragement	
6. *create*	*excitement*	excitable
7. *govern*	government	*governable*
8. *judge*	judgment	
9. *manage*	*management*	manageable
10. *move*	*movement*	movable or moveable
11. *pay*	*payment*	payable
12. *replace*	*replacement*	replaceable

Questions

1. Can you discover, by comparing each noun with its verb form, why *argument* and *judgment* are set in bold type?
2. Compare each adjective form with its verb form. Which verbs have dropped the final *e* before adding *–able?* Which have kept it? Words ending in *–ge* and *–ce* are more likely to keep the *e*. Write the *–able* adjective for *notice*.
3. Write the opposite of five or more of the words in the adjective column, using the dictionary if necessary. One is formed with *ir–*, one is formed with *dis–*, and the others with *un–* in front.
4. Write the noun form (in *–ment*) of: *acknowledge, advance, adjust, amuse, appoint, arrange, assort, assign, astonish, attach, commence, command, conceal, confine, develop, disappoint, engage, enroll, entertain, equip, establish, fulfill, improve, induce, invest, pave, postpone, procure, require, settle, ship.* Which one, like *judgment*, drops the final *e?*

5. Write the past tense and *–ing* form of: *acknowledge, advance, adjust, appoint, assign, employ, equip, excite, require, ship, state.* Use the dictionary, if necessary. Watch out for two which end in a *single* consonant and double that consonant in forming the past tense. (More of this on pages 43–44.)
6. Write the title of the man who governs a state; of the man who employs; of those who are employed.
7. Compose a paragraph using some of the words in this unit.

DICTATION TEST

Write some or all of the following sentences from dictation: *

1. We gladly acknowledge your advance payment.
2. In our judgment you can meet requirements by arranging in advance to obtain enough equipment.
3. Assign six to the project and procure a shipment of material.
4. A building was engaged in which to entertain notables.
5. There was an argument about whom to appoint to settle labor troubles and adjust the differences.
6. One man is too excitable for the job and rather disagreeable. The other is unmanageable.

WORD–BUILDING EXERCISE

Write down for each blank the proper form of the word in parentheses. Watch spelling.

1. How do you like her __?__ (arrange) of the flowers?
2. Mules are famous for __?__ (stubborn) and __?__ (contrary).
3. "Go chase yourself," he answered __?__ (curt).
4. The __?__ (fierce) of the animal made it dangerous.
5. A good man is __?__ (can't replace) on this job; a careless one is __?__ (can't employ) at any price.
6. The bonds are __?__ (retire) in ten years.
7. Have you an __?__ (acknowledge) of your order?

* These sentences contain 20 or more words from this unit. Teachers may grade on the basis of five, ten, or more off for each misspelled word. Each pupil should start a Never-Again list of the words which he misses.

"ONE–CYLINDER" VERBS

Queries

Inspect the list of words at the right. How many of the following questions about them can you answer?

1. Which one is damp?
2. Which are unmanly?
3. Which one is the most polite?
4. Which two would one like to do to an enemy?
5. Which one is selective?
6. Which one is windy?

● *How many of the verbs can you find in the illustration above?*

Verbs

1. cull
2. doff
3. mince
4. moor
5. oust
6. quell
7. raze
8. seep
9. swerve
10. vie
11. waft
12. wince

---

1. CULL . . . . to find and discard

Cull the bad ears as you shuck them.
The culls (discarded ones) will be burned.

2. DOFF . . . . to take off or remove

He learned to doff his cap for a lady.
Doff your coat and roll up your sleeves.

3. MINCE . . . . . to cut into little pieces, tone down

He took short, mincing (cut-into-little-pieces) steps.
She didn't mince words when she told us to leave her yard.
Mincemeat is minced meat or something else chopped very
   small.

4. MOOR . . . . . to tie or anchor (especially a ship)

"A band of exiles moored their bark
   On the wild New England shore."
The ship broke loose from her mooring.
The moor (damp wasteland) was silent and lovely.

5. OUST . . . . to drive out, expel

The effort to oust the mayor failed.
An ouster (order of dispossession) was issued.
Bad manners will ostracize (banish) a person.

6. QUELL . . . . . to put down, suppress, overcome

The police were able to quell the riot quickly.
She tried in vain to quell her tears.

7. RAZE . . . to destroy, tear down, level to the ground

A windstorm razed the barn.
Wreckers razed the old theater in two days.

8. SEEP . . . . to soak through

Water will seep into the basement.
Seepage makes the cellar damp.

9. SWERVE . . to change course or direction (suddenly)

Did the car swerve to avoid an accident?

The cyclone swerved away from the village.

Do not deviate (turn aside) from the course.

10. VIE . . . . to contend, strive in rivalry

The two speakers will vie with each other for first place.

Vying with an experienced rival, he won out.

11. WAFT . . . . to blow, carry along

A gentle breeze wafted the seedlings along.

Waves wafted the houseboat ashore.

12. WINCE . . . to shrink, draw away (as from a blow)

Watch Jerry wince when I pretend to hit him.

Did you wince when you were vaccinated?

Questions

1. Can you name other one-syllable words ending in *–aze*?
2. How many three-letter words ending in *ie* do you know?
3. What words rhyme with *cull*? with *wince*?

FIRST PRACTICE SET

Copy the italicized words and beside each write its meaning in the sentence:

1. Soldiers *quelled* the revolt and *razed* the temple where it had started.
2. Flood waters *seeped* into the grain bins.
3. Why *wince*? The runner will *swerve* if you stand firm.
4. Spring breezes *waft* the perfume of apple blossoms over the countryside.
5. *Doff* your headpiece and *moor* your belongings while the winds *vie* with each other.
6. *Cull* the hens who are poor layers and *oust* the dog from the chicken coop.
7. With *mincing* steps she walked toward us.

SECOND PRACTICE SET

What word fits best in each blank?

1. __?__ the apples which are too small.
2. The balloon broke lose from its __?__ing.
3. What should one do with a mob? __?__ it.
4. A nervous person will __?__ at a loud noise.
5. Puppies __?__ with each other playfully.
6. Waves __?__ the burning oil along.
7. Orators do not __?__ words.
8. Oil will __?__ through the covering.
9. How long did it take to __?__ the city?
10. __?__ the cat from the kitchen.
11. Trucks __?__ to miss dogs.
12. A soldier does not __?__ his cap.

Tidal Wave

Have you read about a Florida hurricane? Write two or three sentences about a hurricane, tidal wave, or thunderstorm, using several of the verbs in this unit.

HOT AND HATEFUL

Teasers

Read over the verbs in the column at the right. Then see how many of the following questions about them you can answer:

Verbs

1. Which one gave the United States more territory?
2. Which is the most painful?
3. Which one is cowardly?
4. Which one protects?
5. Which contains the most hatred?

1. cede
2. chafe
3. cringe
4. loathe
5. scathe
6. secrete
7. seethe
8. sheathe
9. singe
10. tinge
11. wane
12. writhe

1. **CEDE** . . . . **to yield, grant**
   Russia ceded Alaska to the United States.
   He concedes (admits) the value of exercise.

2. **CHAFE** . . . . **to rub, wear away, fret, produce heat**
   The stiff collar chafes his neck.
   A chafing dish is a utensil for warming food at the table.
   Chaff is light stuff like wheat shucks.
   "The ungodly are not so: but are like the chaff which the wind driveth away."

3. **CRINGE** . . . . **to shrink, crouch, cower**
   Jimmie cringes at the sight of the needle.

4. **LOATHE** . . . . **to hate, dislike, detest**
   Robbie loathes spinach.
   Sandra cannot hide her loathing for snakes.
   Leprosy is a loathsome disease.
   He was loath (reluctant) to give up such a good seat.

5. **SCATHE** . . . . **to harm or injure**
   Daddy came through the accident unscathed.
   The coach made some scathing (cutting) remarks.
   Note: *Scathe* is now used only in the participle forms as illustrated.

6. **SECRETE** . . . . **to hide; to generate**
   Joseph tried to secrete himself in a closet.
   Her father is very secretive (inclined to keep secrets).
   Glands near the tongue secrete saliva.

7. **SEETHE** . . . . **to boil, erupt, suffer great agitation**
   The shop began to seethe with activity.
   The basement became a seething mass of flames.
   Seething with anger, the man rushed from the room.

8. SHEATHE . . . to put in protective covering, encase

"Sheathe your swords!" the man commanded.

The trees were sheathed in ice.

The hunting knife is in its sheath.

9. SINGE . . . to scorch, burn slightly (on the surface)

Mother will singe the chicken before dressing it.

Nathan's hands were singed by the flames.

10. TINGE . . . . to color or flavor slightly

Autumn colors began to tinge the leaves.

Even their happy days had a tinge of sadness.

11. WANE . . . . to decrease, die down

"The long day wanes: the slow moon climbs."

Their friendship was on the wane.

12. WRITHE . . . . to twist or turn, especially with pain

The dog writhes in pain.

Writhing with dismay, the man left the building.

Question Games

1. In what ways are the words of this unit alike?
2. Which words contain a silent letter other than final *e?*
3. What word rhymes with *chafe? scathe? sheathe? writhe?*
4. Change one letter of *cringe* and get *a border* (not a boarder); a letter of *singe* or *tinge* and get *a door device;* a letter of *wane* and get *a source of harm.*
5. How many words ending in *–ane* can you list?
6. Can you find *ten* three- or four-letter words inside the base words of this unit — without rearranging the letters? One word contains three and another four of these smaller words.

FIRST PRACTICE SET

Copy the italicized words and beside each write its meaning in the sentence:

1. He should not *chafe* and *cringe* at insults which are merely part of a political campaign.
2. They *loathe* the thought of *ceding* any more territory.
3. The warrior started to *sheathe* his sword as the fighting began to *wane*.
4. His hands were *singed* in his effort to quell the *seething* flames.
5. A *scathing* rebuke made the player *writhe*.
6. The western sky was *tinged* with red, and heavy clouds began to *secrete* the sun.

SECOND PRACTICE SET

What word fits best in each blank? Use each word only once.

1. Do you __?__ castor oil? Does it make you __?__?
2. How do you act when scolded? You __?__.
3. Mexico __?__d land to the United States.
4. A squirrel __?__ his nuts and hopes to remain un__?__d through another hunting season.
5. A volcano __?__ when it is active.
6. What does the moon do every month? It __?__.
7. What is the best thing to do with a sword? __?__ it.
8. She __?__ under his wilting criticism.
9. The candle flame will __?__ her hair.
10. A hint of frost __?__d the September air.

Campfire

Write two or three sentences about having a campfire, using some of the words in this unit. If you prefer, build your fire in the fireplace.

PRONOUNCING PAIRS

Spelling and pronunciation go hand in hand. Often the pronunciation tells you how to spell a word. Read the following pairs two or three times in concert:

Group I

1. can   cane
2. Dan   Dane
3. man   mane (long
                    neck hair)
4. pan   pane
5. wan (pale)   wane (decrease)

Group II

1. pal   pale
2. bit   bite
3. sit   site
4. not   note
5. rot   rote
           (repetition)
6. cut   cute

Group III

1. hast   haste
2. past   paste
3. prim (stiff) prime
4. con   cone
5. human   humane (kind)

Group IV

1. bath   bathe
2. breath   breathe
3. clotn   clothe
4. cloths   clothes
5. lath   lathe
6. loath   loathe
7. sheath   sheathe
8. wreath   wreathe

Questions

1. What is the relation between the spelling and pronunciation of each pair? Three pairs in Group IV differ slightly from the others in this relationship. What are they?
2. How many words can you think of that rhyme with *can?* with *bit* and *sit?* *bite* and *site?*
3. What words rhyme with *prime?*
4. How many pairs can you add to the lists? Make a set with *kin* and *kine, din* and *dine, fin* and *fine.*
5. Write sentences using *mane, wan, wane, rote, prim,* and *humane.* Be sure you know the meaning of each.

SENTENCES FOR PRACTICE

Write some or all of the following from dictation:

1. Please don't waste the paste.
2. He puts his clothes on backward.
3. My pal looks pale this morning.
4. Uncle Ben is *loath* to make haste.
5. The cloths were wrapped in a bathing suit.
6. Do you learn rhymes by *rote?*
7. Does a pinprick make you whine?
8. A *lathe* is not used to make lath.
9. Motes (tiny particles) dance in the *wan* sunshine.
10. A *prim* lady carried a cute paper cutter in a *sheath*.
11. Low-hanging branches chafe the horse's *mane*.
12. The engine breathes like a human being.
13. The old lady *loathes* cats but is very *humane* to them.
14. The warrior refused to *sheathe* his sword.
15. She broke the seal on the envelope in haste.

Copy the italicized words in the sentences above and beside each write its meaning. (Several of the words not defined on page 15 were defined on pages 12–13.)

LITTLE NOUNS

Often

Which of the words at the right often goes with each of the following?

1. Hair
2. Pests
3. Grain
4. Statues
5. A mind that wanders

● *How many of the nouns can you find in the illustration above?*

Nouns

1. breach
2. crest
3. drone
4. gibe (jibe)
5. guise
6. horde
7. lapse
8. niche
9. sheaf
10. stud
11. truss
12. wisp

LITTLE NOUNS—STUDY GUIDE

1. BREACH . . . . a break or opening

Failure to doff one's cap is a breach of etiquette.

The attack made a breach in (breached) the defenses of the city.

2. CREST . . . . top, headpiece, coat-of-arms

Can you see the crest of the waves?

The knight wore a plumed crest.

3. DRONE . . male bee, a lazy person (who lives by the efforts of others)

The worker bees kill the drones.

A good team has no place for drones.

The drone (dull, steady sound) of motors could be heard.

4. GIBE (JIBE) . . . . a taunt, scoffing remark

The gibes (jibes) from the stands did not disturb the batter.

Your words and actions do not always jibe (match, harmonize).

Note: *Jibe* as a verb is a word used in conversation more than in writing.

5. GUISE . . . . . . manner, likeness, appearance

The prince reappeared in the guise of a peddler.

The robber's disguise was detected.

6. HORDE . . . . crowd, mob, swarm

A horde of his followers rushed into the streets.

Hordes of buffaloes roamed the plains.

7. LAPSE . . . . a shortcoming, slip, oversight

A lapse of memory caused the error.

Do not let your insurance policy lapse (cease to be in effect).

8. NICHE .   . a hollowed-out place (for a bust or statue), a place or position (of distinction) just suited to a person

That halfback deserves a niche in football's hall of fame.
The banker made a niche for himself in village society.

9. SHEAF . . . . . a bundle, especially of grain stalks

The ground was covered with sheaves of newly-harvested wheat.
The agent had a sheaf of papers under his arm.

10. STUD .   . a small knob or projection, often ornamental

The stud on his shirt glittered.
The sky was studded with stars.

11. TRUSS . . . . a support or brace

The boy had to wear a truss.
The fence was trussed up (bound together) with wires.

12. WISP . . . . a small bunch or puff

A wisp of cloud clung to the mountainside.
A will-o'-the-wisp (pale glow) hovered over the swamp.

Observations

1. Which of the words have a silent letter other than final *e?*
2. List rhymes for *breach, crest, drone,* and *truss.*
3. Change one letter of *breach* and get *to introduce or bring up* (a topic).
4. Write the plural of *truss* and *breach.*
5. Find out what a will-o'-the-wisp is.

FIRST PRACTICE SET

Copy the italicized words and beside each write its meaning in the sentence.

1. *Hordes* of invaders entered through a *breach* in the walls.
2. The *crest* of the Green Knight appeared above the *niche*.
3. The umpire's *lapse* of memory brought *gibes* from the crowd.
4. A *wisp* of hair clung to the *stud* on the harness.
5. Wearing a *truss*, he escaped in the *guise* of a cripple.
6. A *sheaf* of arrows lay near the lifeless *drone*.

SECOND PRACTICE SET

What word from the unit fits best in each blank?

1. __?__es of etiquette deserve only __?__s.
2. The __?__s on his dress shirts carried the family __?__.
3. A __?__ of smoke appeared near the __?__ of documents.
4. After a __?__ of thirty days, the figure was placed in its __?__ again.
5. __?__s of enemies arrived in the __?__ of refugees.
6. A __?__ held the beam in position, and __?__s lounged under it.

SHORTER ADJECTIVES

Which One?

From the adjectives in the list at the right, choose the one which best describes:

1. A bird that no longer exists.
2. A package undamaged in a wreck.
3. Trees that are few and far between.
4. Habits that pertain to the sea.
5. A boy who looks very pale.

Adjectives

1. chaste
2. dormant
3. extinct
4. ghastly
5. intact
6. lithe
7. nautical
8. prone
9. sallow
10. sparse
11. terse
12. void

SHORTER ADJECTIVES—STUDY GUIDE

1. **CHASTE** . . . . **pure, modest**
She was chaste but not cold-hearted.
Chastity (purity) is an important virtue.
Suffering often chastens (punishes, purifies, refines) a person.

2. **DORMANT** . . . . . **inactive (in sense of sleeping)**
Bears are often dormant during the winter.
The plan lay dormant for months.
The boy remained quiescent (inactive in sense of resting) until his leg healed.

3. **EXTINCT** . . . . . **dead, lifeless, no longer existing**
Mt. Etna is an extinct volcano.
The dodo is an extinct bird which could not fly.
Firemen can extinguish (put out of existence) a blaze if called in time.
Extinction (destruction) of a pest like the Japanese beetle is very difficult.

4. **GHASTLY** . . . . **horrible, ghostlike, deathly, pale**
Shooting his uncle for a burglar was a ghastly mistake.
The ghastliness of her appearance shocked us.
He looked aghast (horrified) at the wreckage.
The murder was a grisly (frightful) crime.
War is grim (stern, forbidding).

5. **INTACT** . . . . **unharmed, undamaged**
The shipment was intact.
The radio station came through the storm intact.

6. **LITHE** . . . . **easily bent, gracefully limber**
An acrobat's muscles are lithe.
She has the litheness of a circus performer.
A pianist has supple (flexible, well-trained) fingers.

7. NAUTICAL . . . . having to do with ships or the sea

Nautical knowledge is hard to get from books.

Bilge is a nautical term for a ship's bottom or water that collects there.

Marine (in-the-sea) life is extremely varied.

8. PRONE . . . inclined, stretched out flat (face down)

Human beings are prone to make mistakes.

He was shooting from a prone position.

The man's proneness (inclination, tendency) to take bribes got him into prison.

Supine means flat on one's back, face up, or effortless and lacking in spirit.

9. SALLOW . . . . yellowish, sickly-looking

A sallow complexion is natural for some persons.

Sallowness may be the result of an illness like jaundice.

10. SPARSE . . . . thinly distributed, scattered

Greenland has a sparse population.

The interior of Australia is sparsely settled.

The sparseness of the peach crop made prices high.

11. TERSE . . . . brief, crisp, pithy

A terse command brought the scouts to his side.

Sailors admire terseness.

12. VOID . . . . empty, of no value

"And the earth was without form, and void."

The check becomes void if altered.

Failure to pay will void (make empty) the agreement.

Her face was devoid (empty) of fear.

Questions

1. What other words end in *–tinct* besides *extinct?*
2. How many words can you obtain by changing the *s* in *sallow* to some other letter? What does each mean?

3. Change *l* in *lithe* to another letter and get a word meaning *a tenth*. Change it again and get a kind of rope or bond.
4. What is the opposite of *chaste?* of *nautical?*

FIRST PRACTICE SET

Copy the italicized words and beside each write its meaning in the sentence:

1. The germs remain *dormant* for weeks without becoming *extinct*.
2. "The ship is *intact*," he announced *tersely*.
3. Her face was *sallow* and *devoid* of color.
4. Uncle Ned's hair is *sparse*, but his legs are still *lithe*.
5. Mother is *prone* to expect a *ghastly* crime.
6. *Chaste* thoughts do not always mix well with *nautical* language.

SECOND PRACTICE SET

Which word in this unit applies most readily to each of the following? Use each word only once.

1. Popeye?
2. A telegram?
3. Space between stars?
4. Lilies in winter?
5. A sickly boy?
6. A volcano that will never erupt again?
7. A figure skater?
8. Population in Nevada?
9. A girl on her stomach?
10. A nun?
11. The electric chair?
12. A piano unharmed in a cyclone?

A SPELLING PROBLEM

GROUP I

Quite a few words end in *–ar*. Those below are among the most common. Read them aloud several times. Exaggerate the pronunciation, especially the *–ar* endings. Write them down or use them in sentences until you are sure you can spell them even when mixed up with other words.

beggar	circular	particular	scholar
burglar	collar	peculiar	similar
calendar	familiar	poplar (a tree)	singular
cedar	grammar	popular	vinegar
cellar	liar	regular	vulgar

Questions

1. What letter comes in front of the *–ar* ending most often? This observation may help you spell the words.
2. Which words contain a double letter? which two a *liar?*
3. The vowel in front of a *single* consonant in front of *–ar* is long (or almost long) in most cases. What are the exceptions?
4. Write the adverb or *–ly* form of eight of the words.
5. Study the following words ending in *–ary* as you did the *–ar* words above: *boundary, customary, diary, dictionary, elementary, literary, military, primary, revolutionary, salary, sanitary, stationary* (fixed, not moving), *temporary, voluntary.*

Exaggerate the pronunciation, especially the *–or* endings, **and** study the spelling of the following:

actor	elevator	janitor	radiator
author	emperor	liquor	rumor
aviator	error	major	scissors
bachelor	favor	minor	senator
conductor	flavor	mirror	tenor
director	honor	motor	terror
doctor	horror	odor	traitor
ᵣditor	humor	pastor	vigor

Questions

1. What letter comes in front of the *–or* most often?
2. Can you reduce or transform *elevator, error, horror, radiator,* and *terror* into verbs?
3. What do *anterior, behavior, exterior, junior, inferior, interior, prior* (before), *senior,* and *superior* have in common? Pronounce them carefully, and make sure you can spell them.
4. Study the following familiar *–ory* words: *advisory, directory, dormitory, history, inventory, memory, territory, victory.*

SENTENCES FOR PRACTICE

Write some or all of the following sentences from dictation:

1. The janitor found a beggar wearing his collar.
2. The scholar talked about a temporary boundary.
3. The Senator broke the actor's mirror.
4. His diary is a history of military planning.
5. The odor in the dormitory was a familiar one.
6. A burglar stole a calendar in error.
7. A senior's grammar should be superior.
8. The traitor's humor was vulgar.
9. The rumor about the doctor's behavior is false.
10. It is customary for the tenor to receive a salary.
11. The motor and radiator are stationary.
12. Liars often display a singular lack of memory.

STORY WORDS

Characters

Of the words at the right:

1. Which one is in the Navy?
2. Which one lives underground?
3. Which one is almost a king?
4. Which would scare a girl the most?
5. Which is the most powerful?

Story Words

1. ballad
2. chalice
3. changeling
4. fantasy
5. ghoul
6. gnome
7. parable
8. phantom
9. pixie
10. regent
11. sorcerer
12. yeoman

STORY WORDS—STUDY GUIDE

1. BALLAD . . . . a simple story in poem form

The teacher brought a book of ballads to class.

A *ballet* (*BAL-lay* or *bal-LAY*) is a kind of artistic dance.

2. CHALICE . . . . a drinking cup or goblet

The Holy Grail was the chalice used by Christ at the Last Supper.

3. CHANGELING . . a child secretly substituted for another in infancy

According to a legend, the stupid prince was a fairy changeling.

4. FANTASY . . . . . something unreal or imagined

The side-hill gopher is a creature of fantasy.

The story that the girl is a witch is fantastic (fanciful).

A *phantasm* is a fantasy or specter.

5. GHOUL . . . . a fiend, evil creature

Only a ghoul could commit such a crime.

There was a ghoulish leer on the man's face.

The landlord was an ogre (hideous or cruel person).

6. GNOME . . . . a dwarf

Gnomes are story-book creatures who live underground and protect mines or treasures.

A gnomelike (dwarfish) little man lived in the cabin.

7. PARABLE . . a brief story which illustrates a truth by making a comparison

The parable of the talents is in the Book of Matthew.

A *parabola* is a hairpin-like curve.

A *fable,* like a parable, is a story intended to impart a truth, but more unreal and often having animal characters that talk.

A *legend* is a story that has some factual or historical basis, but a *myth* may have none at all.

8. PHANTOM . . . . a ghost, specter

A phantom horseman could be seen each evening in the moonlight.

9. PIXIE . . . . a fairy or elf

Pixies appeared in the late afternoon.
The pixie-faced girl is my cousin.
Water sprites (elves) danced in the sunshine.

10. REGENT . . . . acting ruler, governor

The kingdom was under a regent.
During his regency the country was attacked.
One of the regents of the university died.

11. SORCERER . . . . . one who practices witchcraft

The old man was a sorcerer.
Fairy stories are full of sorcery.
A wizard is a sorcerer.

12. YEOMAN . . a man of the common people; small land-owner

A yeoman won the archery contest.
Brave yeomen were England's pride.
A yeoman in the United States Navy is a petty officer who types letters and performs clerical duties.

Questions

1. What word which rhymes with *ballet* means a Swiss cottage (one *l*)?
2. Can you think of three other words besides *ghoul* which begin with *gh*?
3. Can you write four or five words besides *gnome* which begin with *gn* — all quite familiar?
4. Can you think of two or three ghost adjectives?
5. How many three and four-letter words can you find in the base words of this unit without rearranging letters?

FIRST PRACTICE SET

Copy the italicized words and beside each write its meaning in the sentence:

1. The *regent,* some said, was a *changeling* from the home of a *yeoman.*
2. The girl in the *ballad* smiled a *pixie* smile and drank from a flowered *chalice.*
3. A *ghoul* was the villain of the *fantasy.*
4. The *gnome* was a *sorcerer.*
5. The *phantom* in the *parable* represents fear.

SECOND PRACTICE SET

Can you fill the blanks correctly, using each base word at least once? Fill first the blanks you are sure about, and then go back, rearranging, if necessary, to get each word where it fits best.

The following tale is a __?__:

A __?__ met a __?__ one day. She was running very fast. "My fairy friend," he said, "what frightened you?"

"I don't know," she cried, "whether it was a __?__, a __?__, a __?__, or a __?__. It looked like a little old man."

"It must have been a __?__," the honest __?__ replied.

"He tried to bewitch me," she wailed.

"Then it was a __?__."

This story is not a __?__ because it is not in poem form, and it is not a __?__ because it does not illustrate a truth. It happened during the time of a __?__ who later became the Knight of the Golden __?__. The king, who was only ten, was said by some to be a __?__ because he was lame.

Creative Exercise

Write briefly about getting lost in the forest. Be sure to use several of the words in this unit.

PART ONE   **UNIT 9**

PERSONALITIES

Which Are Which?

Of the characters at the right:

1. Which are the most religious?
2. Which are the most traveled?
3. Which are the youngest?
4. Which are the wealthiest?
5. Which is the best businessman?

● *How many of the personalities in the list can you find in the illustration above?*

Personalities

1. buccaneer
2. friar
3. huckster
4. magi
5. mendicant
6. pauper
7. pilgrim
8. stowaway
9. stripling
10. urchin
11. vagabond
12. waif

1. BUCCANEER . . . . **a pirate**

Captain Kidd was a bold buccaneer.

A Turkish corsair (pirate) seized the cargo.

A privateer was a pirate vessel or the commander of one.

2. FRIAR . . . . . . **member of a male religious order**

A poor friar found the princess.

Monks live in retirement in monasteries.

Note: Friars went about preaching. Monks stayed in the monastery
   to pray, think, and work.

3. HUCKSTER . . . . **a peddler or hawker**

We buy vegetables from a huckster who comes around every
   week.

Those who sell goods by radio advertising are now called
   hucksters.

4. MAGI . . . . **the wise men from the East**

"The Gift of the Magi" was written by O. Henry.

Mage (wise man, wizard) Merlin knew the secret of King
   Arthur's birth.

5. MENDICANT . . . . **a beggar**

A horde of mendicants overran the town when it became
   known that food was plentiful there.

A hobo is a tramp or mendicant.

6. PAUPER . . **a very poor person (dependent on charity)**

Laziness and disease had made paupers of the entire family.

High prices and no work will pauperize thousands.

7. PILGRIM . . . . **a traveler or wayfarer**

The pilgrim was on his way to visit a shrine.

Life is a pilgrimage (a long journey).

8. **STOWAWAY** . . **a hidden, illegal passenger (especially in ships or aircraft)**

The stowaway was arrested when the ship docked.

The documents were given the safest possible stowage (storage).

9. **STRIPLING** . . . . **a youth**

The task is too difficult for a stripling.

10. **URCHIN** . . . . . . **a prankish child, ragamuffin**

Street urchins crowded around the huckster.

A sea urchin is a small sea creature covered with prickly spines.

Note: The French word for urchin is *gamin.*

11. **VAGABOND** . . . . **a wanderer, vagrant**

Autumn "calls and calls each vagabond by name."

A migrant (traveling-from-place-to-place) worker was killed by lightning.

12. **WAIF** . . **a homeless person or animal, especially a child**

The waif was very hungry when we found him.

Questions for Study

1. Why were the Pilgrim Fathers so named? Who were the pilgrims in "Pilgrim's Chorus" from *Tannhäuser?*
2. What is the relation between *migrant* and *immigrant? emigrant? migrate?*
3. What else can you find out about friars and monks? What does *cloister* mean?
4. What do paupers, mendicants, and waifs have in common?
5. What is a vagrancy charge?

FIRST PRACTICE SET

What is the meaning of each italicized word in the sentences below?

1. The *Magi* were *pilgrims* seeking the Christ child.
2. A Dutch *urchin* tried to reach America as a *stowaway*.
3. The king, while disguised as a *vagabond*, was insulted by a *mendicant*.
4. The *friar* rescued a *waif* in the forest.
5. The *stripling* pretended to be a *buccaneer*.
6. The *huckster* paid no attention to the *pauper*.

SECOND PRACTICE SET

Which of the personalities in this unit would you be most likely to find:

1. Riding on camels?
2. Sailing a ship?
3. Hidden in a plane?
4. Riding in a box car?
5. Traveling to a shrine?
6. Lost in the woods?
7. Running a truck farm?
8. On a playground?
9. At a youth camp?
10. Living in a hovel?
11. Kneeling in his cell?
12. Begging on the street?

WORD BUILDING

Sometimes you think of a word you want to use, but it does not fit into the sentence. For example, suppose you want to say that Joe was absent yesterday and that you lost the ball game because he wasn't there. You could say:

"Joe's not being there made us lose the game."

It is simpler and more punchy to say:

"Joe's absence made us lose the game."

If you want to tell the teacher that Daddy talked last night as if his mind was on something a long way off, you could say it in three words:

"Daddy talked absently."

This unit is an activity in thinking of several different forms of a word — and spelling them correctly. Copy the guide words and for each blank supply a word that ends like the other words in the column:

GROUP I

Adjective	*Noun*	*Adverb*
Example: absent	absence	absently
1. abundant	__?__	__?__
2. __?__	distance	__?__
3. __?__	__?__	evidently
4. convenient	__?__	__?__
5. __?__	magnificence	__?__
6. __?__	__?__	obediently
7. patient	__?__	__?__
8. __?__	__?__	presently
9. __?__	permanence	__?__
10. __?__	__?__	violently

Questions

1. What is the verb for *defiantly, excellently, obediently, presently, silently,* and *violently?* the adjective and noun for *instantly, defiantly,* and *excellently?*
2. Can you write the opposite of the adjective in lines 4, 6, 7, and 10 of Group I by putting *in–, im–, dis–,* or *non–* in front?
3. Write the *–cy* noun form for *agent, recent, accurate, decent. frequent, vacant.*

GROUP II

Can you fill each blank in the following:

Verb	Noun
1. admire	_ _ ? _ _
2. _ _ ? _ _	cancellation
3. confirm	_ _ ? _ _
4. _ _ ? _ _	consideration
5. converse (to talk)	_ _ ? _ _
6. _ _ ? _ _	expectation
7. _ _ ? _ _	explanation
8. initiate	_ _ ? _ _
9. observe	_ _ ? _ _
10. _ _ ? _ _	organization

Questions

1. What is the noun ending in *–tion* for: *accuse,* combine, consult, examine,* declare, destine, explore,* identify, imagine, inform,* inspire, install, irrigate, invite, limit, oblige, prepare, register, quote, represent, reserve, salute, situate, tempt*?* for *expedite** and *render?*
2. Change the verb for lines 1, 9, and 10 of Group II to a person by adding one letter. In the same way make a person or agent noun from the starred verbs in the first question above. Example: *give — giver.*

3. Write the past tense of *cancel, consider, limit, examine, organize, prepare, oblige, register, quote, render, represent.*
4. Can you write an adjective (ending in *–able* or *–tive*) for the verb in lines 1, 4, 7, and 9? for *imagine, inform,* and *quote?* Use dictionary, if needed.

GROUP III

Can you fill all the blanks correctly? Watch the center column especially, and use the dictionary if you are not sure.

Verb	Person or Agent Noun	Regular Noun
1. __?__	celebrator	__?__
2. __?__	competitor	__?__
3. __?__	communicator	__?__
4. __?__	__?__	cultivation
5. __?__	decorator	__?__
6. demonstrate	__?__	__?__
7. generate	__?__	__?__
8. __?__	__?__	navigation
9. operate	__?__	__?__
10. __?__	__?__	solicitation

Questions

1. What is remarkable about the endings of the words in the second column? Is there anything in Unit Seven which would lead you to expect this?
2. Write the verb form for *association, affection, appreciation, anticipation, collection, completion, cooperation, conviction, desperation, devotion, distribution, education, elimination, graduation, imitation, indication, investigation, location, population, prohibition, visitor.*
3. Can you think of an adjective ending in *–tive* for five of the verbs in the table and for four of the words in question 2?

SENTENCES FOR PRACTICE

Write some or all of the following from dictation:

1. A lending organization will investigate the plan to irrigate the field.
2. Your cooperation in keeping silent is much appreciated.
3. The speaker at graduation quoted an explorer.
4. Did you observe the location of the Indian reservation?
5. There was an abundance of appreciative celebrators.
6. "I want to set up a permanent agency," he declared.
7. Evidently they are excellently prepared.
8. She is patient, affectionate, and obedient.
9. He was tempted to cancel the plan to operate a bus.
10. A letter confirmed the conversation with his competitor.

WORD–BUILDING EXERCISE

Can you fill each of the blanks correctly, using a form of the word in parentheses?

1. The captain yelled __?__ (defy). There was a __?__ (defy) look on the halfback's face.
2. House-to-house __?__ (solicit) is prohibited.
3. There is a law against __?__ (not decent) books. The Legion of D__?__ (decent) opposes bad movies.
4. His father was once the __?__ (navigate) of a B-17.
5. *Bungalow* has a Hindu __?__ (derive).
6. The __?__ (devastate) was hard to believe.
7. The serpent was the __?__ (tempt) in the Garden of Eden.
8. My __?__ (inform) was a nurse at the hospital.
9. From the mountain one can see __?__ (no limit) stretches of prairie land.
10. They lived in hourly __?__ (expect) that the ship would founder.

SPARK PLUGS

The verb is the spark plug of a sentence.

Actions

In terms of the verbs at the right:

1. What does one do with a captive?
2. What do boats sometimes do?
3. Which one means *to walk*?
4. Which pertains to harvests?
5. Which is the most affectionate?

Verbs

1. banish
2. burnish
3. capsize
4. cherish
5. foster
6. garner
7. imbibe
8. mingle
9. relish
10. saunter
11. shackle
12. warrant

1. **BANISH** . . . . . . **to drive or send away; expel**
   Laughter will banish worry.
   The decree of banishment was revoked.
   The king's son went into exile (banishment).

2. **BURNISH** . . **to polish to brightness, especially a metal**
   surface
   The handle was burnished brass.
   A burnisher will make the radiator lustrous.
   The refinished cabinet has a high luster (gloss).

3. **CAPSIZE** . . . . **to upset, overturn**
   The car capsized after hitting the curb.
   Ships sometimes capsize in a storm.

4. **CHERISH** . . . . **to treat with fondness**
   A bicycle is a gift he will cherish.
   Jerry likes to fondle (caress) his pet rabbit.

5. **FOSTER** . . . . . . **to sustain, encourage, nurture**
   The school fosters good sportsmanship.
   The boy's foster parents were quite wealthy.
   The school will sponsor (assume responsibility for) a carni-
   val.

6. **GARNER** . . . . . **to gather for storage, to harvest**
   Vending machines garner nickels by the hundred.
   Grain is garnered in the autumn.

7. **IMBIBE** . . . . **to drink, drink in, absorb**
   Flowers imbibe the sunshine.
   The man is a habitual imbiber.
   Quaff (drink) the potion bravely.

8. **MINGLE** . . . . **to mix**
   Oil and water do not mingle readily.

9. RELISH . . . . . . to enjoy (the taste or flavor of)

The teacher does not relish excuses.

"It hath no relish [taste or flavor] of salvation in it."

Mary plays with real zest (hearty enjoyment).

Boys often eat with great *gusto* (zest or relish).

10. SAUNTER . . . . to walk or wander slowly, meander

I watched Maisie saunter down the street.

A dog meandered across the meadow.

Together they stroll (ramble, roam) toward town.

11. SHACKLE . . . . to bind, fetter, enslave

He tried to shackle a free nation.

The prisoners threw off their shackles (fetters).

The convict's manacles (handcuffs) were cumbersome.

12. WARRANT . . . . to justify, guarantee

Does the condition of the car warrant the cost of repairs?

There is no warrant (justification) for thinking that the plan will succeed.

(See dictionary for other forms and meanings of *warrant*.)

Questions

1. What word(s) can you find to rhyme with each of the following, changing only the first letter or the first two?

banish	mingle
burnish	shackle
cherish	

2. Change the first letter of *garner* twice and get a familiar proper name each time. Change the first letter of *foster* and get a placard.

PRACTICE SET

Copy the italicized words and beside each write its meaning in the sentence:

1. The cowboy *sauntered* over to see the canoe which had *capsized*.
2. Do you *cherish* the idea that we must not *shackle* free speech?
3. The captain *garnered* eighteen points before he was *banished* from the game on fouls.
4. Custom *fosters* the use of *burnished* silverware.
5. The detective *mingled* with the gamblers but did not *relish* the idea of joining their gang.
6. I *warrant* he will not *imbibe* too freely.

THE RECEPTION

What verb from this unit fits best in each blank below? Fill first the ones you are sure about and rearrange, if necessary.

I thought the car would __?__ before we got there. As we arrived, I saw our host __?__ over to greet us. He was doing his best to __?__ sociability, __?__ bashfulness, and break the __?__s of self-consciousness. Soon the guests began to __?__ freely and some to __?__. Harold __?__ed the hope of meeting an author who was present, but I did not __?__ the idea because I did not know what to say to an author. Circumstances did not __?__ our staying too late, but I managed to __?__ quite a bit of exciting information. On the way out I stumbled into a __?__ed andiron and barked my shins.

PRONOUNCING AND SPELLING

Were you shining your shoes or shinning them? Anybody who said you were "shinning" them would be fooling — or crazy. Yet in writing, pupils sometimes mix up *shining* and *shinning* without realizing that *the way you pronounce it tells you how to spell it.*

Read the following sets aloud several times:

file, filing a fingernail	hope, hoping for good weather
fill, filling the gas tank	hop, hopping across the room
pine, pining for farm life	cube, cubing the number three
pin, pinning a map on the wall	cub, cubbing in a scout troop
mate, mating of birds in spring	plane, planing a pine board
mat, matting on the porch floor	plan, planning a long hike

What is the difference between *filing* and *filling*? One has a single *l* with a LONG vowel in front while the other has a *double* consonant with a SHORT vowel in front. Thus, you show by the way you pronounce it how each of the *–ing* forms is spelled.

The *i* in *file* is long just as in *filing*, and the *i* in *fill* or *pin* is short. In fact, you may have noticed (page 15) that if a word ends in an *e* with *one* consonant in front of it, the vowel or double vowel in front of the consonant is almost always long. There are thousands of examples: *fate, late, Pete, complete, bite, site, divide, decide, note, rote, mute, lute.* Omit the *e*, and each vowel is pronounced *short: fat, slat, pet, booklet, bit, sit, David, acid, not, rot, mutt,* and *slut.*

ACTIVITIES

A. Write the missing word for each pair below:

1. whine	__?__		6. can	__?__
2. sin	__?__		7. mine	__?__
3. tube	__?__		8. __?__	gaping
4. __?__	dining		9. __?__	tapping
5. win	__?__		10. define	__?__

B. Make a list of sets such as: *dine, dining — din, dinning; gripe, griping — grip, gripping; write, writing — written; later — latter; unite — unit.*

C. Write the past tense and *–ing* form of: *combine, commit, dim, line, mine, omit, skim, submit, worship.**

D. Many words are not spelled correctly because they are pronounced incorrectly or carelessly. Read the following groups aloud several times, carefully. Exaggerate the pronunciation of each to show clearly what the spelling is:

1. *because, poem, quiet, quite, whether, twentieth*
2. *chairman, fragrant, freshman, furnace, human, image, message, salad, servant, shortage, standard, storage, vacant, Satan*
3. *closet, comedy, hundred, modest, mystery, parent, poetry, remedy, specimen, student, talent, travel, wondering*
4. *difficult, evidence, fugitive, hesitate, horrible, horrid, spirit, splendid, timid, victim, selfish, satin*
5. *ballot, harmony, hover, method, pilot, sermon*

SENTENCES FOR PRACTICE

Read the following sentences aloud two or three times. Then write some or all of them from dictation:

1. Full of spirit, the players hoped they were winning.
2. The mystery of the timid tapping was never solved.
3. Servants are human, civil, and modest.
4. Satan is selfish and fond of travel.
5. Satin in a quiet color is quite bewitching.
6. The fugitive's victim was buried in a filing cabinet.
7. Stopping a hundred feet from the ballot box, he grinned at the chairman.
8. The new method of trimming a tree is quite difficult.
9. The glass tube was hidden in a basket of knitting.
10. In the latter part of the inning the bases were filled.

* *Worship, kidnap, travel,* and a few others no longer require the double consonant.

PINT–SIZED NOUNS

Short Short Short Short Story

What word from the list at the right fits best in each blank?

The __?__ had no __?__ but to drink the deadly poison. The king was a __?__ and the __?__ of his __?__s was known all over the world.

Nouns

1. acme
2. baton
3. culprit
4. edict
5. facet
6. luster
7. mettle
8. morsel
9. option
10. pagan
11. profile
12. rigor

1. ACME . . . . **peak or highest point**

His playing is the acme of perfection.

2. BATON . . . . **a stick or wand**

The orchestra leader waved his baton.

The second runner in the relay race passed his baton to the third.

3. CULPRIT . . . . **wrongdoer, offender, guilty person**

"Are you the culprit?" Father demanded.

4. EDICT . . . . **decree, fiat**

The edict banished Garth from the kingdom.

Daddy rules the household by fiat.

Fiat means literally, in Latin, "Let it be done."

5. FACET . . **one of the surfaces of a stone or gem; one aspect of a situation**

Each facet of the diamond glitters and sparkles.

Her personality has many facets.

6. LUSTER . . . . . . **glowing or shiny appearance**

There was a soft luster in her eyes.

The luster of a waxed floor is treacherous.

Sunday was a cloudy, lusterless day.

Synonyms: *gloss, sheen, polish.* See *burnish,* page 40.

7. METTLE . . **courage, spirit, ability to rise to a situation**

The new selling plan will be a test of his mettle.

Garth was a mettlesome (spirited) youth.

Note: Do not confuse *mettlesome* with *meddlesome.*

8. MORSEL . . . . **particle, fragment**

Not a morsel of food fell on the floor.

The letter brought a morsel or two of hope.

9. OPTION . . . . . . choice, first right to buy or use

You have the option of taking the money now or leaving it with the company at 4% interest.

Her mother has an option on the blue house.

(Often one pays for the first right to buy or use something.)

10. PAGAN . . . a heathen or a person of no religious beliefs

The Roman religion was pagan in that it was not a one-god religion like the Christian or Jewish worship.

Modern pagans often have no religion at all.

11. PROFILE . . . . tracing or outline, side view

The profile of the mountaintops against the sky was like a row of saw teeth.

A silhouette shows one's profile.

12. RIGOR . . . . stiffness, severity

Few could endure the rigors of frontier life.

Army life is often rigorous.

Rigor mortis (stiffness of death) sets in an hour or two after a person dies.

WORD GAME

Who can finish it first — and get it perfect?

1. Change one letter of *acme* and get a plot of land.
2. Change one in *baton* and have an overlord.
3. Change one in *edict* and drive a family out of its lodging.
4. Add a letter to *luster* and get wind and noise. Interchange two letters and get a long cloak. Substitute one different letter and get another long outer garment. What other words can you obtain by changing a letter or two?
5. Change a letter of *mettle* and you will have a kitchen utensil. What other word can you get?
6. Change a letter of *rigor* and get robust energy.

FIRST PRACTICE SET

Copy the italicized words and beside each write its meaning in the sentence:

1. The *culprit* showed his *mettle* by offering to make amends.
2. According to the *edict*, not a *morsel* was to be wasted.
3. The drum major is the *acme* of skill in twirling a *baton*.
4. The *luster* of each *facet* was dazzling in the sunlight.
5. I watched the *profile* of the *pagan*.
6. His was the *option* of enduring the *rigors* of an Arctic winter or the dangers of an African jungle.

SECOND PRACTICE SET

Can you fill all the blanks? Use each word only once.

1. The __?__ tried to kill his enemy with a __?__ of poisoned meat.
2. The governor issued an __?__ forbidding anyone to harbor the __?__.
3. As the __?__ moved up and down, so did the drum major's __?__.
4. Iron has a __?__ and is a symbol of __?__ or courage.
5. A man who is the __?__ of skill in selling things has many __?__s when he seeks a job.
6. Christmas has many __?__s, and the __?__s of winter are temporarily forgotten.

SPRINGLIKE AND SWAMPY

May Queen

Can you fill the blanks fittingly from the words at the right without using a word twice? Better leave the second blank until last.

After the __?__ days of winter, spring will bring the __?__ rains of April. A few weeks later the crowning of the May Queen will take place amid __?__ displays of __?__ decorations. Joy will be __?__, and the __?__ delights of a summer in our old shack in the country will not be far off.

Adjectives

1. covert
2. fetid
3. floral
4. fragile
5. lavish
6. meager
7. prior
8. rampant
9. rustic
10. somber
11. tepid
12. turbid

1. COVERT (*KUV-ert*) . . . . hidden, secret

The prisoner shot a covert glance of recognition at the judge.
Little brother reached covertly for the jam.

2. FETID (e as in vet) . . . . . . bad-smelling, stinking

The fetid odor of the swamp spread through the night air.

3. FLORAL . . . . consisting of or pertaining to flowers

A floral tribute was presented to the aviator.
A florist raises or deals in flowers.
A florid face is red like some flowers.

What is floriculture? What are florescent trees? Do not confuse *florescent* with *fluorescent*.

4. FRAGILE . . . . easily breakable, delicate

Chinaware is very fragile.
The girl has a fragile appearance.
What is a brittle disposition?

5. LAVISH . . . . . . abundant, generous, bountiful

Uncle George is a lavish giver.
He spends money lavishly.
His unstinted (unbounded) generosity makes him very popular.

6. MEAGER . . . . scanty, scarce, sparing

They kept house on a very meager income.
The meagerness of the vegetation increased as we approached timberline.

7. PRIOR . . . . earlier, before

The old man had a prior claim to the land.
In wartime a priority (first or earlier right) on raw materials is granted to manufacturers who need them to make war goods.

8. RAMPANT . . . . prevalent, unrestrained

Disease and disorder were rampant.

The boys paraded rampantly (unrestrainedly) through the streets.

Trees were uprooted and buildings destroyed when the elephants got free and went on a rampage (reckless behavior).

9. RUSTIC . . . . countrified, unrefined, plain

His rustic behavior was amusing at first.

The rusticity (crudeness) of the furnishings offered a pleasant contrast.

City dwellers like to rusticate (live in the country) during the summer.

10. SOMBER . . . . dreary, gloomy, grave, depressing

The landscape looked somber in the November twilight.

The somberness of the scene made us feel lonely.

11. TEPID . . . . . . lukewarm, neither hot nor cold

The doctor advised tepid baths.

The tepidness of her welcome made him angry.

12. TURBID . . . . muddy, roiled

Floods make rivers turbid.

Turbidity of mind is a confused, unclear condition.

Questions

1. Find in the list three words which rhyme.
2. The first four letters of one of the words mean an incline leading from one level to another. What is it?
3. Remove the first letter from one word and it will mean *ready, willing*. What is it?
4. Remove the last letter of another and you will have a girl's name. What does it mean?
5. Look up *antecedent*. What word on the list has a similar meaning? What is its opposite?

6. What is a lion *rampant* on a coat-of-arms? a lion *couchant?*
7. Can you give the noun form of six of the adjectives on the first page of this unit? Look up the noun forms of four more.

FIRST PRACTICE SET

Copy the italicized words and beside each write its meaning in the sentence:

1. Fear was *rampant* among our enemies *prior* to the battle.
2. A funeral is a *somber* affair in spite of the *floral* displays.
3. The *lavish* use of soap will reduce the *fetid* odor of skunk on his hands.
4. The *turbid* water swept away our *meager* supply of food.
5. A *rustic* tune from a *covert* nook under the tree enlivened the air.
6. The *fragile* crystalware was washed in *tepid* water.

SECOND PRACTICE SET

Which of the adjectives in this unit goes best with each of the following phrases? Fill in first those you are sure about.

1. Daniel Boone
2. Uncle Sam
3. A city in ruins
4. Dishwater
5. Onion breath
6. Your allowance
7. Your older brother's birth
8. A prank you wish to play
9. A pair of glasses
10. The river in April
11. Baseball enthusiasm in May
12. May as a month

SPELLING INTERLUDE

GROUP I

Read the following pairs of sentences aloud several times. Try to make the differences in meaning clear by your reading.

1. They were *also* sorry. They were all so sorry.
2. We were *almost* happy. We were all most happy.
3. You were *already* outside. You were all ready outside.
4. Scouts are *always* prepared. Scouts are in all ways prepared.
5. Come, *although* you were not invited. Come all, though you were not invited.
6. We are *altogether* satisfied. We are all together satisfied.
7. . . . . Everything is all right.

Write sentences using each italicized word correctly.

GROUP II

Read each of the following columns several times, preferably over a period of two or three days. Exaggerate the pronunciation of each word, especially the final syllable.

central	moral	barrel	repel
equal	normal	cancel	civil
federal	oral	chapel	devil
funeral	physical	expel	evil
general	practical	jewel(ry)	pencil
internal	principal	label	stencil
interval	rival	marvel	until
liberal (generous)	royal	model	
local	rural	Noel	control
loyal	signal	novel	patrol
medal (ornament)	total	parallel	pistol
medical	universal	parcel	
mental	vital	rebel	luxury

EXERCISES

1. Which words contain a double letter?
2. Add *-ly* to each adjective in the lists above and write down the result. (Consider *rival, parallel,* and *novel* as nouns.)
3. Write, if you can, the adjective *-al* form of *crime, critic, economy, electric, fate, form, instrument* (music), *mechanic, music, ornament, nation, nature, politic, technic.*
4. The following have adjectives that end in *-ial.* How many can you do? Two are tricky. Use the dictionary, if necessary, to get each one right: *artifice, commerce, essence, finance, office, part, substance.* How do you explain the *i?*

GROUP III

Review the following nouns and their plurals. Can you discover or recall why some plurals end in *-ys* and some in *-ies?*

baby	babies	jury	juries
country	countries	monkey	monkeys
enemy	enemies	study	studies
factory	factories	turkey	turkeys
galley	galleys	valley	valleys

Write the plural of *alley, apology, battery, colony, company, copy, duty, facility, factory, family, fancy, grocery, gallery, inquiry, pony, quality, quantity, society, supply, testimony, theory, treaty, turnkey.* What is the plural of *banjo, mosquito, formula, memorandum, Negro, potato, scarf, tomato, volcano?*

SENTENCES FOR PRACTICE

Write the following sentences from dictation:

1. We were all ready to cancel the order for supplies.
2. It is vitally important that the principal valleys be open to commercial activity.
3. The stenciled lines are almost parallel.
4. Bring pencils to chapel and also the parcels to send abroad.
5. The factories in which Negroes work will be studied.

FAIRLY FAMILIAR VERBS

How?

Which of the words at the right would you
use to obtain:

F F V's

1. A fire?
2. A larger allowance?
3. More school spirit?
4. A wild bird for a pet?
5. A foolish face?

1. accede
2. allure
3. avow
4. congest
5. distort
6. entreat
7. evade
8. exempt
9. exploit
10. ignite
11. incite
12. revere

FAIRLY FAMILIAR VERBS—STUDY GUIDE

1. ACCEDE (to) . . . . . . **to comply (with), agree**

The police chief will accede to the mayor's request.

Do you have access (means of approach) to the president of the company?

Other *yes* words: *affirm, assent, concur, acquiesce.*

2. ALLURE . . . . **to attract, tempt, entice**

Cheese allures a mouse.

Candy has great allurement for children.

"If sinners entice thee, consent thou not."

No enticement will induce him to betray a trust.

3. AVOW . . . . **to declare or assert openly**

Dad is an avowed Republican.

The candidate will make a frank avowal of his principles.

Opposite: *disavow, disavowal.*

4. CONGEST . . . . **to overcrowd**

Vast throngs congest the stores at Christmas time.

Traffic congestion is an increasing problem.

5. DISTORT . . . . . . **to twist, warp, misrepresent**

Pain had distorted her face.

The speaker distorts the facts.

Modern telephones reduce voice distortion.

6. ENTREAT . . . . **to beg, beseech**

"Entreat me not to leave thee."

Her entreaties persuaded him finally.

"Grant if you can my petition," she implored.

See *implore, supplicate, importune, petition.*

7. EVADE . . . . . . **to avoid, slip away from, elude**

The burglar thinks he can evade the police.

Evasion proved more difficult than he expected.

The witness gave an evasive answer.

8. EXEMPT . . to excuse, release from (a duty to which others are subject)

The law exempts churches from taxation.

The man requested exemption from jury duty.

A clergyman is exempt from military service.

9. EXPLOIT . . . . . to use selfishly or for undue profit

The laws forbid industries to exploit children.

Labor unions oppose exploitation of workers.

The story is about the exploits (deeds, adventures) of Robin Hood.

10. IGNITE . . . . to set afire, kindle

A spark may ignite a forest.

The ignition (spark-furnishing) system in the car was disabled by a snowflake.

11. INCITE . . . . to arouse, stir up

The French tried to incite the Indians to revolt.

Bribes were one means of incitement.

Compare *actuate, impel, spur.*

12. REVERE . . . . to respect or worship

Most Americans revere Abraham Lincoln.

They express their reverence on February 12.

The boy learned to be reverent in church.

Questions

1. List five words that rhyme with *distort.*
2. Change one letter in *allure* to form a word meaning *make a reference to.*
3. Change one letter in *congest* and you will have a struggle.
4. Can you find two or three words that rhyme with *exempt?* with *incite?* with *accede?* Watch spelling.
5. Change one letter of *revere* and it will become harsh or drastic.
6. What is the opposite of *accessible, alluring, congested, distorted, ignited, revered?*

FIRST PRACTICE SET

Copy the italicized words and beside each write its meaning in the sentence:

1. The Senator will *accede* to her plea and take the blame because he is *exempt* from arrest.
2. He *entreats* her not to think him an *avowed* enemy.
3. Did you *distort* your features to *incite* a burst of laughter?
4. Football *allures* men because millions *revere* a good player.
5. Do colleges *exploit* football players?
6. You cannot *evade* the fact that the poorer districts are *congested*.
7. It is dangerous to *ignite* kerosene.

SECOND PRACTICE SET

What word from the unit fits best into each blank?

The company __?__s its employees not to __?__ the entrance at closing time. The employees will __?__ to the request that they work an extra hour on Mondays, but they will not permit the company to __?__ them. Longer hours every day might __?__ the anger of union officers, who would then __?__ the employees to strike even though they all __?__ the president of the company.

The union leader's face __?__s at the idea of __?__ing anyone from paying dues. Even though the idea __?__s him in some ways, he __?__s his dislike for it, and he always __?__s the proposal when it comes up.

THE ANIMAL KINGDOM

Superlatives

Of the words at the right:

1. Which is the best pet?
2. Which is the most useful?
3. Which is the largest?
4. Which is the wildest?
5. Which is the most dangerous?

● *How many of the words can you find in the illustration above?*

Mostly Animals

1. fawn
2. foal
3. mongrel
4. plumage
5. rodent
6. simian
7. swine
8. talon
9. termite
10. vermin
11. viper
12. weasel

THE ANIMAL KINGDOM—STUDY GUIDE

1. FAWN . . . . . . **a yearling deer (buck or doe)**

She was as shy and graceful as a fawn.

She had fawn-colored hair.

The dog fawns (makes a fond display) upon his master when he gets home at night.

A gazelle is a kind of antelope, very swift, famed for its lustrous eyes. What is a stag? What is venison?

Note: A buck is male, a doe female.

2. FOAL . . . . **colt or filly**

This pony is the foal of a race horse.

Mares foal in the spring. A filly is a female colt.

What is a paddock? a corral? a stallion?

3. MONGREL . . . . **of mixed strain, not thoroughbred**

Most dogs are mongrels.

The man is a mongrel (a mixture of good and bad qualities), but his wife is a thoroughbred.

What is a pooch? a mutt?

How many dog varieties can you identify?

4. PLUMAGE . . . . **feathers of a bird**

The cardinal bird has red plumage.

Tropical birds have bright plumage.

5. RODENT (*ROH-dent*) . . . . **small, gnawing animal**

The grain must be protected from rodents.

Beavers, squirrels, and rabbits belong to the rodent family as well as rats and mice.

Hamsters (rat-like rodents) are used in laboratories.

6. SIMIAN . . **monkey or ape (especially man-like type)**

A simian escaped from the zoo.

Children are fond of simian antics.

Can you describe a cheetah? a gorilla? a chimpanzee? an orangutan? a baboon?

7. SWINE . . . . **hog(s)**

The swine rushed into the sea.

The thief had a swinish appearance.

So did Circe's guests.

Eumaeus was a swineherd in Homer's *Odyssey*.

Compare *boar*, male swine; *sow* (pronounced like *plow*), mature female hog. See *porcine*. Can you explain?

8. TALON . . . . . **claw (especially of bird of prey)**

The hawk seized a duckling in its talons.

Human hands are sometimes used like talons.

9. TERMITE . . . . **antlike insect which eats away wood**

The underpinning of the house was weakened by termites.

In what way were the Nazis like termites?

10. VERMIN . . **ugly, harmful creatures (such as rats, lice, bedbugs)**

The first task was to rid the house of vermin.

Bubonic plague is a verminous (vermin-caused) disease.

11. VIPER . . . . **a kind of poisonous snake**

The speaker called his enemies vipers.

"The sucking child shall play on the hole of the asp" (a kind of viper).

The basilisk was a mythical serpent or dragon whose breath or look would kill.

Query: How many kinds of deadly snakes can you name?

12. WEASEL . . **a slender animal that destroys many mice, rats, and birds**

The weasel can crawl into very small places.

"Weasel" words are tricky words that can mean almost anything.

Compare *ferret*. A ferret is a kind of weasel used to drive larger animals out of their holes; hence the expression "to ferret out a mystery."

Questions

1. What is a heifer? a steer? kine? veal? a ram? a mule? a mongoose? a falcon? a cony (daman)? a saurian? a chameleon? a snipe? a cicada?
2. What is the difference between an alligator and a crocodile?
3. How many words ending in *–oal* can you list besides *foal?*
4. Remove a letter from *weasel* and get something an artist uses.
5. What does "playing possum" mean? (See *opossum*.)

FIRST PRACTICE SET

Copy the italicized words and beside each write its meaning in the sentence:

1. A bird with black *plumage* and large *talons* flew over.
2. A startled *fawn* saw a *foal* approaching.
3. Gases which destroy most *vermin* are not effective against *termites*.
4. *Weasels* kill poultry and the smaller *rodents*.
5. *Mongrel* dogs often look somewhat like wild *swine*.
6. *Simians* are sometimes killed by *vipers*.

SECOND PRACTICE SET

On your paper write the numbers 1 through 11 and beside each write the word which best fits each of these descriptive phrases:

1. The snaky one
2. The rodent destroyer
3. The most "human" one
4. The gentlest ones (two words)
5. The mixed-up one
6. The wood-eating one
7. The feathered word
8. The edible ones (two words)
9. The plaguy ones (two words)
10. The grasping one
11. The gnawing one

SOME FAMILIES ARE LARGE

The number of words in the *Mercy* family is amazing:

mercy — merciful — mercifully — mercifulness —
unmerciful — merciless — mercilessly, mercilessness, and so on.

Many common words come from large families, and each member of the family is sometimes a help in saying exactly what one wants to say — without long pauses, delays, or detours.

GROUP I

Copy the guide words and fill in each missing word:

Noun	Adjective	Adverb	Noun
1. __?__	awful	__?__	__?__
2. skill	__?__	__?__	__?__
3. __?__	__?__	__?__	trustfulness
4. __?__	__?__	willfully	__?__

Questions

1. What happened to the *e* in No. 1?
2. Make a similar table with *beauty, bounty, delight, dread, duty, fancy, plenty, regret,* and *respect* in the first column.
3. What is the opposite of the adjective for *skill, trustfulness, duty,* and *respect?*
4. What form of the word *trust* do you find in a college or church? a prison? What *–ful* word means *shy? thankful?*

GROUP II

Copy the guide words below on your paper, and fill each blank:

Noun	Adjective	Adverb	Noun
1. defense	__?__	__?__	__?__
2. __?__ (luck)	hapless	__?__	__?__
3. __?__	__?__	senselessly	__?__
4. __?__	__?__	__?__	witlessness

GROUP III

Many words, like *mercy*, have both *–fulness* and *–lessness*. Copy the following table, filling each blank as you do so.

1. care	_ _ ? _ _	_ _ ? _ _	_ _ ? _ _	_ _ ? _ _
2. _ _ ? _ _	fearless	_ _ ? _ _	_ _ ? _ _	_ _ ? _ _
3. _ _ ? _ _	_ _ ? _ _	joylessly	_ _ ? _ _	_ _ ? _ _
4. _ _ ? _ _	_ _ ? _ _	_ _ ? _ _	pitiful	_ _ ? _ _
5. _ _ ? _ _	_ _ ? _ _	_ _ ? _ _	_ _ ? _ _	tactfully

Make lines for *cheer, doubt, faith, help, hope, pain, sin,* and *soul.*

GROUP IV

Make an Ish family of *ghoul* (page 28), *clan,* and *style.*

Ishness isn't too popular, but it runs in some families. Can you place it in the following? (If you are not doing the exercise orally, copy the table on your paper. Do not write in this book.)

1. fool	_ _ ? _ _	_ _ ? _ _	_ _ ? _ _
2. _ _ ? _ _	girlish	_ _ ? _ _	_ _ ? _ _
3. _ _ ? _ _	_ _ ? _ _	mannishly	_ _ ? _ _
4. _ _ ? _ _	_ _ ? _ _	_ _ ? _ _	peevishness

WORD–BUILDING EXERCISE

For each blank write the most suitable form of the word in parentheses. Watch spelling.

1. The thief took advantage of the girl's _ _ ? _ _ (no defense).
2. Elaine was stubborn and _ _ ? _ _ (will).
3. George Washington is famous for his _ _ ? _ _ (truth).
4. The man failed because of his _ _ ? _ _ (no tact).
5. His _ _ ? _ _ (peeve) makes him unpopular.
6. The _ _ ? _ _ (plenty) of supplies was encouraging.
7. Hubert is _ _ ? _ _ (clan) and unsociable.
8. The explorer's _ _ ? _ _ (no fear) was much admired.
9. Her income was _ _ ? _ _ (pity) small.
10. The account was highly _ _ ? _ _ (fancy).

VARIED VERBS

A Mystery

Can you supply for each blank a word from the list at the right?

Something began to __?__ in the waste basket. Our interest in our lessons suddenly __?__d. The teacher was __?__d at first. She sent for the janitor, who __?__d into the room as we marched out, __?__ing because it was cold outside.

Verbs

1. accrue
2. baffle
3. chasten
4. clamor
5. cower
6. dwindle
7. garble
8. hamper
9. smolder
10. sojourn
11. stalk
12. swathe

VARIED VERBS—STUDY GUIDE

1. ACCRUE . . . . to accumulate, increase

Interest accrues at the rate of three per cent.

The accrual on the investment amounted to six hundred dollars a year.

2. BAFFLE . . . . to perplex, foil, balk

This case will baffle the police.

Their state of bafflement may last for months.

A balky car often baffles its owner.

3. CHASTEN . . . to punish, discipline, purify, refine (by suffering)

Birch rods were used to chasten wayward children.

The illness had a chastening effect.

Compare *chaste* (page 22).

4. CLAMOR . . . to cry or complain noisily, to raise an outcry

Starving men clamor for food at first.

The strikers began to clamor for action.

The clamor for equal rights continued.

A clamorous throng gathered.

5. COWER . . . . to shrink (quivering)

The little dog cowers when a big dog comes near.

The mouse was "a wee, cowering, timorous beastie."

A quavering voice is unsteady, usually from cold, illness, fear, or age.

Compare *wince* (page 9) and *cringe* (page 12).

6. DWINDLE . . . . to decrease, diminish, waste away

Will our Indian population continue to dwindle?

Our 15-point lead in the game soon dwindled to three points.

Compare *wane* (page 13).

---

7. GARBLE . . . . to mix up, twist, mutilate

The newspaper account was badly garbled.

Her version of the story was garbled.

Note: *Distortion* (page 56) suggests intentional twisting, but garbling is usually careless or accidental.

8. HAMPER . . . . . . to hinder, obstruct, impede

Rain hampers our work on the new house.

Strikes often impede production.

George's desire to play ball was stymied (blocked) by his leg injury.

9. SMOLDER . . . . to burn slowly

A log will smolder (without flame) on the hearth for hours.

There was a look of smoldering rage in his eyes.

10. SOJOURN . . . . to dwell, stay

They decided to sojourn for a while on the edge of the desert.

Their sojourn (brief residence) in Illinois was eventful.

11. STALK . . to walk (or approach) stealthily or haughtily

Death and disease stalked unchecked.

Hunters stalk their game in the forest.

12. SWATHE . . . . to wrap or envelop

The burned man was swathed in bandages.

The heiress was swathed in furs.

The cyclone cut a swath (path like that of a sickle) through the town.

Questions

1. Change a letter in *baffle* and get a kind of lottery.
2. Drop a letter in *chasten* and get *hurry*.
3. Change a letter in *clamor* and get *attractiveness*.
4. Change a letter in *cower* and have *one who arrives*.
5. Change the first two letters of *dwindle* and have a *reel*.

6. How many different words can you get by changing the first letter of *hamper?*
7. List words that rhyme with *smolder.*
8. Find a unit already studied which contains several pairs like *swathe* and *swath.*

FIRST PRACTICE SET

Copy the italicized words and beside each write its meaning in the sentence:

1. His displeasure *smolders* and *accrues* until there is an explosion.
2. Poisonous gas in the mine shaft *hampers* and *baffles* the rescue party.
3. Danger *stalks* abroad, courage *dwindles,* and thousands *cower* in fear.
4. *Swathed* in woolen clothing, he was ready to *sojourn* on an Arctic island.
5. The *clamor* about *garbled* facts had a *chastening* effect on the editor.

SECOND PRACTICE SET

What is each of the following most likely to do, in terms of the words in this unit?

1. Overheated wood? __?__
2. Hungry children? __?__ for food.
3. Explorers and travelers? __?__ a few days.
4. Muddy roads? __?__
5. Village gossips? __?__ the facts.
6. Men condemned to die? __?__
7. An angry man? __?__ out of the house.
8. A nurse to a burned arm? __?__ it in dressings.
9. Hailstones in July? __?__
10. Interest in government bonds? __?__
11. A strange new illness? __?__ the doctors.
12. Loss of one's allowance? __?__ the culprit.

ADVENTURE WORDS

Where?

Nouns

1. Where would you find a quagmire?
2. What would you do with a turret?
3. What is a scion?
4. Who would use a bludgeon?
5. Where would you put a rampart?

1. bludgeon
2. cult
3. defile
4. ember
5. grace
6. prowess
7. quagmire
8. rampart
9. scion
10. sinew
11. turret
12. vigil

ADVENTURE WORDS—STUDY GUIDE

1. **BLUDGEON** . . . . **a thick club**
   The man was felled with a bludgeon.
   The police bludgeoned (forced) him into yielding.

2. **CULT** . . . . **a religious system, a sect**
   Animal worship is an African cult.
   Some make a cult of hero worship.
   The rites (religious ceremony or a ritual) were held Thursday.

3. **DEFILE (de-FILE)** . . . . **a narrow chasm or passage**
   The men marched through a defile in the mountainside.
   A gorge or glen, if narrow enough, is a defile. So is a canyon.

4. **EMBER** . . **glowing coal or fuel fragment (among ashes)**
   Nothing was left of the fire but embers.

5. **GRACE** . . . . **(1) favor, mercy, kindness**
                           (2) attractiveness, charm
   By the grace of God, he escaped injury.
   Her airy grace captivated everybody.
   Compare *disgrace, scapegrace, gracious.*

6. **PROWESS** . . . . **superior bravery, skill**
   Have you heard of Custer's prowess as an Indian fighter?

7. **QUAGMIRE** . . . . . **soft, muddy ground, a bog**
   The covered wagon was stuck in a quagmire.
   Politics is sometimes called a quagmire.

8. **RAMPART** . . . . **a barrier or bulwark**
   The ramparts of the fortress were guarded fiercely.
   An embankment may be one form of rampart.

9. SCION (*SIGH-un*) . . . . descendant, heir

The story is about a scion of the house of Rothschild.

Note: The word means *sprout* or *bud*, literally.

10. SINEW . . . . . strength, in a muscular sense; tendon

He had the sinews of an ox.

The blacksmith has a sinewy arm.

11. TURRET . . . . a small tower

The turrets of the castle were visible in the distance.

The gun turrets were fully manned.

12. VIGIL . . . . wakeful watching

The vigil at the bedside lasted all night.

Vigilance (watchfulness) is especially necessary in enemy country.

"Be vigilant [watchful] at all times," the speaker warned.

Questions

1. Change one letter of *cult* and get *sharp, almost rude* (page 4).
2. What meaning does *defile* have as a verb?
3. What adjective does *bludgeon* suggest to you? Can you think of other words ending in *–geon?*
4. Change one letter of *sinew* and get a two-word exclamation pertaining to novelty.
5. Add three letters to *ember* and get a month. Do it again.

FIRST PRACTICE SET

Copy the italicized words and beside each write its meaning in the sentence:

The Indian of great *prowess* and *sinew* waited in the *defile* with a *bludgeon*. He belonged to a fire-worshiping *cult* which told fortunes by watching *embers*. His horse had been lost in the *quagmire* near the *ramparts* of an English fort while he was maintaining a *vigil* for his chieftain. An English officer, the *scion* of a wealthy British family, was watching anxiously from a *turret* of the fort while he invoked Divine *grace*.

SECOND PRACTICE SET

Which word on the list is most likely to be connected with each of the following? Fill in first the ones you are sure about, and rearrange as necessary.

1. Athlete
2. Doctor (on a night case)
3. Colorado
4. Florida Everglades
5. Circus strongman
6. Castle walls

7. Fireplace
8. May Queen
9. African voodoo
10. A killer
11. Our national anthem
12. Son of a famous family

ITSY–BITSY *ITY*

"Are you sure?" the reporter asked.
"Certain," she replied.

Her knowing without any doubt about the depth of the pool saved everybody a lot of trouble.

. . . .

What word could be used in place of *knowing without any doubt* — assuming that she *was* certain and not merely positive about it? The word is *certainty*. Noun, verb, or adverb forms of common adjectives will often save needless, awkward, time-wasting verbal detours. Knowing them is important in acquiring a good command of English.

Sometimes you need only to add –*y* or –*ty* to an adjective to get a noun. More often Itsy-Bitsy *Ity* is required. Frequently the final *e* on the adjective becomes the *i* of *Ity*. In many cases the spelling changes. What word goes in each blank below?

Adjective	*Adverb*	*Noun*
1. __?__	certainly	__?__
2. __?__		difficulty
3. honest	__?__	__?__
1. __?__	absurdly	__?__
2. minor		__?__
3. __?__	__?__	personality
4. public	__?__	__?__
5. __?__	__?__	solemnity
1. curious	__?__	__?__
2. __?__	humbly	__?__
3. __?__	__?__	profanity
1. able	__?__	__?__
2. __?__	__?__	probability

Questions

1. Write the adverb and noun forms of *acid, active, electric, equal, false, fatal, fraternal, immense, modern, modest, native, necessary, original, possible, real, reliable, responsible, sane, secure, severe, simple, sincere, vain.* What is the *–ity* noun for *captive? liable? major? prior* (page 50)? *senior?*

2. List five familiar prefix-formed opposites from the adjectives in the table on the preceding page and ten from the words in question 1.

3. Under what conditions does a double *l* appear in the adverbs above? Note that the final *e* of an adjective is usually *not* dropped in forming the adverb.

WORD–BUILDING EXERCISE

For each blank supply the correct form of the word in parentheses:

1. "__?__ [vain] of __?__ [vain-plu.], all is __?__ [vain]."
2. Railroad men have __?__ (senior) in their jobs.
3. The __?__ (not probable) of the tale was apparent.
4. The Labor Day weekend brought many __?__ (fatal-plu.).
5. A person who is __?__ (not responsible) is not __?__ (necessary) __?__ (not sane).
6. It is __?__ (not noble) to be __?__ (not sincere).
7. The contractor was worried by the __?__ (immense) of the task and the __?__ (not certain) about obtaining materials.
8. The __?__ (severe) of the storm created a feeling of __?__ (solemn).
9. His __?__ (humble) is sometimes mistaken for __?__ (not able).
10. Treating a man __?__ (fraternal) gives him a feeling of __?__ (secure).

US AND US—NESS

Another word pastime consists of collecting families that belong to a tribe known as the –*ous*sians and pronounced *ussians* but in no way related to the Russians. Can you supply the word which goes into each blank in the following and spell it correctly?

Base Word	Adjective — Adverb	Noun
1. danger	_ _ ? _ _	_ _ ? _ _
2. humor	_ _ ? _ _	_ _ ? _ _
3. _ _ ? _ _	perilous (ly)	_ _ ? _ _
4. _ _ ? _ _	poisonous (ly)	_ _ ? _ _
5. _ _ ? _ _	_ _ ? _ _	vigorousness
6. _ _ ? _ _	_ _ ? _ _	villainousness

The following have slight variations in spelling. Be careful as you write down the guide words and fill the blanks:

1. _ _ ? _ _	_ _ ? _ _	famousness
2. _ _ ? _ _	_ _ ? _ _	gloriousness
3. _ _ ? _ _	gracious (ly)	_ _ ? _ _
4. harmony	_ _ ? _ _	_ _ ? _ _

Questions

1. What are the spelling changes? The one in *gracious* is needed to keep the *c* soft.
2. Expand each of the following into a line like the ones above, using the dictionary if you are doubtful: *ambition, bile, continue, curiosity, envy, fury, industry, injury, marvel, mystery, nerve, prosper, ridicule, space, study, treachery, vary.* Bile behaves like *grace* even though it does not have a *c*. Write the opposite of four of the adjective forms.
3. Write a line for *advantage* and *courage* remembering that a *g* needs its *e* to keep it soft. Do *conscience*, remembering *essential* on page 54. What is the –*ous* adjective of *anxiety? courtesy? generosity?*
4. What –*ous* word means *before? delightful to taste? huge?*
5. What is the opposite of *gracious? glorious? harmony?*

A FINAL –FLING

Write the word which goes in each blank:

1. __?__	sparkled	__?__
2. __?__	__?__	tackling
3. tickle	__?__	__?__

Construct a similar table from *grumbling, handle, resembled, ruffling, sampling, stumbling, tangled, trembling, trifled,* and *tumble.*

Write the *–le* word for the name of a book; a finger cover used in sewing; a place of worship; plenty large enough; a write-up in a magazine. Watch spelling.

WORD–BUILDING EXERCISE

Write for each blank the correct form of the word in parentheses:

1. Murder is a __?__ (villain) crime.
2. "I won't do it!" is an __?__ (not grace) remark.
3. The __?__ (poison) of the drug is so great that one drop will kill a man.
4. The __?__ (space) of the new library pleased us.
5. An attack of __?__ (bile) kept him out of school.
6. The letter was a __?__ (humor) account of our trip.
7. __?__ (not harmony) sounds are very disturbing.
8. The runner was __?__ (tackle) behind the goal line.
9. __?__ (study) habits will help you in college.
10. The new method proved quite __?__ (advantage).

THE SEA AND SHIPS

Seascape

Which word, from the list at the right, goes in each blank?

1. A __?__ was better than a __?__ for an ocean voyage because it was larger.
2. A __?__ usually indicates danger.
3. __?__ is foam and __?__ is wreckage.
4. Which is the larboard side of a ship?

● *How many of the base words can you find in the illustration above?*

Base Words
1. bight
2. buoy
3. doldrums
4. flotsam
5. frigate
6. galleon
7. keel
8. larboard
9. lee(ward)
10. mariner
11. spume
12. tarpaulin

1. **BIGHT** . . . . **loop, bend, bay**

   A bight in the line was slipped over the mooring post.
   The boat was anchored near a bight in the coastline.

2. **BUOY (BOO-ey)** . . . . **a floating marker**

   The lighted buoy marks a shoal (shallow area) not far from
   the channel.
   A buoyant person floats lightly on the surface of things.
   Cork has unusual buoyancy.

3. **DOLDRUMS (DOLL-drums)** . . **very calm area (near the
   equator)**

   Once in the doldrums, it was difficult for a sailing ship to get
   out again.
   A person who feels listless and tired is said to be in the doldrums.

4. **FLOTSAM (pronounced like *plot*)** . . **drifting wreckage
   (and other floating refuse)**

   What looked like a rock was merely flotsam.
   Jetsam is goods tossed overboard to lighten a ship in trouble.

5. **FRIGATE** . . . . **a light (war)ship**

   A frigate is larger than a *corvette* and smaller than a destroyer.
   A frigate was once a ship propelled by sails *and* oars.

6. **GALLEON** . . **a sailing vessel of the time of Columbus**

   The Spanish galleon had four decks.

7. **KEEL** . . . . **bottom centerpiece of a ship**

   Laying the keel is the first step in building a ship.
   A pirate ship would sometimes keelhaul a victim — that is,
   drag him under the keel of the ship.

8. **LARBOARD** . . left or port side (as one faces the prow)

An island was sighted to larboard.

The setting sun was just touching the horizon to starboard (right side).

9. **LEE(WARD)** . . side away from the wind (or protected from it)

The leeward deck was already awash.

The windward side is the side toward the wind.

The flotsam was alee.

Jason stands in the lee (protection) of the teacher's favor.

10. **MARINER** . . . . . . sailor, one who goes to sea

My mariners are brave, devoted men.

We shall make a study of marine (sea) life.

11. **SPUME** (rhymes with *fume*) . . . . . . foam, spray

Sea spume makes one's hands sticky.

12. **TARPAULIN** . . . . waterproofed canvas

The hatches were covered with tarpaulins.

The sailors wore tarpaulin coats and hats.

Questions

1. How many words ending in *–ight* can you list?
2. Change a letter of *buoy* and get a word meaning *to put underground*.
3. What word rhymes with *doldrums* and means *temper spasms?*
4. Can you find five boys' names in the base words of this unit?
5. Can you think of two-syllable words which rhyme with *spume?*
6. How deep is a fathom? What nautical terms can you add to this list? Perhaps you would like to make a collection. See Part Two, Unit 18, pages 157–160, if you would like to do another unit on ships right away.

FIRST PRACTICE SET

Copy the italicized words and beside each write its meaning in the sentence:

1. The *buoy* was hidden by *flotsam*.
2. A *frigate* had advantages over a *galleon* in the *doldrums*.
3. A wise *mariner* keeps in the *lee* of an island.
4. A *tarpaulin* is a protection against the salty *spume*.
5. He headed for the *bight* to *larboard* and hoped that the *keel* would not touch bottom.

SECOND PRACTICE SET

Can you fill each blank correctly with a word from the unit without repeating?

A __?__ was becalmed in the __?__. Its crew could hear the bell on a distant __?__. A __?__ approached from the __?__ on the __?__ side, put out a line (with a __?__ in it), and towed the helpless ship. No __?__ came over the side to wet the __?__s because there was so little wind; and because of the heat they wore no __?__ clothing. The __?__s of the ships cut silently through the water, and only patches of __?__ from a wrecked ship could be seen on the smooth surface.

A SEA STORY

Write a brief story about an adventure at sea, using several of the words in this unit.

UPLAND AND LOWLAND

Sound, Shape, and Smell

Of the words at the right:

1. Which one makes the most noise?
2. Which two are often round and smooth?
3. Which are likely to have a pleasant odor?
4. Which is the most extensive?
5. Which are dangerous? In what ways?

Base Words

1. avalanche
2. boulder
3. cataract
4. chasm
5. cove
6. dell
7. firmament
8. foliage
9. glade
10. gloaming
11. knoll
12. morass

1. AVALANCHE . . . a sliding or falling mass, landslide

An avalanche destroyed the house on the mountainside.

The button factory received an avalanche of orders.

2. BOULDER . . a large rock (detached, water smooth or weatherworn)

He sat on a boulder and ate his lunch.

3. CATARACT . . . . waterfall (usually a large one)

The noise of the cataract is thunderous.

A cataract on the eye makes the lens whitish and hard to see through like the white foam of a waterfall.

A *cascade* is a small or rippling waterfall (or series) or something resembling one in appearance.

4. CHASM (*cazm*) . . . . . . a gap, gorge, or abyss

The chasm has great scenic beauty.

There was a chasm between the father and his son.

Other *chasm* words: *cleft, canyon, fissure, rift.*
Compare *defile*, page 70.

5. COVE . . . . sheltered nook or inlet

He headed his canoe into a cove nearby.

She dreamed of islands with lazy lagoons (little ponds or lakes).

6. DELL . . . . . . a glen or small, secluded valley

The hikers spent the morning in a mossy dell.

A glen is a delightful place to spend a summer day.

7. FIRMAMENT . . . . the sky or heavens

"The spacious firmament on high!" they sang.

She was the only star in his firmament.

8. FOLIAGE . . . . . leafy growth of trees and plants (including flowers)

The foliage is fresh and green in May.
No foliage grows in the desert.

9. GLADE . . grassy plot in a forest (sometimes swampy)

The hunter crossed a quiet, sunny glade.
The Everglades is a swampy area.

10. GLOAMING . . . . . . dusk, twilight, sundown

"Roaming in the Gloaming" is a lively song.
The afterglow is the final stage of twilight when the sun has
gone down but its light is reflected from the clouds.

11. KNOLL . . . . a mound or hillock

"Round Top" is a knoll on the Gettysburg battlefield.

12. MORASS (mo-RASS) . . . . . . swamp or marsh

The travelers were lost in a morass.
A savage's mind is a morass of ignorance.

Review *quagmire*, page 70.

Questions

1. Can you think of a girl's name that rhymes with *avalanche?*
   It means *white.*
2. Change a letter of *boulder* and get *one who shapes clay or
   plastics* (alternative spelling).
3. CATA– in *cataract* means *down.* What other words begin
   with *cata–?* See dictionary.
4. What word used in connection with blood rhymes perfectly
   with chasm if you remove the final letter?
5. Change two letters of *firmament* to one letter and get *war
   equipment.*
6. What word meaning *lots of words* has the same four letters at
   the end as *foliage?*
7. List five or six words which begin with *kn.*
8. Change two letters of *morass* and get a word meaning *to annoy.*

FIRST PRACTICE SET

Copy the italicized words and beside each write its meaning in the sentence:

1. The train was wrecked by a *boulder* and buried by an *avalanche*.
2. The *cataract* had cut a *chasm* in the hillside.
3. We hid the boat in a *cove* and explored a *dell* not far away.
4. The *firmament* seems to change in the *gloaming*.
5. The *foliage* in the *glade* was luxuriant.
6. From a *knoll* we could see that the glade merged into a dank *morass*.

SECOND PRACTICE SET

Which word in the unit is best described by each of the following phrases?

1. Deep and narrow
2. Miniature mountain
3. Studded with stars
4. Painful to toes
5. Crushing and crunchy
6. Close to bed time
7. Refuge for canoes
8. Noisy and misty
9. Found in a forest
10. Rampant in Maytime
11. Damp and unwholesome
12. Damp but refreshing

BASHFUL LETTERS

Many words contain a letter that is timid and shy. It never speaks up, and it never says much of anything. One almost forgets that it is there. Some words, like *knowledge,* have three or four silent letters. Study each of the following groups. Pronounce the words carefully. Mispronounce them so as to make the shy letters speak out. Divide the longer words into syllables. Write sentences containing at least one word from each group.

B words: *debt, debtor, dumb, tomb, womb*

G words: *campaign, foreign, foreigner, gnash, gnome* (page 28), *resign, sign(ed), strength*

H words: *ache, anchor, architect, character(istic), chasm* (page 82), *chemical, chemistry, chord, ghost, orchestra, rheumatism, rhythm, stomach*

GH words: *bough, height, high(ly), naughty, neigh, neighbor(ing), right, straight, thorough, twilight*

L words: *balm, calm, folks, palm, psalm, stalk* (page 67)

MN words: *autumn, column, condemn, hymn, solemn.* Once there was an extra syllable at the end — *autumn* was *autumnus,* for example.

U words: *guarantee, guard, guardian, guest, source*

UE words: *avenue, bouquet, catalogue, conquer, continue, due, issue, league, pursue, rescue, revenue, value, virtue.* Which letter is silent in each word?

Note: One UI and several UE words not having a silent letter should be included at this point: *banquet, duel, fuel, request, exquisite.* What letter always follows *q?*

UI words: *biscuit, bruise, building, circuit, disguise, guile, guise* (page 18), *juicy, pursuit, suit.* Sometimes the *i* is silent, sometimes the *u.*

Tricky words: *arctic, beyond, bosom, business, ceremony, hygiene, knowledge, laughter, prairie, praise, twelfth.* Why is each one tricky?

ACTIVITIES

1. Do any words on the preceding page contain a double letter?
2. What words can you add to each of the groups?
3. Make a scramble of several groups and see whether you can sort them out again.
4. Use the words for a spell-down, if time permits.
5. What spelling difficulties have you found other than the silent or almost silent letters?
6. Make a list of all the other forms you can (adjectives, nouns, past and present verb forms, and so on) of the words in the MN or one or more of the other groups.
7. Which is the longest word containing only one vowel? Which two words on the preceding page contain no *a, e, i, o,* or *u?*

SENTENCES FOR PRACTICE

Write some or all of the following from dictation:

1. The column of troops served as a guard on the avenue.
2. The foreign orchestra has unusual rhythm.
3. The architect planned a building of great strength.
4. My neighbor rode calmly away in the twilight.
5. A guest issued forth in hot pursuit.
6. A ghost hovered over the tomb of the condemned man.
7. The naughty boy looked guileless as he ate the biscuit.
8. The fall into the chasm gave him a stomach-ache.
9. In the autumn the league paid its debts and disbanded.
10. The campaign aims at a better knowledge of hygiene.
11. Each character wore a disguise at the banquet.
12. The hymn is a psalm about the beauty of virtue.

IT'S FUNNY

Comic Relief

Can you find a word in the list at the right which fits in each blank aptly?

Animated cartoons __?__ people we all know. In some ways they __?__ animals quite well. They are full of __?__ and __?__. Many of them contain a __?__ which gets one of the characters into trouble. Often there is a __?__ of a nursery rhyme.

Verb-Nouns
1. banter
2. burlesque
3. caper
4. gambol
5. jest
6. mimic

Nouns
1. buffoon
2. drivel
3. farce
4. frivolity
5. hoax
6. parody

1. BANTER . . to make fun of (in a good-natured manner)

Sue likes to banter her brother about his girl friends.
The two spent an hour in light-hearted banter yesterday.

2. BURLESQUE (*bur-LESK*) . . to mock by imitating (in an exaggerated manner)

Dick likes to burlesque his sister's behavior at a party.
His sister enjoys the burlesque too.

3. CAPER . . . . to romp, frolic, cavort

Monkeys like to caper.
Kitten capers are amusing to watch.
A playful horse cavorts gracefully.

4. GAMBOL . . . . to leap about playfully

Lambs gambol happily in the pasture.
Their gambols are joyful and carefree.

Note: *Gambol* and *caper* have about the same meaning except perhaps that capers are lighter and less dignified than gambols.

5. JEST . . . . to joke, make witty remarks

It is bad taste to jest about sacred subjects.
What radio comedian's jests do you enjoy the most?

6. MIMIC . . to imitate, usually for fun (or with humorous effect)

Dick sometimes mimics his sister's way of using the telephone. He is a skillful mimic.
Mimicry is an entertaining hobby.

Note: Mimicry is more precise and not so "broad" as burlesque.

---

1. BUFFOON . . . . a clown or jester

Uncle Herb is quite a buffoon at times.
We all enjoy his buffoonery.

Compare *harlequin*.

2. DRIVEL . . . . nonsense, silly talk, twaddle

That political speech was mostly drivel.

Note: *Drivel* literally is saliva flowing from one's mouth or the foam around a horse's bridle.

3. FARCE . . hollow or empty imitation (of the real thing)

The trial was a farce.
Life without friends would be a farce.

Note: *Farce* is also a term for a light, humorous, exaggerated play.

4. FRIVOLITY . . . . light-hearted fun

Frivolity makes a party enjoyable.
Girls are often frivolous (giddy, fond of trifling).

Note: Frivolity is gayer and not so stupid as drivel.

5. HOAX . . . something which fools, a practical joke

The telephone call was a hoax by which Dick made his sister look ridiculous.

6. PARODY . . . humorous imitation of a song or poem

Sue knows a clever parody of "Jingle Bells."
The comedian parodied Kipling's "If."

Badinage —~~female~~ small talk
Persuflage —

Questions

1. In what ways is *buffoon* like *balloon?*
2. How does *gamble* differ from *gambol* in spelling and meaning?
3. Change a letter in *caper* and go into business furnishing food at parties; change another and have a candle.
4. How many words can you get by changing a letter of *banter?* of *jest?* of *hoax?* of *drivel?*
5. Can you name two other words besides *burlesque* which end in —*esque?*

PRACTICE SET

Copy the italicized words and beside each write its meaning in the sentence:

1. Uncle Joe likes to *banter* with his nieces and *mimic* their actions but not to *caper* with them.
2. Do not *jest* about sacred matters or *burlesque* religious ceremonies.
3. The two *buffoons* added to the *frivolity* by showing how an elephant *gambols* in a china shop.
4. The campaign for longer vacations was a *farce,* and the arguments mostly *drivel.*
5. The *parody* on "John Brown's Body" is part of the *hoax.*

A FERRY DANCE

What word from this unit fits best in each blank? Fill in first the ones you are sure about and rearrange as necessary.

It __?__s a fairy dance. A fullback weighing 250 pounds __?__s across the stage, and a basketball center weighing 150 pounds who is six and a half feet tall __?__s about, making __?__ing remarks to the fullback. His __?__s amuse the audience because he is a good __?__ even though what he says is merely __?__ and not so light-hearted as __?__ really should be. The fullback recites a __?__ entitled "The Bearfoot Boy" and fixes up a little __?__ to make the tall boy bump his head. The whole act is a __?__. Neither one can dance at all, but the fullback can __?__ an elephant cleverly.

FINAL TESTS ON REGULAR UNITS

Copy the italicized words and beside each write its meaning in the sentence:

Unit 2

1. *Cull* the bad ones and do not *wince.*
2. *Doff* your jacket before you *moor* the boat.
3. *Oust* the governor if he fails to *quell* the uprising.
4. When politicians *vie,* they do not *mince* words.
5. Unless the truck *swerves,* it will *raze* the old mill.

Unit 3

1. He *loathes* stiff shoes which *chafe* his toes.
2. Try never to *cringe* in fear or *seethe* with rage.
3. He will get a *scathing* rebuke if he *singes* my coat.
4. My energy *wanes* when spring breezes *tinge* the air.
5. Efforts to *secrete* the money made us *writhe.*

Unit 5

1. He will protect his *crest* from any *breach* of honor.
2. The comment was a *gibe* in the *guise* of a friendly tip.
3. A *horde* of ants milled about the dead *drones.*
4. That *sheaf* of bills indicates a *lapse* of some kind.
5. A *wisp* of grass had caught in the *truss.*

Unit 6

1. His strength remained *intact,* but hope was *extinct.*
2. The ballet dancer is *lithe* and *chaste.*
3. *Nautical* men are fond of *terse* remarks.
4. His face was *sallow* and *ghastly.*
5. Life is *dormant* and the population *sparse* up there.

Unit 8

1. The *ballad* was about a *yeoman*.
2. A *changeling* is a creature of *fantasy*.
3. A *ghoul* crushed the *chalice* with his foot.
4. He mistook the *gnome* for a *phantom*.
5. The *parable* is about a *sorcerer*.

Unit 9

1. The *huckster* dreamed he was a *buccaneer*.
2. The *friar* told the story of the *Magi*.
3. This *pilgrim* is not a *mendicant*.
4. A mere *stripling*, he got to Africa as a *stowaway*.
5. The *vagabond* and the *urchin* became friends.

Unit 11

1. She did not *relish* having to *mingle* with slaves.
2. Try to *cherish* courage and *banish* fear.
3. *Garner* knowledge and do not *shackle* curiosity.
4. He will *foster* the plan if circumstances *warrant*.
5. He *sauntered* over when he saw the wagon *capsize*.

Unit 13

1. The *culprit* is not a *pagan*.
2. He had the *mettle* to defy the *edict*.
3. We watched the drum major wave his *baton*, and saw the *luster* of his satin shirt.
4. His sharp *profile* suggested the *rigor* of the life he led.
5. A *morsel* of cheese is the *acme* of delight for a mouse.

Unit 14

1. She is *lavish* with praise and *meager* with blame.
2. Insects were *rampant* and the kitchen *fetid*.
3. *Prior* to the war, *floral* displays were more elaborate.
4. *Rustic* manners are sometimes *somber*.
5. The bath water was *tepid* and also *turbid*.

Unit 16

1. I *entreat* you not to *distort* the truth.
2. You *avow* your defiance, yet *accede* to the demand.
3. It is better to *evade* the dangers which *allure* you.
4. To *incite* an outburst is to *ignite* a rebellion.
5. A man who *exploits* a widow does not *revere* women.

Unit 17

1. *Swine* do not have *talons*.
2. A *viper* is less destructive than a *weasel*.
3. *Termites* are much smaller than *rodents*.
4. A *mongrel* dog had a *simian* for a playmate.
5. A *fawn* and a *foal* are about the same age.

Unit 19

1. Do your savings *accrue* or *dwindle*?
2. The *fumes* hamper and the smoke *baffles* the firemen.
3. Did you *cower* or did you *stalk* out of the room?
4. Crowds *clamor* and fires *smolder* everywhere.
5. Try not to *garble* the reports of your *sojourn*.

Unit 20

1. The *bludgeon* was reduced to *embers*.
2. The *quagmire* served as a *rampart* on one side.
3. The *cult* has its shrine in a mountain *defile*.
4. Your *prowess* does credit to a *scion* of the Maxwells.
5. The guide kept his *vigil* in a *turret* of the castle.

Unit 22

1. The *keel* of the *galleon* was broken.
2. A *frigate* was sighted to *larboard*.
3. In the *doldrums* *flotsam* could be seen for miles.
4. The sailor slipped a *bight* over the *buoy*.
5. Look to *leeward*, my *mariners*!

Unit 23

1. The little *cove* almost shut out the *firmament*.
2. The *cataract* was hidden by *foliage*.
3. An *avalanche* deposited this *boulder*.
4. There is a quiet *dell* at the bottom of the *chasm*.
5. There is a *knoll* in the middle of the *morass*.

Unit 25

1. Do you like to *banter* your friends and *mimic* your elders?
2. Elephants *gambol* and comedians *jest*.
3. Puppies *caper*, and children love *frivolity*.
4. A *buffoon* likes to *burlesque* important people.
5. The *parody* made school appear to be a *farce*.

DIVISION TEST (BASE WORDS ONLY) REGULAR UNITS

Copy the italicized words and beside each write its meaning in the sentence:

1. Why not *raze* the building? Everybody *loathes* it.
2. The *jibes* of enemies made him *writhe*.
3. Once there were *hordes* of them. Now they are *extinct*.
4. Seeds lie *dormant* until the rain *seeps* in.
5. The *mendicant* saw a *phantom* hovering near.
6. The *vagabond* found himself in *shackles*.
7. The *regent* does not *relish* his responsibility.
8. The *pilgrim* was a victim of *sorcery*.
9. He traveled in the *guise* of a *friar*.
10. "Do *pixies garner* cobwebs?" she asked.
11. When we *vie*, he never *cringes*.
12. His treachery was a *ghastly breach* of honor.
13. The *culprit* could not *evade* me.
14. Life was *somber* then and full of *rigor*.
15. Nothing could *allure* him into giving up his *option*.
16. He was *meager* in his praise of *mongrels*.
17. It is *fragile*, but it is *exempt* from the tax.

18. The number of *rodents* began to *dwindle*.
19. The lamb *cowered* as the *talons* reached for it.
20. She plays in the *spume* with the *grace* of a mermaid.
21. The brush in the *defile* looked like *flotsam*.
22. He spread a *tarpaulin* between the *boulders*.
23. There was no *frivolity* while we were in the *doldrums*.
24. Fawns *gambol* in the *glade*.
25. The tale about the *morass* was a *hoax*.

DIVISION TEST—SUPPLEMENTARY WORDS IN REGULAR UNITS

Copy the italicized words in the sentences below and beside each write its meaning in the sentence:

1. He was *ostracized* because he had been a *privateer*.
2. Great Salt Lake is almost *devoid* of *marine* life.
3. The *migrant* laborer has *supple* fingers.
4. The *wizard* went on a *rampage*.
5. Do you *concede* your ignorance of *floriculture*?
6. The *vagrant's disavowal* was disregarded.
7. Would you prefer a *filly* or a *stallion* for a pet?
8. *Venison* is more of a delicacy than *veal*.
9. Do tales of the *basilisk entice* you?
10. The Indian *rites* took place in the *canyon*.

DIVISION TEST — WORD-BUILDING UNITS

Write for each blank the correct form of the key word(s) in parentheses. Spelling counts.

1. She was completely __?__ (courage gone).
2. The horse became __?__ (couldn't be managed).
3. No __?__ (acknowledge) of the __?__ (appoint) has come.
4. A cow is stolid and __?__ (doesn't get excited).
5. Let there be no __?__ (not pleasant) when I leave.
6. The __?__ (not convenient) is very great.
7. We plan to __?__ (make vacant) the house tomorrow.
8. The __?__ (quote) about __?__ (represent) is famous.

---

9. Byrd's __?__s (explore) required expert __?__ (navigate).
10. The boy's __?__ (no respect) was a sign of __?__ (fool).
11. It was ignoble to disturb __?__ (without help) women.
12. We began to realize the __?__ (no hope) of the situation.
13. He dislikes __?__ (making public) about his affairs.
14. Real __?__ (being humble) is a beautiful quality.
15. The man was __?__ (fatal) injured while __?__ (not sane).
16. Wild animals do not thrive in __?__ (captive).
17. The team went down to __?__ (not glory) defeat.
18. The __?__ (ridicule) of the idea made everyone laugh.
19. The plan of attack seems __?__ (advantage).
20. "Why are you __?__ [tremble] ?" he asked.

DIVISION TEST—SPELLING

These sentences contain more than fifty words covered in the special units of Part One. Write some or all from dictation.

1. The argument about the paste on the envelope was silly.
2. She appeared in the dining room with new clothes on.
3. The cellar is equipped with movable tubs.
4. A grammar book is less popular than a history text.
5. The dictionary is a familiar and honorable volume.
6. The operator is an obedient organizer.
7. The explorer's accusation proves him a liar.
8. She became an interior decorator after graduation.
9. The doctor submitted the plan in writing.
10. He refused the poem because it was badly written.
11. One hundred quiet freshmen are quite a mystery.
12. The fugitive had a message from the physician.
13. Will the jewelry be all right until I get back?
14. The two valleys are almost parallel.
15. She is unusually skillful at peeling potatoes.
16. The condemned man was bruised and severely burned.
17. He reached the prairie on the twelfth day.
18. We do not guarantee the remedy for stomach trouble.
19. Psalms often have an exquisite rhythm.
20. He is business manager of the building campaign.

WORD WEALTH JUNIOR

PART TWO

DO WORDS

What, in terms of the words at the right, would you do with:

Base Words

1. A bomb? __?__ it. Why?
2. A maniac? __?__ him.
3. A boy with polio? __?__ him.
4. A chocolate milk shake? __?__.
5. A war hero? __?__ him.
6. A murder clue? __?__ it.
7. A gavel? __?__ it.

1. emit
2. exhort
3. extol
4. immerse
5. indulge
6. intern
7. invoke
8. obviate
9. portray
10. ransom
11. recoil
12. rescind
13. segregate
14. verify
15. wield

● *How many of the base words can you find in the illustration above?*

DO WORDS—STUDY GUIDE

1. EMIT . . . . **to give forth, to voice**

The foghorn emits a sleepy grunt.

Soup noises are unpleasant emissions.

2. EXHORT . . . . **to urge, entreat**

"I exhort you to be patient," he pleaded.

The exhortations had no effect.

3. EXTOL (ex-*TAHL*) . . . . . **to praise, laud, glorify**

We extol the courage of George Washington.

Extolment often comes only after a hero has died.

4. IMMERSE . . . . **to dip, plunge into a fluid**

Immerse the bearing in kerosene.

What is baptism by immersion?

Are you ever immersed in a book?

Other words from the same root: *submerge, submersion, emerge.*

5. INDULGE . . . . **to yield to (a desire)**

Do you often indulge your fondness for candy?

He is thick in the middle because he indulges too often in steak dinners and gets little exercise.

An indulgent parent is one who usually lets you do what you please.

6. INTERN . . . . **to confine, imprison, detain**

Enemy aliens were interned when war broke out.

Do you know someone who was in an internment camp?

7. INVOKE . . **to call upon (for aid), make an appeal to**

The Negro invoked the protection of the police.

A chaplain will offer the invocation (opening prayer).

8. OBVIATE . . . . . **to remove, take out of the way**

A big breakfast will obviate the need of stopping for lunch.

The answer is obvious (evident, easy to see).

9. PORTRAY . . . . . **to describe, depict, represent**

The book portrays the fate of a criminal.

Portrayal of royalty on the stage was forbidden in England.

Query: What related noun means *a picture?*

10. RANSOM . . . . . **to redeem, buy back, liberate**

The king refused to ransom his former tutor.

Have you ever read "The Ransom of Red Chief"?

11. RECOIL . . . . **to spring back, rebound**

She recoiled in horror from the body.

The rifle's recoil made his shoulder sore.

12. RESCIND . . . . . . **to cancel, annul, make void**

The club voted to rescind the motion raising the dues to
$2.00.

13. SEGREGATE . . . . **to separate, isolate, set apart**

Doctors segregate those who have the disease.

Segregation of Negroes is common in the South.

14. VERIFY . . . . **to confirm, make certain**

Did you verify the figures you gave?

The court will demand verification.

15. WIELD . . . . **to handle, use with skill**

Can all lumbermen wield an ax?

The principal wields his influence wisely.

Questions

1. List a few words that rhyme well with *exhort, immerse, indulge, segregate, portray.*
2. What words can you get by changing the first letter of *wield?*

Copy the italicized words and beside each write its meaning in the sentence:

1. The fife *emits* a shrill sound to *portray* a boat's whistle.
2. The coach *exhorts* the players not to *indulge* in rich desserts.
3. He was *immersed* in his work when the boys tried to *invoke* his aid.
4. The town council will *rescind* its decision to *segregate* the boys.
5. "Do not *recoil* at my threat. You may *ransom* your child," the outlaw declared.
6. The president *wields* great authority because he *verifies* his facts. Even his enemies *extol* his accomplishments.
7. There was no way to *obviate* the danger of being *interned*.

SECOND PRACTICE SET

What is each of the following most likely to do, in terms of the base words of this unit? Place each word where it fits best, filling first the blanks you are sure about. Use each word only once.

1. A girl confronted by a mouse? __?__ and __?__ a yell.
2. A doughnut, near a cup of coffee? __?__ itself.
3. Angry lady with rolling pin? __?__ it.
4. Legislature, with bad law? __?__ it.
5. A novel about life in Africa? __?__ it.
6. Girl with a quart of strawberries? __?__.
7. The police with a probable firebug? __?__ him and __?__ the danger.
8. Father of a kidnaped boy? __?__ him.
9. Man, who thinks he has inherited $1,000,000? __?__.
10. Farmer, with six sick sheep? __?__ them.
11. A Republican orator, on February 12? __?__ Abraham Lincoln.
12. A minister in his church service? __?__ his people and __?__ Divine aid.

WHAT IS (S)HE LIKE?

Selling Things

How would you fill the blanks?

Competition is sometimes __?__, but if I am very __?__ and __?__ I feel sure I shall succeed. I must not be __?__ about meeting prospects, and I should not be too __?__ when they make excuses for not buying. Women customers may be more __?__ than men.

Traits

1. affable
2. boisterous
3. canny
4. coy
5. diligent
6. fickle
7. gullible
8. haughty
9. impulsive
10. pliable
11. prudent
12. ruthless
13. stolid
14. timorous
15. wayward

WHAT IS (S)HE LIKE?—STUDY GUIDE

1. AFFABLE . . . . . . **pleasant, friendly, amiable**
George is an affable companion.
His affability makes him popular.
Friendly words to look up: *genial, congenial, amicable.*

2. BOISTEROUS . . . . . . **noisy, disorderly, violent**
The two newsboys are a boisterous pair.
Their boisterousness broke up the scout meeting.
Boisterous winds drove the ship ashore.
Compare *blatant, raucous, vociferous.*

3. CANNY . . . . **knowing, shrewd, wary**
The Yankee trader is a canny merchant.
The Indian eyed us warily.

4. COY . . . . . **shy or pretending to be shy, demure**
Boys are sometimes bashful; girls are often coy.
Coyness is charming if not too much pretended.
A demure girl is shyly modest.

5. DILIGENT . . . . . . **hard-working, industrious**
A diligent person will get along well.
The boy's diligence won him the prize.
Compare *assiduous, sedulous, zealous.*

6. FICKLE . . . **changeable, variable, given to whims**
Her tastes are fickle.
He understood the fickleness of the crowds.

7. GULLIBLE . . **willing to believe almost anything; easily deceived**
Quack doctors get rich on people who are gullible.
Circus sideshows often exploit (page 57) one's gullibility.

8. HAUGHTY . . . . **proud, disdainful**
"Pride goeth before destruction and a haughty spirit before a fall." No one likes haughtiness.

9. IMPULSIVE . . . quick to speak or act, very responsive

Peter was an impulsive person.

Impulsiveness is a tendency to say or do the first thing that comes to mind.

10. PLIABLE . . . . easily influenced, flexible

Father is more pliable than Mother.

He is grateful for his father's pliability.

11. PRUDENT . . . . wise, cautious, discreet

It was prudent of you to ask for advice.

Is prudence always a virtue?

12. RUTHLESS . . . . merciless, cruel, pitiless

Germany waged ruthless warfare.

The ruler's ruthlessness caused a revolt.

Note: If your name is *Ruth*, it means *sympathy, pity, compassion*.

13. STOLID . . . . . . impassive, not easily excited

Though accused of murder, the prisoner remained stolid.

Compare *obtuse, callous, phlegmatic*.

14. TIMOROUS . . . . nervously afraid, timid

A timorous mouse darted under the baseboard.

The lady's timorousness was very amusing.

15. WAYWARD . . . . . unruly, disobedient, contrary

The teachers thought me very wayward.

Waywardness in the Army leads to the guardhouse.

Compare *froward* (a Biblical word), *perverse* (stubborn or contrary), *willful* (determined to have one's own way).

Questions

1. How many words ending in *–pulsive* can you list? What do they mean? Can you list three other words (besides *timorous*) ending in *–orous*?
2. What is the prefix opposite of *pliable? prudent?*
3. Find rhymes for *haughty, prudent, wayward, fickle*.

4. How many words can you add to those given in the unit for describing a person's temperament? The following are a few:

affected, altruistic, blunt, brusque, buoyant (page 78), *capricious, chivalrous* (page 120), *compassionate, complacent, composed, constant, curt* (page 4), *dynamic, erratic, frivolous* (page 89), *gallant, gracious* (pages 70, 75), *indulgent* (page 100), *judicious, listless, nonchalant, sedate, shrewish, sprightly, temperate, tolerant, vivacious, volatile.*

How many can you explain? What is the noun form of each?

FIRST PRACTICE SET

Copy the italicized words and beside each write its meaning in the sentence:

The catcher is *affable,* but the pitcher is rather *haughty* at times. He is *ruthless* when in good form but *prudent* about arguing with the umpire. The first baseman is *impulsive* and *pliable.* The shortstop is *stolid* and somewhat *wayward.* He attracts many *coy* smiles from the bleachers. The third baseman is *canny* and *diligent.* The second baseman is rather *boisterous* and *gullible* off the field. The coach keeps everybody at his best by seeming *fickle.* He acts *timorous* about our playing at times.

SECOND PRACTICE SET

Which of the base words in this unit applies most readily to the following? Answer first the ones you are sure about and later rearrange as necessary. Use each word once.

1. A friendly salesman
2. Boys in a reform school
3. An ox
4. A believer in Santa Claus
5. A cautious banker
6. A fawn in the woods
7. A tame fawn
8. A Halloween party
9. A slow driver
10. Quick generosity
11. Spring winds
12. A lordly peacock
13. A bold gangster
14. An overfond parent
15. A hive of bees

HOW DID (S)HE ACT?

Uncle Theodore

Can you fill the blanks properly from the list of words at the right?

He became very __?__ when his wife died, and his daughter was __?__ at times. It was very __?__ of her friends to say that she was __?__ because of her spells of grief-stricken excitement. They became very __?__ when they began to understand. She was often __?__ too, but they learned to overlook her irritability and to understand the __?__ look in her eyes.

Manner Words

1. callous
2. casual
3. contrite
4. deliberate
5. demented
6. despondent
7. flippant
8. hysterical
9. irate
10. passive
11. peevish
12. resolute
13. stealthy
14. surly
15. wistful

1. CALLOUS . . unfeeling, hardened, having a thickened skin

Could anyone be callous in the presence of starvation? Callousness would be almost criminal.

Compare *callus*, skin thickened by pressure or rubbing.

2. CASUAL . . . . . . offhand, occurring by chance

A casual inspection showed that the frame was cracked.
The casualness of her manner disarmed us.

3. CONTRITE . . . . . deeply sorry for a sin or wrong

"A broken and a contrite heart, O God, thou wilt not despise."

Her contriteness (contrition) made it easy to forgive her.

4. DELIBERATE . . . intentional, done on purpose, unhurried

The remark was a deliberate insult.
Her answer was careful and deliberate.

5. DEMENTED . . . . insane, unbalanced

The violinist was apparently demented.
Senile dementia is the "madness" of old age.

6. DESPONDENT . . . . discouraged, disheartened

Losing the race made him despondent for a while, but his despondency was short-lived.

Compare *disconsolate, doleful, dejected.*

7. FLIPPANT . . . . not serious enough, silly, frivolous

Doctors dislike flippant remarks about incurable diseases. Flippancy is not amusing.

I would not give a flip (snap) of my finger for a coward.

8. HYSTERICAL . . . . highly excited

Does a mouse make her hysterical?
War hysteria is dangerous.

9. IRATE . . . . angry, enraged, indignant

My refusal to pay made him irate.
The dog barked irately, his ire (wrath) aroused by a cat.

10. PASSIVE . . . . inactive, indifferent

In the rush for seats, he remained passive.
Passiveness is not an American trait.
A cow is very impassive (unemotional).

11. PEEVISH . . . . fretful, irritable, cross

Illness makes her peevish.
Peevishness destroys friendships.

Cross words: *pettish, petulant, waspish, splenetic.* Can you think of others?

12. RESOLUTE . . . . determined, steadfast

As a leader he is quietly resolute.
Resoluteness commands respect.

13. STEALTHY . . . . sly, sneaky, secret

A stealthy footstep was heard in the kitchen.
The thief's stealth(iness) did not save him.

Query: What familiar five-letter word is the base?

14. SURLY . . . . crabby, snappy, ill-natured

A surly answer makes him irate.
The guard's surliness got him into trouble.

Compare churlish, curt (page 4), *glum, morose, peevish* (above).

15. WISTFUL . . . . . . thoughtful, wishful, yearning

His wistful eyes stared into space.
Wistfulness is one of her charms.

Questions

1. What is the prefix opposite of *resolute?*
2. List five other words ending in *–ful.*
3. What words rhyme with *stealthy* and are spelled similarly? *passive? surly? despondent?*

4. What do *callous, flippant, passive, peevish* have in common?
5. List other words for the way (s)he acted. Here are a few for study or review: *baffle(d)* (page 66), *bellicose, brash, brisk.*

PRACTICE SET

Copy the italicized words and beside each write its meaning in the sentence:

1. The Chinese wise man was ~~passive~~ and ~~wistful~~.
2. The German general was *resolute* and rather *callous*.
3. The cat was ~~stealthy~~ and ~~deliberate~~ as she waited.
4. Junior is very ~~contrite~~ about the *flippant* letter he wrote to his *irate* father.
5. The man is *peevish* but not ~~demented~~.
6. A ~~surly~~ policeman made a woman driver ~~hysterical~~.
7. A ~~casual~~ remark about bad breath made her ~~despondent~~.

A PRANK

Can you fill each blank appropriately in the anecdote below? Put in the words you are sure about first. Some rearranging may be necessary before each word fits properly.

"You must have been __?__ when you bought it!" Sue exclaimed when she saw Sammy's new suit. Her manner was __?__ but quite __?__. Sammy was __?__ and, being in the opposite of a __?__ mood, decided to get even.

After a long search, he found a snake in a ditch, made a __?__ entry into his sister's room, and slowly, with __?__ care, arranged it in her bed. She became __?__ when she found it and ran away so fast she collided with Dad, knocking him downstairs.

Dad was unhurt but __?__. Sammy, when he saw what had happened, became very __?__ and rather __?__, for he realized how seriously his father might have been hurt. Sue, however, acted __?__ and rather __?__ because Dad did not get out of her way. Mother was __?__ and rather __?__.

VERB MAKING

GROUP I

Many useful verbs are formed by adding *–ize* to a familiar adjective or simple noun. For example:

Base	*Verb*	*Noun*
real	realize, *to make real*	realization

Reality or *unreality* is a condition whereas *realization* is an achievement. Copy the guide words below and fill each blank.

1. general   __?__, *to make general*   __?__ or __?__

2. __?__   __?__, *make harmonious*   harmonization

3. organ   __?__, *make an organization*   __?__ (watch pron.)

Write a line for each of the following words, placing it where it belongs in the line: *authorization, civil, commercialization, dramatization, fertile, mobile, public* (noun is shortened), *visualize.* Write lines for *critic* and *patron.*

What is the opposite of *civil?* of *mobile?* of the *adjective* for *fertilization, commercialization, harmony,* and *critic?*

GROUP II

Other verbs are formed in various ways with *–ify,* using an adjective or noun as a base. Can you fill the blanks below?

1. __?__   __?__, *to make larger*   amplification

2. certain   __?__, *to guarantee*   __?__

3. __?__   verify, *to make sure*   __?__

Write a line for each of the following words, placing it where it belongs in the line: *deity* (a god), *false, intense, just, magnification* (no word for first column), *note, sign, verse.*

Use some of the *–fy* verbs in sentences. What *–fy* verb means *make contented?* Write its adjective, adverb, and noun.

GROUP III

A third verb ending is –*ate*. Complete the following:

Base	*Verb*	*Noun*
1. captive	__?__, *to charm*	__?__
2. __?__	designate, *to name*	__?__
3. __?__	__?__, *to start something new*	origination

Write a line for *activate, complex, domestication, motivate, vacant.* Change each verb to past tense and then to its opposite with a prefix. Write sentences.

Here are four words to which a syllable must be added at the beginning to form a verb in –*ate*. Can you do them?

1. brief, brevity	__?__, *make brief*	__?__
2. fury	__?__, *make furious*	__?__
3. timid	__?__, *make timid*	__?__
4. vigor	__?__, *make vigorous*	__?__

WORD–BUILDING EXERCISE

For each blank supply the correct form of the word in parentheses:

1. To say that most criminals are foreigners is to __?__ (false) the facts and make a dangerous __?__ (general).
2. In case of war the National Guard will be __?__ (mobile).
3. He hates to see famous buildings __?__ (commercial).
4. Whom did he __?__ (design) as his executor?
5. The movers required a __?__ (certain) check in payment.
6. The two views could not be __?__ (harmony).
7. Pickets tried to __?__ (timid) men who wanted to work.
8. The Gordons received a __?__ (note) to __?__ (vacant) their apartment.
9. Father's skill in __?__ (verse) is unusual.
10. Junior was __?__ (captive) by the antics of the monkeys.

FACING THE MULTITUDE

The Basketball Situation

Can you fill each blank fittingly from the list at the right?

The basketball team gets a big __?__ whenever it appears in assembly and the coach __?__s each player. This year the __?__ of six-footers made it hard to find a center. The one who was chosen does not __?__ himself as he should when his opponent __?__s him, but we are winning our games because our cheerleader can __?__ the low spirits which sometimes haunt us when we play.

Verbs

1. abash
2. assert
3. beguile
4. commend
5. confront
6. divest
7. exorcise

Nouns

1. myriad
2. orifice
3. ovation
4. paucity
5. pinion
6. portal
7. qualm
8. rabble

1. ABASH . . . to embarrass, destroy one's composure

The visits of the boss always abash him.

Notice her abashment in the presence of strangers.

Compare *confound, discomfit, disconcert, abase* — and *bashful.*

2. ASSERT . . . . to declare, state, aver

Father should assert his authority.

Are all of those assertions true?

3. BEGUILE . . . . to charm, deceive, ensnare

Can we beguile you into going?

We can beguile the time away by telling stories.

The stranger's beguilements induced her to betray us.

Compare *allure* on page 56.

4. COMMEND . . . . to praise, approve, compliment

I commend your bravery.

The coach's commendation was merited.

Review *extol* and *laud* on page 100.

5. CONFRONT . . . . to face, oppose

The man will confront his accuser in court.

Let us confront our enemies boldly.

6. DIVEST . . to separate (oneself) from, put off or away

He will divest himself of all responsibilities.

The law divests criminals of the right to vote.

7. EXORCISE . . . . . . to drive out or deliver from

The witch doctor tries to exorcise demons by a magic formula.

Can you exorcise the gloom that hangs over us?

---

1. **MYRIAD** . . . . . ten thousand, a very large number
A myriad voices chattered and babbled below.
Myriads of flies buzzed around the jar.

2. **ORIFICE** . . . . . . a small opening, vent, or nozzle
The ear is one of the body's orifices.
Gasoline is sprayed through an orifice in the carburetor.

3. **OVATION** . . . . . applause or enthusiastic popular demonstration
The candidate received a tremendous ovation as he entered
the auditorium.

4. **PAUCITY** . . . . smallness, fewness, dearth
The paucity of contestants was discouraging.
There was a paucity of boys at the party.

5. **PINION** . . (1) small(est) gear (of two or three which mesh)
(2) bird's wing or part of wing
A broken pinion crippled the machine.
The bird with the broken pinion could not fly.
It is possible to pinion (bind the arms of) an assailant by
pulling his coat down over his arms.

6. **PORTAL** . . . . gate or entrance
"Portal of Paradise" is the title of a poem.
The miners prefer portal-to-portal pay.

7. **QUALM** . . . . misgiving, uneasiness, scruple
The boy had many qualms about taking the bicycle without
permission.

8. **RABBLE** . . . . noisy mob or crowd
The Roman rabble filled the arena.
What is a rabble-rouser today?

Questions

1. Can you think of any words with an *–iad* ending like *myriad?*
2. Can you think of any words which begin with the same three letters as *paucity?*
3. Change one letter of *divest* and get *to turn aside.*
4. List words ending in *–mend, –front, –cise, –alm, –sert.*

PRACTICE SET

Copy the italicized words and beside each write its meaning in the sentence:

1. *Myriads* of invaders swarmed through the *portals* of the city.
2. The *rabble* wanted to *divest* the traitor of all his medals.
3. The mechanic was *abashed* when *confronted* with the defective *pinion.*
4. A big *ovation* will *beguile* the singer into giving an encore.
5. Have you no *qualms* about filling the *orifice* with clay?
6. He *asserts* that he can *exorcise* the family ghost.
7. *Commend* him for the *paucity* of his mistakes.

THE MULTITUDE

Which of the base words of this unit fits best in each blank?

The governor-general was __?__ed when he saw how many peasants had assembled, and he had __?__s about addressing the __?__s who had gathered. He knew he must __?__ his authority when the spokesman for the __?__ __?__ed him. He managed by his oratory to __?__ them into applauding, and the __?__ which he got gave him courage to soar even higher on word __?__s, even, so it seemed, to the __?__s of heaven itself. The newspapers would not __?__ his action, he knew, but he hoped he could __?__ them of their readers by his eloquence. No one would suspect the __?__ of his courage at the outset. Truly he had __?__ed the evil spirit that animated the mob, and he had done it largely by skillful use of that facial __?__ which houses the tongue.

EE—I—EE—I—OH!

Is it *ei* or *ie?* How can I always remember? Is there a rule?

There is a rule, but you must work it out for yourself — and then perhaps you will remember it! Study the two groups of words below and answer the questions which follow them. You will notice that all but one of the words in List A come from a single root — *ceive–cept.*

List A	*List B*	
ceiling	achieve	apiece
deceive	believe	belief
deceit	brief	chief
conceive	field	fierce
conceit	fiend	frontier
receive	grieve	grief
receipt	pierce	priest
perceive	relieve	relief
	retrieve	shriek
	shield	siege
	thief	tier
	view	yield

What letter comes in front of *ei* in List A? Does it come in front of *ie,* in any of the words in List B? How are both *ei* and *ie* sounded? Can you think of a simple rule to guide you when the *ei* or *ie* is pronounced *ee?*

The following words are *exceptions* to the rule you have (we hope) worked out:

leisure   weird   seize   (n)either

Can you devise a catchy sentence containing all four words that you may use to help you remember that they are exceptions?

Note: *Financier* is another exception, but it need not bother you because *–ier* is a word *ending,* and endings pronounced *–eer* are sometimes spelled *–ier,* but rarely with an *e* before an *i.*

Now let's look at the *ei* and *ie* words in which the *ei* and *ie* are NOT pronounced *ee.* Here are some of the *ei* words, which we shall call List C:

feign, feint	reign, rein	Sinn Fein
freight	skein	geisha
heir, height	sleigh	vein
neighbor	chow mein	weigh, weight

How is *ei* pronounced in most cases? What does *feign* mean? *geisha? skein?* Distinguish between *reign* and *rein.*

Other *ie* words include *friend, sieve,* and three-letter words such as *die, fie, hie, lie, pie,* and *tie.* Mispronounce (*fry-end, sy-eve*) a few times and write any of these or any *ei* words you are inclined to misspell.

SENTENCES FOR PRACTICE

Write some or all of the following sentences from dictation to measure your mastery of *ie* and *ei* words:

1. Do you believe in signing a receipt for a neighbor?
2. He perceived that the thief would seize the chow mein.
3. The ceiling fell during the brief reign of Catherine.
4. Conceit kept him from yielding to the besiegers.
5. The fierce fiend shrieked and ran across the field with a skein of yarn.
6. His heir tried to feign insanity, but he deceived no one.
7. The thief failed to retrieve either the sieve or the handkerchief.
8. Neither the financier nor his friend could find the sleigh.
9. The priest saw a weird view of a human vein.
10. Each tier weighs ten tons and was shipped by freight.

LOOKING BACKWARD

Far Away or Long Ago

Base Words

Can you fill the blanks and defend your choices?

1. The Chinese worship their __?__s.
2. A wife's __?__ helped her husband get established in business.
3. Knights liked to take part in __?__s.
4. A __?__ is a kind of indoor cemetery.
5. The __?__ was a Moslem weapon.

Base Words
1. ancestor
2. chivalry
3. crypt
4. dowry
5. esquire
6. gauntlet
7. joust
8. lineage
9. minstrel
10. moat
11. parchment
12. scimitar
13. steed
14. vassal
15. visor

● *How many of the base words can you find in the illustration above?*

LOOKING BACKWARD—STUDY GUIDE

1. **ANCESTOR . . a forefather, person from whom one is descended**

   One of his ancestors was a Danish king.
   Millions trace their ancestry to William the Conqueror.

2. **CHIVALRY . . (practices of) knighthood; courtesy to women (often heroic)**

   Sir Galahad was a model of chivalry.
   The boy is very chivalrous (gallant).

3. **CRYPT . . a vault, all or partly underground (usually part of a church)**

   Woodrow Wilson is buried in the crypt of the National Cathedral in Washington.
   "My knees are bowed in crypt and shrine."
   The teacher made a cryptic (mysterious) remark.

4. **DOWRY . . property a woman brought to her husband when married**

   A homely girl needed a large dowry.
   "With all my worldly goods I thee endow [enrich]."
   Compare *dower, dowager, endowment.*

5. **ESQUIRE . . . a (landed) gentleman, shield-bearer**

   A boy from a noble family became first a page or attendant to a knight. Later he became a squire (esquire) or shield-bearer and finally — *perhaps* — a full-fledged knight.

   Note: Today *esquire* means a gentleman or important citizen. Such a man's name may be written George F. Adams, Esq.

6. **GAUNTLET . . . a glove of mail or leather, challenge**

   The knight tossed his gauntlet down as a challenge.
   "Running the gantlet" was an Indian punishment.

7. **JOUST . . . combat or mock combat between knights**

   Jousts (on horseback) were part of a tournament.
   Sir Andrew jousted (tilted) with Sir Percy.

---

8. LINEAGE (*LIN-ee-ij*) . . . . ancestry
Joseph was of the lineage of David.

9. MINSTREL . . . . a wandering singer
Troubadours were minstrels of Southern France.
Minstrels today are comedians, usually made up to look like Negroes.

10. MOAT . . a deep ditch (especially around a castle and filled with water to give protection)
One of the attackers fell into the moat and was drowned.

11. PARCHMENT . . a kind of fine paper (once made from animal skins)
The story was written on parchment.
A few copies of *The New York Times* are printed on parchment each day.
Compare *papyrus, vellum.*

12. SCIMITAR . . . . a curved sword used by Moslems
This scimitar was used in defending Jerusalem.
Other weapons: *lance, poniard, saber, dagger.*

13. STEED . . . . horse, charger
Sir Henry mounted his steed and rode proudly away.
Note: *Steed* is a literary, rather poetic word.
Other *horse* words: *mare, stallion, courser, mount, charger.*

14. VASSAL . . . . . an underling, servant, bondman
The knight on the steed was a vassal of King Henry.
A small country is often the vassal of a great power.
Compare *serf, fief, feudalism.*

15. VISOR . . . . front part of a helmet or cap
The knight put down his visor before entering the lists.
The visor on a cap today may be traced to the visor on a knight's helmet.
Other *armor* words: *casque, cuirass, greaves.* See pictures in encyclopedia or dictionaries.

Questions

1. What three-letter words stand out in the base words of this unit? One is an animal, one is a kind of electric light, and one means wrath.
2. How many four-letter words can you find? One means to drive out. There are three five-letter words, one being a quantity of paper.
3. Can you name a tooth that rhymes with *visor?* A word for mounted soldiers to rhyme with *chivalry?*

PRACTICE SET

Copy the italicized words and beside each write its meaning in the sentence:

1. A jeweled *scimitar* was part of the bride's *dowry.*
2. Her male *ancestors* were *vassals* of French kings.
3. The class visited the *crypt* of the church and saw the *moat* of the old castle.
4. The knight dismounted from his *steed* and raised his *visor.*
5. Write the *minstrel's* tale on *parchment* after the *joust.*
6. The *squire* handed a *gauntlet* to the knight.
7. In the days of *chivalry* a man's *lineage* was very important.

THE TOURNAMENT

Which of the base words of this unit fits best in each blank?

Each knight put on his __?__s, mounted his __?__, adjusted his __?__, took leave of his __?__, and entered the lists. Sir Humphrey, who considered King John one of his __?__s and who traced his __?__ back to King Arthur, thought himself a fine specimen of __?__. He used his wife's __?__ to buy the best armor there was, induced a __?__ to glorify his brave deeds, and had them recorded on __?__ and preserved in a __?__. He was proud of the __?__ he had captured in Palestine but said little about the time his horse stumbled into a __?__. He won his first __?__ in the tournament but lost the second. He was a __?__ of the English king.

HOPES AND FEARS

Our Puppy

Can you fill the blanks fittingly from the words at the right?

He __?__s from under the bed, __?__s on the floor and in a tussle with a stuffed rabbit creates a __?__ in the middle of the room. His eagerness never seems to __?__, and he has what Dad calls __?__.

Verbs

1. diminish
2. emerge
3. encumber
4. endorse
5. gainsay
6. grovel
7. imbue
8. imply

Nouns

1. rebate
2. residue
3. rift
4. spouse
5. stamina
6. trance
7. vortex

1. DIMINISH . . . . to lessen, decrease, reduce
The number of calls will soon diminish.
Only by undiminished effort can he win.

2. EMERGE . . . . . to appear, come forth, rise from
She will emerge from the stage door in a moment.
The emergence of new problems delayed the work.
Compare *emergency*.

3. ENCUMBER . . . . to burden, weigh down
Worry should not encumber you.
Armor was very cumbersome (burdensome).
Remain, if you can, unencumbered by debt.

4. ENDORSE (INDORSE) . . . . to approve, sign over
Does the mayor endorse the candidate? Does his endorsement mean his active support?
Did you endorse the check? Endorsement is necessary before it can be cashed.

5. GAINSAY . . . . . . to contradict, speak against
No one will gainsay him when he says we must work.

6. GROVEL . . . . . . to crawl (abjectly), lie prone
Slaves were accustomed to grovel before a king.
He is inclined to grovel before his employer.

7. IMBUE . . . . to saturate, tinge deeply
A summer out of doors will imbue him with vigor.
The man is imbued with patriotism.

8. IMPLY . . . . to hint, involve
Does silence imply approval?
Does Halloween fun imply destruction of property?
The implications of his refusal are clear.
Note: *Imply* means literally *to fold in.* Compare *pliable* (page 105).
The root *–plic, –plex* is presented on page 243.

1. **REBATE . . . . . . a refund or return (usually partial)**
   There is a rebate of ten cents on tickets purchased before the
   price was reduced.

2. **RESIDUE . . . . a remainder, part left behind**
   Water boiled away leaves a residue in the pan.
   Soot is a residual deposit in a furnace.

3. **RIFT . . . . a split, break, opening, cleft**
   There is a rift in the clouds already.
   A rift in the Democratic party enabled the Republicans to
   win.
   The "thunder-riven" tree was split by lightning.
   Compare *cleave, cleavage, cleft.*

4. **SPOUSE . . . . wife, mate**
   His faithful spouse accompanied him everywhere.
   Milton espoused (embraced) the ideals of freedom.

5. **STAMINA . . . . endurance, vigor**
   It takes stamina to resist evil.
   It takes stamina to be a good miler.

6. **TRANCE . . . . . a dream, transported condition**
   She seemed to be in a trance.
   She was entranced (delighted, enraptured) with the idea of
   going to Switzerland.

7. **VORTEX . . . . a whirlpool, eddy**
   The tub lingered a moment on the edge of the vortex before
   it was swallowed up.
   The vortex of the cyclone veered suddenly toward us.

Questions

1. Find and list, if you can, ten or more verbs formed with *es–* or
   en– in front of a word, such as *gross — engross, trench — en-*
   trench, mesh — enmesh, and *strange — estrange.*

---

2. List other words, especially verbs, ending in *–ue, –vel, –ply, –umber*.

3. List a few other nouns ending in *–ex, –ouse, –ift*.

PRACTICE SET

Copy the italicized words and beside each write its meaning in the sentence:

1. Uncle Herb, though *imbued* with the spirit of Christmas, is *encumbered* with extra duties and will not be the one who *emerges* as Santa Claus at the party.
2. His words *imply* that one must *grovel* to please him.
3. Has she the *stamina* to hold her own in the *vortex* of school activities?
4. There was a *rift* between him and his *spouse*.
5. This act will *diminish* our willingness to *endorse* him.
6. I do not *gainsay* your claim about the enormous value of the *residue*. The very thought puts one in a *trance*.
7. We get a *rebate* on our fare if the train is late.

HOPES AND FEARS

Can you fill all the blanks correctly, using each base word in this unit once?

Dad hopes for a __?__ on his income tax, a change in the price level, and the __?__ to resist his competitors successfully in the __?__ of business. He wants the sales manager to become __?__d with his enthusiasm and to __?__ his advertising plan. Incidentally, he expects to __?__ as bowling champion in the Winter League.

Dad is often afraid that sales will __?__, even though the reports do not __?__ that they will. He worries about a __?__ between the sales manager and himself, about having too large a __?__ of unsold goods, and about the bills with which his __?__ sometimes __?__s him after a shopping trip to New York. "Were you in a __?__?" he demands, and she does not __?__ that she was, but she refuses to __?__, nevertheless.

SPEAK RIGHT

The words in this paragraph are often mispronounced. Divide them into syllables. Practice reading them, together and individually, until it seems natural to accent them as indicated — and be sure you can spell them correctly:

Accent FIRST syllable: *absolutely,* cannot, comparable, contrary, decade* (ten-year period), *deficit* (debt, shortage), *dirigible, harass** (annoy), *hospitable, influence, obsequies* (funeral rites), *positively, preferable, puerile* (childish)

Accent SECOND syllable: *acclimate** (accustom), *adult,* ally, defile, detail,* detour,* distribute, entire, excess, grimace, horizon, inquiry,* pianist,* research,* resource,* robust, romance**

Accent FINAL syllable: *amateur,* magazine**

Many words contain a short *i* which is often mispronounced, and so is the long *a* in several very common words. Practice them, and be sure you can spell each one:

Short *i* as in *hit: fertile, fragile, juvenile,* puerile, reptile,* textile *; genuine, Italian*
Note: *Infantile* and *senile* (*SEE-nile*) prefer *i* as in *smile.**
Long *a* as in *hay: apparatus,* data,* strata,* tomato **

You will spell the following words better if you speak them more accurately. Practice them carefully, giving each consonant, vowel, and syllable its full value — and *more:*

banquet (BANG-kwet),* *chocolate* (CHAWK-o-lit), *countenance, dairy* (cows), *diary* (journal), *distinctly, environment, family, government, librarian, period, privilege, partner, recognize, reelection, shepherd, surprise, traveler, accidentally, electrically, equally, generally, incidentally, usually*

* Preferred in *Webster's New Collegiate Dictionary,* but one or more other pronunciations are also allowed.

A few are misspelled because of an extra letter that ISN'T there.

Practice: athletics   elm   film   grievous   lightning

Most of the words below have a tricky *e, i,* or *o* that needs watching — among other things. Divide them into syllables if there is time. Find similar pairs. Practice the words patiently — and exaggerate the pronunciation:

List A: *bachelor, bulletin, cabinet, celebrate, college, despair* (compare *repair*), *diet, different, elevator, England, expedition, federal, fiery, item, kindergarten, luncheon, offering, opera, pattern, pigeons, rotten, scarlet, secretary, surgeon, telegram, vegetable, vessel, wondering*

List B: *ancient, basis, brilliant, champion, Christian, companion, cordial, cushion, diploma, experience, favorite, genius, margin, musician, opinion, physician, policy, region, religion, ruin, sentiment, suspicion, uniform, university, vicinity*

Ice words: *justice, prejudice, sacrifice, service*

O words: *corporation, decorate, history, ivory, laboratory, memory, temporary, theory, victory*

SENTENCES FOR PRACTICE

Read them aloud. Write some or all from dictation.

1. The history lesson is about an Italian expedition.
2. The Federal Government will share the cost equally.
3. College students naturally celebrate athletic victories.
4. The family is using its influence to reelect you.
5. The bachelor attended the opera in spite of the telegram.
6. A fiery speech may help eliminate juvenile crimes.
7. The bulletin in the elevator is about tripping accidentally.
8. The musician has talents that are distinctly different.
9. The remedy, incidentally, depends on memory alone.
10. The magazine has an article on the Christian religion.

WEAR WORDS

Her Apparel

What word from the list at the right would *you* put in each blank?

On her head she wore a __?__. Around her neck was a __?__ similar to a boy's, and her dress was made of __?__. Her gloves were __?__, and her cheeks were __?__. She carried a __?__ in her hand.

● *How many of the garments and materials can you find in the illustration above?*

Garments
1. apparel
2. chapeau
3. cravat
4. haberdashery
5. lingerie
6. mantle
7. oxfords
8. trousseau
9. valise

Materials
1. chenille
2. damask
3. satin
4. serge
5. suede
6. textile

WEAR WORDS—STUDY GUIDE

1. APPAREL . . . . **clothing, garments, attire**

"The apparel oft proclaims the man."
He came to the wedding suitably appareled.

Other *apparel* words: *vestments, habiliments, raiment, garb, ensemble.* Which are familiar?

2. CHAPEAU (*shah-PO*) . . . . **hat**

Her new chapeau is very gay.

Other *hat* words to study: *beret, fedora, sombrero, fez, biretta, havelock* (page 290).

3. CRAVAT . . . . **necktie**

One of his presents was a bright-colored cravat.

4. HABERDASHERY . . **men's furnishings or store selling**
them

The shirts are from the new haberdashery on Winslow Street.

Note: Haberdasher(y) has a different meaning in England.

5. LINGERIE (*LAHN-zhuh-ree*) . . . **ladies' underwear**

Men do not like to buy lingerie for their wives.

Note: *Lingerie* is really a French term for linen goods, but it has taken on a new meaning in English.
See *camisole, chemise, negligee, bodice,* if time permits. *Camisole* is now used in state hospitals instead of *straitjacket* for the canvas garment used to restrain disturbed patients.

6. MANTLE . . . . . **cloak, sleeveless outer garment**

The mantle reached to the ground.
The ground had a mantle (covering) of snow.
The mantle (symbol of responsibility) passed from Elijah to Elisha.

Compare *mantel,* ledge over a fireplace.

7. OXFORD(S) . . . . **low shoe(s)**

Do you need a new pair of oxfords?

8. TROUSSEAU (*true-SO*) . . bride's outfit or wardrobe

Mother helped buy her trousseau.

9. VALISE . . . . grip, satchel, traveling bag

The valise is old and worn.

In England, a large suitcase is often called a *portmanteau*.

---

1. CHENILLE (*sheh-NEEL*) . . tufted cord (usually cotton)
or fabric "filled" with it

We saw chenille bedspreads for sale in the South.

Other cotton fabrics: *muslin, organdie, percale, broadcloth, madras,* and often *seersucker*.

2. DAMASK . . a figured tablecloth fabric (especially
linen); a shade of red

The cover was made of the finest damask.
Here is a bouquet of damask roses.

3. SATIN . . . . a glossy silken cloth

The lining of the coat is satin.

Rayon and nylon, artificial fabrics, have replaced silk to a large extent.

4. SERGE . . a cloth (often of wool) used for coats, suits,
and dresses

Millions wear serge suits.

Compare *worsted* (from Worstead, England), a kind of wool yarn, and *twill*.

5. SUEDE (pronounced *swayd*) . . a soft leather from a
tanned skin

A suede jacket is very warm.

"Leather" words: *morocco, alligator, calfskin, kid(skin)*.

6. TEXTILE . . . . any woven fabric

One of the newer textiles is cloth made of spun glass. It wears well and has a definite luster.

Questions

1. Look up the incidental fabric words in this unit if time permits. The class might make a collection of clothing materials and prepare an exhibit.
2. What is gabardine? sharkskin? a cardigan? Other wear words to consider are: *smock, frock, ulster, jerkin, surplice, cassock, tunic, toga, tulle.*
3. Read the words of this unit in concert with the teacher several times to get the pronunciation correct. From what language do most of them come? How do you explain this fact?
4. Which words contain a double letter and what is it?

PRACTICE SET

Copy the italicized words and beside each write its meaning in the sentence:

1. The *cravat* is made of *satin.*
2. *Suede* is warmer than *serge,* usually.
3. A *haberdashery* does not sell *lingerie.*
4. *Valises* and *oxfords* usually contain leather.
5. A snappy *chapeau* sets off one's *apparel* nicely.
6. The *damask* serves as a *mantle,* concealing the burned spots.
7. *Chenille* is a *textile* found in a *trousseau.*

THE TROUSSEAU

Can you fill the blanks correctly, using each of the base words once?

It included a __?__ suit with a __?__ lining. There was plenty of other __?__ including new __?__, a bright purple __?__ in an oval box, a pair of __?__s, a pair of __?__ gloves, and a kind of __?__ for cool days in April and May. Another of the bulkier articles was a __?__ dressing gown. There were, of course, no __?__s or other __?__. Most of these articles were packed in a __?__ to take on the trip. Though not really a part of her __?__, the bride-to-be had three __?__ tablecloths. She also had one made of rayon, a less expensive __?__.

SOUP TO NUTS

The Banquet

Can you fill each blank edibly?

1. The __?__ potatoes looked like a game of jack straws.
2. The __?__ on the pie was at least two inches thick.
3. The weather is too cold for a __?__.
4. Coffee was served __?__.
5. All in all, the meal will be a fine __?__.

Dishes and Ways

1. au gratin
2. demitasse
3. éclair
4. fricassee
5. julienne
6. lyonnaise
7. meringue
8. mousse
9. repast
10. sauté

Adjectives of Taste

1. brackish
2. delectable
3. potable
4. rancid
5. saline

SOUP TO NUTS—STUDY GUIDE

(Read in concert several times for correct pronunciation.)

1. **AU GRATIN** (*oh-GRAHT'n*) . . . covered with bread crumbs (browned) or cheese

   Au gratin potatoes were listed on the menu.

2. **DEMITASSE** (*DEM-ih-tass*) . . . a small cup (of black coffee)

   Demitasse is served with the dessert.

   In French *demi–* means *half* and *tasse* is *cup*.

3. **ÉCLAIR** (*aye-CLARE*) . . . bun-shaped shell filled with cream; cream puff

   The bakery had some fresh éclairs.

4. **FRICASSEE** (*fric-ah-SEE*) . . . meat cut in pieces and cooked in gravy; a kind of stew

   Do you like fricassee of veal?
   Fricassee of chicken is fried chicken.

   Fricassee means *fried* in French.

5. **JULIENNE** (*joo-lih-ENN*) . . cut in thin strips; soup containing thin strips of vegetable

   The carrots were served julienne (in slender strips).
   The soup was julienne that day.

6. **LYONNAISE** (*lie-uh-NAZE*) . . . cooked with onions

   Men like lyonnaise potatoes.

   The word in French means *as in Lyon.*

7. **MERINGUE** (*meh-RANG*) . . . frothy egg-white-and-sugar covering

   She ate the meringue off her pie first.
   A meringue looks like whipped cream.

8. MOUSSE (pronounced *moose*) . . a frozen mixture of gelatin and cream

For dessert one could have a chocolate éclair or a strawberry mousse.

9. REPAST . . . . a meal, feast

He omits the noonday repast.
What a repast that dinner was!

10. SAUTÉ (*so-TAY*) . . . . . . to fry lightly all over

Do you intend to sauté the onions in butter?
Sautéed liver is delicious.

---

1. BRACKISH . . . . flat, somewhat salty

The water from the spring turned brackish.
How do you explain its brackishness?

2. DELECTABLE . . . . . . delightful, very pleasing

An éclair makes a delectable dessert.

3. POTABLE (*PO-tah-bul*) . . . . . . fit for drinking

River water is not potable.
Horse meat is edible (fit to eat), but dogs are considered inedible.

4. RANCID . . . . . having a "strong" or sour taste

Butter becomes rancid in hot weather.

5. SALINE (*SAY-line*) . . . . salty

Gargling a saline solution helps a sore throat.
Can you explain the name Salina Street in Syracuse, N. Y.?

Questions

1. What is the source of most of the words? Can you explain?
2. Change *gr* in *gratin* to one letter and it will be *morning*.

---

3. Can you think of other words or phrases that end in *–asse?* in *–aise?* in *–ienne?* in *–ee?*
4. Where are double letters found in the words of this unit? How many three- and four-letter words are within the base words?
5. Name two or three other adjectives ending in *–cid* besides *rancid.*
6. How many of the following eat-words do you recognize? *hors d'oeuvre, giblet, glutton, toffee, treacle?*

PRACTICE SET

Copy the italicized words and beside each write its meaning in the sentence:

1. The *julienne* soup, oysters *au gratin, demitasse,* and strawberry *mousse* made a splendid *repast.*
2. Susie ate the *meringue* off the pudding and helped herself to an *éclair.*
3. We ordered *fricassee* of lamb and *lyonnaise* potatoes.
4. Kippered herring is rather *saline.*
5. Swamp water is not *potable,* but frogs living in the swamp are edible.
6. Cod-liver oil sometimes becomes *rancid,* and stale ginger ale is rather *brackish.*
7. *Sautéed* mushrooms make a *delectable* dish.

HIS LAST MEAL

For his final __?__ the condemned man ordered __?__ of chicken, potatoes __?__ because he did not like onions, and __?__ beets. He requested chocolate pie with a thick __?__ rather than a cherry __?__ because he did not like frozen desserts. A __?__ of coffee would have been much too small for him.

He complained that the water was __?__ and the butter __?__. The coffee, he said, had a __?__ flavor but the pie was truly __?__.

His death-house companion had __?__ed liver, __?__ potatoes, and fried eggplant with an __?__ for dessert. He complained that the coffee was as __?__ as dishwater.

NOUNS AND VERBS

A Summer Evening

Can you fill the blanks appropriately?

We like to watch the waves __?_ along the shore while we __?_ about the stars and wonder what __?__s on Mars. We'd like to __?__ some of our pennies into gold coins and forget forever the __?__ which says, "A penny saved is a penny earned." Tomorrow's work will come all too soon to __?__ these pleasant fancies.

Nouns
1. adage
2. apostle
3. caldron
4. compact
5. courier
6. damsel
7. edifice

Verbs
1. pervert _turn aside_
2. ratify
3. reinstate
4. speculate
5. supplant
6. transmute
7. transpire
8. undulate

NOUNS AND VERBS—STUDY GUIDE

1. ADAGE . . . . . . wise saying, proverb, maxim
"Murder will out" is a familiar adage.

2. APOSTLE . . one of the disciples of Christ; one who promotes a great idea or undertaking
Paul was an apostle to the Gentiles.
The Senator went abroad as an apostle of good will.

3. CALDRON . . . . . . a large kettle (for boiling)
"Double, double, toil and trouble,
Fire burn and caldron bubble."

4. COMPACT . . . . a solemn agreement or contract
What was the Mayflower Compact?
A *covenant* is also a solemn agreement, often with religious implications.

5. COURIER . . . . runner, messenger
The courier arrived at dawn.
The Marines communicated by means of couriers.

6. DAMSEL . . . . girl, maiden
Who will rescue the damsel?

7. EDIFICE . . . . . . (large) building or structure
The Colosseum is still an imposing edifice.
Grand Central Station is quite an edifice, too.

---

1. PERVERT . . . . to lead astray, turn aside
The banker tried to pervert justice.
Jealousy is a form of perversion in the soul.
A perverse (wayward) tongue causes much trouble.
Her little perversities (mock-wayward acts) are very amusing.

2. RATIFY . . . . to approve or confirm

The Senate would not ratify the treaty.
Ratification of the agreement may affect prices.

3. REINSTATE . . to restore to original place or standing

The man was discharged, but later reinstated. A court ordered his reinstatement.

4. SPECULATE . . . . . . to guess, wonder, theorize

She likes to speculate about the future.
Speculation in stocks is buying on the *expectation* or *theory* that they will go up in value.

5. SUPPLANT . . . . . to take the place of, supersede

A new government will supplant the old.
Why can't love supplant hate in our lives?

6. TRANSMUTE . . . . to change into something finer, transform

The alchemists tried to transmute baser metals into gold.
Transmutation of hate into love is not uncommon.

7. TRANSPIRE . . to happen, come to pass, become known

Events transpired so as to bring about an agreement.
It transpired that the king was in league with the enemy.

8. UNDULATE . . . . to rise up and down like waves, fluctuate

The tall grass began to undulate softly in the breeze.
He ran his fingers over the undulations (wavy surface) of the windowpane.

Questions

1. How many words can you list ending in *–vert, –plant, –spire, –fice, –pact?*
2. Why are there two p's in *supplant?* See dictionary.

PRACTICE SET

Copy the italicized words and beside each write its meaning in the sentence:

1. The *apostle* saved a *damsel's* life.
2. The witches' *caldron* is a *perverted* piece of heavy hardware.
3. All but two unions were ready to *ratify* the *compact*.
4. A new manager will *supplant* the present one when the new *edifice* is completed.
5. Why *speculate* about what will *transpire* when the *courier* arrives?
6. If the board *reinstates* him, he must *transmute* some of his foolishness into good ideas for selling soap.
7. The surface *undulates* as the *adage* says it should.

QUIZ

Can you fill the blanks correctly, using each of the base words in this unit once?

1. "All's well that ends well" is an __?__ that could __?__ one's judgment.
2. He was called "the __?__ of freedom" because he arranged a __?__ providing for equal rights.
3. Buckingham Palace is a London __?__. What __?__s there is front-page news.
4. A __?__ is used to heat large quantities of water.
5. The company will __?__ the guarantee it discontinued or __?__ it with a better one if the directors __?__ the new plan.
6. Those who __?__ in stocks know that the market __?__s considerably.
7. The __?__ fell in love with the __?__ who brought the message.
8. The human body can __?__ coarse food into beautiful eyes and lovely hair.

WORD CONSTRUCTION AHEAD

The leading characters in this little drama are Ance and Ence. Each is the head of a tribe which includes several families or parts of families, and each is rather jealous of the other. The Sure words, for example, belong to Ance, and the Sist words to Ence — all but two, Resistance and Assistance.

We'll present the tribes *separately* at first. If you can find a simple, sure rule to tell them apart once they mingle, you will go down in history with Christopher Columbus.

TABLE I

Can you copy the guide words below accurately and fill all the blanks *correctly?* Use a dictionary, if necessary.

	Verb	Noun	Adjective	Adj.-Opposite
1.	_ _ ? _ _	_ _ ? _ _	_ _ ? _ _	unacceptable
2.	allow	_ _ ? _ _	_ _ ? _ _	_ _ ? _ _
3.	_ _ ? _ _	avoidance	_ _ ? _ _	_ _ ? _ _
4.	_ _ ? _ _	_ _ ? _ _	endurable	_ _ ? _ _
5.	_ _ ? _ _	_ _ ? _ _	_ _ ? _ _	uninsurable
6.	_ _ ? _ _	_ _ ? _ _	resistible	_ _ ? _ _
7.	rely	_ _ ? _ _	_ _ ? _ _	_ _ ? _ _
8.	_ _ ? _ _	variance	_ _ ? _ _	_ _ ? _ _

Questions

1. Read the completed tabulation of the Ances, exaggerating the endings to fix them in mind for the ear as well as the eye.
2. Write the noun form of *annoy, comply, convey, ignore, maintain, persevere, prevail, resemble.* Two lose an eye.
3. What is the noun and past tense opposite of *assist, remember, sever* (cut), *acquaint, appear, apply, attend, enter, issue, perform,* and *suffer?* Three lose an e. Be careful.

TABLE II

The second table is part of the family tree of the Ence Tribe. Can you fill all the blanks — without writing in them? Two of the adjectives are Able and the rest are Ent:

Verb	Noun	Adjective	Adj.-Opposite
1. confide	_ _?_ _	_ _?_ _	
2. _ _?_ _	difference	_ _?_ _	_ _?_ _
3. _ _?_ _	_ _?_ _	existent	_ _?_ _
4. _ _?_ _	_ _?_ _	_ _?_ _	independent
5. _ _?_ _	insistence	_ _?_ _	
6. _ _?_ _	_ _?_ _	preferable	
7. reside	_ _?_ _	_ _?_ _	_ _?_ _
8. _ _?_ _	_ _?_ _	_ _?_ _	untransferable

Exercises

1. What is the noun form of *confer* (hold a consultation), *correspond, defer* (yield to authority), *interfere, persist, refer, revere?* The past tense of *transfer?*
2. Read the Ence Chart several times, with suitable exaggeration, just as you did the Ance Chart. Which is the larger tribe?
3. Compose sentences containing fifteen or more *Ance* and *Ence* words. Dictate them to each other in pairs and correct them, or the teacher will dictate one set to the entire group.

WORD–BUILDING EXERCISE

Can you fill each blank correctly?

1. The two are at _ _?_ _ (vary) over a trifling matter.
2. The new janitor is _ _?_ _ (can't be relied upon).
3. Her _ _?_ _ (insist) on a new trial won out.
4. A fishing license for _ _?_ _s (not residents) costs more.
5. A man with heart trouble is _ _?_ _ (can't get insurance).
6. The ticket is not _ _?_ _ (can't transfer).
7. The original document is no longer in _ _?_ _ (exist).
8. _ _?_ _ (comply) with the new law is very difficult.
9. The accident was _ _?_ _ (couldn't avoid).
10. Tony is _ _?_ _ (not acquainted) with American ways.

WORKADAY WORDS

Housing Project

Can you fill the blanks sensibly from the list of words at the right?

Wood is __?__. It will __?__ if exposed to the weather for thirty or forty years. Brick is more __?__, but it is less __?__. It will not __?__ as readily as wood or a painted surface.

Verbs
1. anneal
2. baste
3. bevel
4. congeal
5. erode
6. fuse
7. glaze
8. gyrate
9. tarnish

Adjectives
1. acrid
2. ductile
3. durable
4. porous
5. resilient
6. viscous

1. ANNEAL . . to toughen and temper by heat treatment

We anneal each frame to make it less brittle.

Education is a mind-annealing process.

2. BASTE . . . . (1) to sew loosely (with long stitches)
               (2) to moisten (roasting meat)
               (3) to hit, strike, beat

Mother bastes a dress before sewing it on her machine.

At intervals while the Thanksgiving turkey is roasting, it is necessary to baste it with melted fat from the pan.

The boy promised to baste him if he did it again.

3. BEVEL . . . . to cut on a slant or at an angle

Be sure to bevel the ends of the boards.

Look up *bevel* gear, if possible.

4. CONGEAL . . . . to freeze, stiffen

Does a murder story congeal your blood?

Zero weather has a congealing effect on the grease in a car.

5. ERODE . . . . to wear away, eat away

Strong acid tends to erode one's teeth.

The hills are barren because of soil erosion.

6. FUSE . . . . . to melt (together), to blend by heat

Sugar crystals will fuse when heated.

Sand and soda fuse to form glass.

7. GLAZE . . . . to coat with glass

Glazed porcelain is porcelain coated with glass.

His eyes were glazed (glassy) in death.

8. GYRATE . . . . to whirl, revolve

The place fairly gyrates with activity.

The dancer gyrates gracefully on one foot.

The pitcher's gyrations confused the batter.

9. TARNISH . . to discolor, lose its luster, smirch or sully

Stainless steel will not tarnish.

Silverware tarnishes readily.

His reputation began to tarnish.

---

1. ACRID . . . . sharp, bitter, biting

Vinegar has an acrid taste.

Acrid remarks make enemies.

2. DUCTILE . . easily drawn out (as into wire) or hammered thin

Copper is very ductile.

A ductile person is very compliant or pliable.

3. DURABLE . . . . lasting, long-wearing

Canvas is very durable.

The speaker discussed the durability of our friendship with England.

4. POROUS . . having many tiny openings (that water can soak into)

Unglazed earthenware is very porous.

The porousness of a sponge makes it very useful.

5. RESILIENT . . . springy, coming back readily to its original shape

Rubber is very resilient.

The resiliency of car springs saves much discomfort.

6. VISCOUS . . . . . sticky, not flowing freely, thick

Molasses is very viscous.

Heavy oil has a high viscosity.

Questions

1. Change a letter in *congeal* and get *hide;* a letter in *fuse* and get a vapor or a trick; a letter in *bevel* and get noisy fun; a letter in *baste* and get the curse of India.

2. Change two letters of *durable* and get a short short short short story; two in *resilient* and get *one who receives*.
3. Review the *–ile* words on page 127. Can you add any?

PRACTICE SET

Copy the italicized words and beside each write its meaning in the sentence:

1. An *annealing* oven is hot enough to *fuse* glass.
2. *Bevel* the cloth and then *baste* it.
3. Silver is *ductile* and quite *durable*.
4. Rain will *tarnish* a metal roof, and it will *erode* a shingle roof in time.
5. Sponge rubber is both *porous* and *resilient*.
6. The dessert will *congeal* and take on a *glazed* appearance.
7. The *viscous* stuff in the jar gives off an *acrid* odor.
8. The winds *gyrate* ceaselessly around the peak.

TWELVE REMARKS

Can you fill each blank correctly? Use each base word once. Rearrange if necessary.

1. Milk on a zero morning will __?__.
2. Frost will often __?__ the pond in late October.
3. Cheap mirrors __?__ quickly.
4. __?__ a casting to toughen it.
5. Rocks __?__ through the centuries.
6. The bantams __?__ as they fight.
7. A boy's clothes must be extremely __?__. Summer underwear should be very __?__.
8. Wooden bleachers are more __?__ than brick would be.
9. Medicine usually tastes __?__ and cough medicine with honey in it is quite __?__.
10. Red-hot coals have a tendency to __?__, and glass is more __?__ than most persons realize.
11. Rafters must be __?__ed to fit.
12. __?__ the meat two or three times every hour.

VILLAINY

Jesse James

Can you fill the blanks appropriately?

He was a famous __?__ who committed the crime of __?__ on a large scale many times. His daring robberies caused many to __?__ the skill of law-enforcement officers. Clearly he was no __?__, and his __?__ is overlooked somewhat by admirers of his boldness and daring.

Verbs
1. assault
2. avenge
3. blaspheme
4. encroach
5. impugn
6. malinger
7. pilfer
8. ravage

Nouns
1. brigand
2. dastard
3. depredation
4. infamy
5. larceny
6. marauder
7. turpitude

1. ASSAULT . . . . to hit, strike, attack

Did you see the hobo assault the barber?

The suspect was charged with assault.

2. AVENGE . . . to repay, retaliate, exact punishment

Hamlet vowed he would avenge the murder of his father.
Thus, he became an avenger.

3. BLASPHEME . . to curse, abuse, swear, utter profanity

"Do not blaspheme," the stranger warned.

Blasphemy is irreligious and in bad taste.

A blasphemous ejaculation escaped his lips.

4. ENCROACH . . . . to trespass, intrude

Does Ellen ever encroach upon her brother's rights?

He will find a way to punish her encroachments.

5. IMPUGN (*im-PEWN*) . . . . to assail, call in question

Why do you impugn her honesty?

Note: *Impugn* means *fight against*, literally. Compare *pugnacious*.
Villify and *malign* (to *defame* or *slander*) are more forceful.

6. MALINGER . . to pretend illness (to avoid duty), to shirk

The new hand is inclined to malinger on Mondays.

Physical weakness makes her a malingerer.

7. PILFER . . . . . . to swipe, steal (small quantities)

Sam tried to pilfer fruit from a market.

A pilferer was arrested — and charged with pilferage.

"The Purloined [stolen] Letter" is the title of a story by
Edgar Allan Poe.

8. RAVAGE . . . . to lay waste, destroy

Epidemics began to ravage Europe.

Stone houses resist the ravages of time remarkably.

Compare *pillage*, to plunder.

1. **BRIGAND** . . . . . . **robber, bandit, plunderer**

A notorious brigand was shot by the police.
Brigandage once flourished in England.

Compare *desperado*, a reckless or especially daring lawbreaker.

2. **DASTARD** . . . . **base, malicious, or sneaky coward**

Only a dastard would run away from his duty like that.
Betraying the woman was a dastardly act.

Compare *pillage*, to plunder.

3. **DEPREDATION(S)** . . . . . . **despoilment, pillage**

The depredations of the rats ruined the stored food.

4. **INFAMY** . . . . . . **disgrace, dishonor, reproach**

Long will that day live in infamy!
Treason is an infamous crime.

5. **LARCENY** . . . . **(legal term for) theft**

The man was charged with larceny.
Petty or petit (page 263) larceny involves a small sum, grand
 larceny a large one.

6. **MARAUDER** . . **one who raids and plunders (or goes
about with such intentions)**

A skunk in a chicken house is a marauder.
We trailed the marauder all night.

7. **TURPITUDE** . . . . **baseness, shameful wickedness**

Was it turpitude or weakness that made him do it?

Questions

1. What other words end in *–ault? –oach? –ard? –tude?*
2. Which words contain two a's? a double letter?
3. Although you have not had such units as No. 21 and No. 11,
 Part Three, can you explain why some words ending in *–fer*
 have a double *f* and not others (*offer, differ, prefer, refer*)?
4. How many three-letter words can you find within the base
 words of this unit?

PRACTICE SET

Copy the italicized words and beside each write its meaning in the sentence:

1. The *brigand* was a *dastard* to *assault* an old man.
2. Who will *avenge* the *depredations* of the *marauder?*
3. Is it *turpitude* that makes him willing to *malinger* and *blaspheme?*
4. The accusation *impugns* my honor and *encroaches* upon my civil rights.
5. *Pilfering* pennies is a form of *larceny*.
6. The *infamy* of the idea lay in planning to *ravage* a neutral country.

THE CRIMINAL

Can you fill the blanks, using each base word once — where it fits best?

He early learned to __?__ candy from a store. Bad company taught him to __?__ the church, to __?__ upon the rights of others, and to __?__ the motives of his own parents. He also learned to __?__ when he was supposed to be working. At first his __?__s were confined to a neighbor's fruit trees, but he became more and more of a __?__ in the neighborhood, until at length he was serving a prison term for __?__. He even tried to __?__ an officer of the law.

When he got older he became an out-and-out __?__ who held up banks. He was no __?__ when it came to courage. He kept wishing he were a conqueror who could __?__ whole cities. When his __?__ reached the point of murdering an old woman, her son resolved to __?__ his mother's death. The bandit was shot in a gun battle, and the tragic story of his increasing __?__ thus came to a fitting end.

SHYNESS AND SILENCE

Talkative children sometimes become quiet adults. Wives sometimes let their husbands do most of the talking, but more often it is the other way around. In a similar way many words have pairs of letters, one of which now does most of the talking.

Year is an example. A thousand years ago it was probably pronounced *yea–air,* but the *a* became more and more silent until now it serves only to make the *e* longer than it might be otherwise.

Each word in the groups below has at least one letter which no longer talks. Study them carefully. Pronounce the words as they should be. Mispronounce them so as to make the silent letters speak. Divide the longer words into syllables. Write sentences containing one or more from each group.

A words: *beacon, beard, creature, deaf, dreary, eagle, endeavor, feature, increase, league, reason, search, sweat, treason, weapon, weary; decrease, defeat, disease, ease, easier, easily, increase, release, retreat, steamer, threat(en), treasure, treasury; abroad, boast, broadcast, groan, loan; aisle, carriage, cocoa, diamond, marriage, parliament*

D-T words: *badge, patch, snatch; (know)ledge, pledge, sketch, stretch; bridge, cartridge, ridge; hodge-podge, lodge; budge, judge, grudge*

E words: *bearing, determine, fiery, heart(ily), vengeance; aerial, bade* (pronounced *bad*), *foreign, forestall, foretell, height, ninety*

I words: *bier* (coffin), *brigadier, cashier, financier, frontier, pier* (a dock), *tier* (a layer). Review pages 117–118.

P words: *pneumatic, pneumonia, psalm, psychology*

SC words: *ascend, conscious, conscience, descent, discipline, scene, science, scientist, scissors*

W words: *answer, borrow, fellow(s), knowledge, narrow, shadow, toward(s); whole, whoop, widow, window, wrench, wrest, wretched, wringer, write*

Miscellaneous and tricky: *depot, mortgage, rhythmic, schedule, scheme, Wednesday, wholly*

ACTIVITIES

1. List the words which contain a double letter.
2. What word(s) can you add to each group?
3. Make a scramble of several groups and see whether you can sort them out again.
4. Use the words for a spell down, if time permits.
5. What spelling difficulties have you discovered, other than the silent or almost silent letters?
6. Take one group and make a list of all the other forms you can think of for each word.

SENTENCES FOR PRACTICE

Write some or all of the following from dictation:

1. The financier's knowledge of psychology helped him.
2. Hold the scissors downward as you ascend the narrow stairs.
3. The foreigner is deaf and wears a beard.
4. His conscience made him wholly wretched.
5. The brigadier hoped to forestall aerial attacks.
6. The widow stricken with pneumonia was still conscious.
7. Last Wednesday a bandit snatched the diamond and ran.
8. The heavy work on the bridge made us sweat and groan.
9. Scientists are doing research work on cartridges.
10. A carriage could be driven down the aisle easily.

PART TWO   UNIT 17

"YOU'RE IN THE ARMY NOW"

Questionnaire

Which word from the column at the right gives the best answer to each of the following questions?

1. What got you in? _ _ ? _ _ ion.
2. Where do you live?
3. What makes the most noise?
4. What do you wear on your uniform?
5. Where do you spend free time?
6. What are you often ordered to do on maneuvers?

● *How many of the nouns and verbs of this unit can you find in the illustration above?*

Nouns

1. artillery
2. barracks
3. canteen
4. cavalry
5. hostage
6. infantry
7. insignia
8. munitions
9. platoon
10. truce

Verbs

1. conscript
2. deploy
3. infiltrate
4. muster
5. ricochet

1. **ARTILLERY . . . . mounted guns, ordnance**
Our heavy artillery began the attack.
The man had been an artilleryman in World War I.

2. **BARRACKS . . . building(s) for housing military personnel**
We keep the barracks nice and clean.

3. **CANTEEN . . place for refreshment or recreation of military personnel**
The canteen (post exchange) sells candy.
He visited the Red Cross canteen often.

Note: *Canteen* also means a container to carry drinking water, hence its connection with refreshment(s).

4. **CAVALRY . . . . mounted force(s)**
Cavalry was important in the Battle of Waterloo.
A cavalryman was hurt.

5. **HOSTAGE . . . . . . person held as a guarantee**
Bandits seized the man's wife as a hostage.

6. **INFANTRY . . . . foot soldiers**
Infantry is the mainstay of any army.
Infantrymen must walk, but they get there.

7. **INSIGNIA . . . . badges or emblems**
Military insignia show a man's division and his rank.

8. **MUNITIONS . . . . . military stores, ammunition**
The ship carried munitions.
A munitions factory blew up.

9. **PLATOON . . small military unit (part of a company)**
Several platoons went out for rifle practice.
The platoon leader will be promoted.
A company consists of several platoons, and a battalion is made up of several companies.

10. TRUCE . . . . a halt (by agreement) in fighting; an armistice

A truce was arranged in order to bury the dead.
The armistice saved bloodshed while peace was arranged.

---

1. CONSCRIPT . . . . . to draft (for military service)

Should the government conscript men during peacetime?
A million conscripts were needed.
Conscription was necessary in both wars.

2. DEPLOY . . to spread out (a military force), take positions for battle

The 89th was ordered to deploy and surround the village.
The deployment of our artillery confused the enemy at first.

3. INFILTRATE . . . to slip through (singly or gradually)

Enemy troops began to infiltrate our lines.
Our position was weakened by enemy infiltration.

4. MUSTER . . . . . . to assemble, summon, gather

The troops will muster at dawn.
Shirley could not muster the courage to speak.

5. RICOCHET (rik-o-SHAY) . . to glance off, rebound, skip

The bullet will ricochet if fired at the water.

Questions

1. How many three- and four-letter words can you find in the base words of the unit without rearranging letters?
2. List other words (one or two) ending in *–trate, –ploy, –et* (pronounced like *a* in *day*), *–alry, –oon.*
3. Change three letters in *infantry* and get *hard work*; one letter in *hostage* and get *mailing cost.* How many different words can you get from *muster* by changing one letter each time?
4. Other military words include *reveille* (page 259), *caisson* (artillery ammunition wagon), and *latrine* (toilet).

PRACTICE SET

Copy the italicized words and beside each write its meaning in the sentence:

1. *Artillery* fire destroyed our *barracks* and a *munitions* dump.
2. The lady at the *canteen* recognized the *insignia* of a *cavalry* division.
3. The *platoon* leader was held as a *hostage* when he went to arrange a *truce*.
4. The *infantry* division is made up mostly of men who were *conscripted*.
5. We shall *deploy* before the attack and *muster* afterward.
6. Bullets began to *ricochet* around them as they tried to *infiltrate* the enemy position.

UNHORSED

Can you fill the blanks, using each base word where it fits best?

An ex-jockey wanted to join the __?__, but he found himself on foot in the __?__ instead. He became the leader of a __?__ which guarded a __?__ plant. Every morning he __?__ed his little force of __?__s in front of the __?__ where they were quartered. Off duty they spent much time in the __?__.

Later the ex-jockey was transferred to an __?__ division and became a gunner. He liked to watch shells __?__ from the rocks where enemy soldiers were __?__ed as they tried to __?__ our position. He was proud of the __?__ on his shoulder. Once he was captured and held as a __?__ before the __?__ came which turned out to be the end of the war.

Army Life

Write a paragraph, if time permits, on experiences in the army based on imagination, reading, or the disclosures of a relative. Use a few of the words in this unit.

"ANCHORS AWEIGH"

If

1. If a storm comes up, we may have to __?__ part of the cargo.
2. If a man-o'-war challenges, we will scuttle the ship because it is loaded with __?__.
3. As the __?__ rises in the hull, it must be pumped out.
4. If we get seasick, we lean over the __?__.
5. If we look in the __?__, we find a compass.

Nouns
1. armada
2. barge
3. barnacle
4. bilge
5. binnacle
6. boatswain
7. contraband
8. corvette
9. ensign
10. gunwale

Verbs
1. convoy
2. debark
3. jettison
4. navigate
5. scuttle

1. ARMADA (*ar-MAH-da*) . . . **an array of armed ships, large fleet**

The enemy armada sailed toward Midway.
The Spanish Armada was defeated and destroyed.

2. BARGE . . **a large, flat-bottomed ship (chiefly on rivers and canals)**

The barge was loaded with iron ore.
A barge may be a pleasure boat or houseboat.
He barged (pushed his way) in ahead of me.

3. BARNACLE . . **a form of marine life which clings to ship bottoms and rocks**

Barnacles on a ship's hull slow it down.
Bad habits are like barnacles.

4. BILGE . . **bottom of hull or dirty water which collects there**

A loose bilge plate let in water.
Bilge is like dishwater in some ways.

5. BINNACLE . . . . . **case containing ship's compass**

The binnacle is near the ship's wheel.

6. BOATSWAIN (*BO-s'n*) . . . **a minor officer who has charge of rigging, anchors, and cables**

The boatswain uses a "pipe" to call the crew to duty.
The coxswain is the crewman who steers a racing shell.

7. CONTRABAND . . . **forbidden or smuggled goods**

Opium shipments are listed as contraband.
The ship was carrying contraband of war.

8. CORVETTE . . . . **a small warship**

A corvette is smaller than a frigate (page 78).

9. ENSIGN . . . (1) the national flag
(2) lowest commissioned naval officer *

Officers and men all salute the national ensign as they board or leave the ship.

They also salute the officer of the deck, who on a small ship may be an ensign.

10. GUNWALE (*GUN'l*) . . . upper edge of ship's side, deck railing

Sailors were leaning over the gunwale.

Originally the gunwale served as a support for the guns.

---

1. CONVOY . . . to conduct or escort (for protection)

The corvette was directed to convoy a small merchant ship through the danger zone.

A large convoy assembled (could be land or sea).

2. DEBARK . . . . to land (after voyage), disembark

A landing party will debark in the morning.

Le Havre was the port of debarkation.

3. JETTISON . . . . to throw overboard

Before long we had to jettison extra clothing and equipment.

Review *jetsam* and *flotsam* on page 78.

4. NAVIGATE . . . . . . to sail, plot one's course

No one could navigate the ship.

A navigator came aboard. He had studied navigation for many years.

5. SCUTTLE . . . . to sink one's own ship; to run briskly

A Nazi crew scuttled the *Columbus* to prevent its capture.

A gray dog scuttled past the open doorway.

Scuttlebutt (means *drinking fountain*) is rumor or gossip, which is often circulated at the drinking fountain on a warship.

* (Except for a few commissioned warrant officers.)

Questions

1. How many naval words or expressions such as *capstan, pelorus, crow's nest,* and *pipe down* can you list? Review *starboard, larboard,* and other sea terms in Part One, Unit 22. What do the following sea terms mean: *shoal, keel, holystone, coaming?* What time(s) is eight bells?
2. Can you find fifteen three-letter words contained within the base words of this unit?
3. Change one letter of *binnacle* and get a peak.

PRACTICE SET

Copy the italicized words and beside each write its meaning in the sentence:

1. The *boatswain* of the wrecked merchantman ordered the crew to *jettison* the *contraband* before *debarking.*
2. The light near the *binnacle* could be seen from the *gunwale* of the *barge.*
3. It was necessary to *scuttle* the *corvette* sent to *convoy* the tanker because it could not *navigate* in shallow water.
4. The *ensign* thought the ship was covered with *barnacles.*
5. Each ship of the *armada* was pumping out *bilge.*

ALL AT SEA

Which of the base words of this unit goes in each blank? Use each once — where it fits best.

1. __?__s are found on the outside of the hull's bottom, __?__ on the inside. The __?__ is located in the pilothouse.
2. A __?__ can be used to __?__ a merchant ship but is not large enough to fight a battleship; a __?__ is not a fighting ship at all, and is awkward to __?__ in a narrow channel.
3. Our huge __?__ will __?__ every ship if it does not triumph.
4. The __?__ leaned on the __?__. He was telling how to board a merchant ship in searching for __?__.
5. Should we __?__ the compass before we strike (lower) the __?__ and __?__ from the stranded ship?

PAIRED PERILS

What is the difference between an angle and an angel?

That is a foolish question if you can read, but the boy who wrote, "The streets make an obtuse angel at that point," would not admit he was a fool.

Read the following pairs several times, noting the definitions and the differences. Exaggerate the pronunciation enough to show the differences:

1. **angle** — figure formed by lines that meet   **angel** — heavenly being
2. **carrot** — a vegetable   **caret** — omission mark (∧);
   carat — unit of jewel weight
3. **cease** — stop   **seize** — grasp
4. **cemetery** — burial park   **seminary** — training school
5. **dairy** — cow institution   **diary** — daily record
6. **envelop** — enfold   **envelope** — container
7. **formerly** — before   **formally** — in a formal manner
8. **loose** — not tight   **lose** — suffer loss of
9. **route** — path or road   **rout** — drive forth
10. **sphere** — globe   **spear** — a sharp weapon

Questions

1. Write sentences using, first, the words in the first column, and then the words in the second column. Or write sentences using different pairs in contrast.
2. Write the following words in two columns. Be sure you can pronounce each and explain the differences in meaning: *adapt, adopt; advise, advice; bough, bow; carless, careless; celery, salary; decease, disease; duly, dully; facet, faucet; later, latter; liable, libel; profit, prophet; roomer, rumor; series, serious; sole, soul; suit, suite; trail, trial.*

HOMONYMS

Homonyms, words spelled differently but pronounced alike, are plentiful in English. Study or review the following:

1. **coarse** — rough, unrefined   **course** — path, route, or study
2. **canvas** — cloth   **canvass** — sell or solicit
3. **compliment** — a bit of praise   **complement** — something that completes
4. **council** — a group   **counsel** — advice or a lawyer
5. **current** — in motion   **currant** — red fruit
6. **desert** — dry land   **dessert** — tasty food
7. **metal** — cold, shiny stuff   **mettle** — courage (page 46)
8. **principal** — money, chief   **principle** — a rule, generality
9. **stationary** — immovable   **stationery** — writing paper
10. **troop** — group or collection   **troupe** — actors, usually

Questions

1. Write sentences using the homonyms above correctly.
2. Write a homonym for: *base, birth, boarder, capitol, foreword* (to a book), *hanger, kernel, night, meddle, morn, piece, cent, stake, strait, throne, vale, vain, weakly.* Be sure you can spell, define, and pronounce each pair correctly.

SENTENCES FOR PRACTICE

Practice reading the following sentences and write some or all from dictation:

1. The advice about the suite of rooms came later.
2. An angel left an envelope in the cemetery.
3. The colonel's trial came in the latter part of August.
4. The detour made us lose the route past the seminary.
5. He will loose a series of libel suits.
6. The diary tells of a troupe of actors living in a dairy.
7. A carrot lay beside the hollow metal sphere.
8. The disease formerly made it dangerous to view the deceased.
9. The principal would not offer a coarse compliment.
10. His principal use for stationery is in offering counsel.

VERBS AND NOUNS

Public Affairs

Can you fill the blanks correctly?

1. What should we do about graft? __?__ it.
2. What about the Red Cross drive? Give it greater __?__.
3. What about new industries? Encourage their __?__.
4. What about prosperity? Our town should __?__ it.
5. What about the school system? __?__ it and find out what is needed.
6. What do speakers like to stand on? A __?__.

Verbs

1. agitate
2. appraise
3. commute
4. comprise
5. engender
6. eradicate
7. exude

Nouns

1. dais
2. facsimile
3. gamut
4. gravity
5. hovel
6. impetus
7. influx
8. inkling

VERBS AND NOUNS—STUDY GUIDE

1. AGITATE . . . . **to stir up, excite**

The old man was greatly agitated.

A labor agitator came to town.

Agitation for a pension plan has begun.

2. APPRAISE . . . . **to estimate the value of**

Ask him to appraise our car.

The appraiser shook his head sadly.

The appraisal was disappointing.

3. COMMUTE . . **(1) to reduce or lessen (a sentence)**
(2) to travel regularly (especially to and from one's work in a city)

The governor will commute the sentence to life imprisonment. Commutation will bring joy to the man's parents. The bank president lives in Bugville and commutes to the city. He has been a commuter for thirteen years.

4. COMPRISE . . . . . **to make up, include, embrace**

Ten towns comprised the region known as Decapolis.

Guns taken from criminals comprise the F.B.I. collection.

5. ENGENDER . . . . . **to breed, generate, produce**

Criticism engenders ill will.

6. ERADICATE . . . . **to remove, wipe out**

Can we eradicate race prejudice?

An ink eradicator is often useful.

Eradication of crime is difficult.

Note: *Eradicate* means literally *to tear out by the roots.* Compare *extirpate, exterminate.*

7. EXUDE . . . . **to give forth**

His face exudes perspiration when he thinks hard.

A happy person exudes cheerfulness.

Note: *Exude* literally means *to sweat out* (through the pores).

---

1. **DAIS** (*DAY-iss*) . . . . a small platform

   Sandra stepped onto the dais to sing.

   Compare *rostrum*. Look up the derivation, if possible.

2. **FACSIMILE** . . . an exact likeness (in photographic sense)

   The document on exhibit is a facsimile of the Declaration of Independence.

   Find out, if possible, what facsimile transmission is.

3. **GAMUT** . . . . whole range or series

   The novel covers the entire gamut of human emotions.

4. **GRAVITY** . . . . seriousness, solemnity

   The gravity of the world situation worried us.

   The gravity with which the President spoke made his words hard to forget.

   Gravity is also the pull of the earth and of other bodies.

5. **HOVEL** . . . . a hut, very poor dwelling

   The family lived in a hovel.

   Compare *hostel, domicile, abode.*

6. **IMPETUS** . . . . . . momentum, drive, incentive

   The impetus of the attack made it successful.

   The inventor worked under the impetus of his new idea.

7. **INFLUX** . . . . inflowing, inpouring

   The new factory brought an influx of metal workers.

8. **INKLING** . . . . . . hint, intimation, indication

   The police had an inkling that the man would be murdered.

Questions

1. Can you explain the double letter in *appraise* and *commute?*
2. How many three- and four-letter words can you find in the base words without rearranging letters?

3. *Ex–* usually means *out (from)*. How many *ex–* words can you list? Has the *ex–* changed its meaning in any?
4. *Simil(e)* in *facsimile* means *like*. Can you think of five other words in which it appears? *Simile* (page 213) is one.

PRACTICE SET

Copy the italicized words and beside each write its meaning in the sentence:

1. We had no *inkling* that the bank would *appraise* the house.
2. Uncle George could not *eradicate* from his mind the notion that we lived in a *hovel*.
3. Will an *influx* of new pupils *agitate* the teacher?
4. Will the governor *commute* the sentence of a man who has run the *gamut* of crimes as this man has?
5. The *gravity* of the danger should *engender* caution.
6. He *exudes* confidence, and his experiences *comprise* a fine preparation for his new work.
7. A *facsimile* of the *dais* will be made.
8. The *impetus* of the movement grew.

THE MAN WHO KEPT CHICKENS

Which of the base words fits best in each blank?

The recent __?__ of new people included a man who keeps chickens. His yard soon began to __?__ an unpleasant odor. The neighbors' complaints, gathering __?__ day by day, served only to __?__ him and __?__ bad feeling. As a matter of fact, the complaints __?__d a just cause for police action. He had no __?__, however, that we planned a meeting to denounce him from the __?__, so to speak, but we sent him a copy of the charges and a __?__ of his chicken coop as a joke. Our meeting ran the __?__ from silly fun to long-faced __?__ and violent hatred.

At length a real estate agent came to __?__ his home. He sold it, moved to a __?__ in the country, and began to __?__ to his job in the city. Thus the great evil of keeping chickens in our neighborhood was __?__d.

KNOTTY NOTS

A combat is a fight, and a person who participates in a fight is a combatant or participant. Anyone who is not a fighter or refuses to fight becomes a *noncombatant* or *nonparticipant.* Thus a three-letter prefix *non–* has changed a fighter into a person who does not fight. Prefixes are an easy, swift, and efficient way of making words fit our needs when we want to say something a trifle complicated.

The English language has a dozen or more prefixes that denote the *negative* or *opposite* of a word or *root.* They deny, they separate, they divorce something or somebody. This unit presents twelve such prefixes and shows how they work. The exercise below will help you discover how skillful you already are in using them to find a word you need.

Opposites

Can you make each sentence contradict itself by putting the correct prefix from the list at the right in each blank?

1. The material was __?__usable.
2. The dog is __?__contented in the house.
3. This book is strongly __?__-Communist.
4. Do you ever __?__spell the word *rhythm?*
5. Public executions are __?__grading.
6. Gandhi believed in __?__violent resistance.

Prefixes

1. anti–
   contra–
   counter–
2. non–
   un–
   in–
3. mis–

   _____

1. ab–
2. de–
3. dis–
4. ex-, ec–
5. se–

KNOTTY NOTS—STUDY GUIDE

1. ANTI–, CONTRA–, COUNTER– . . . against, opposing, opposite

An *anti*toxin works *against* a poison.
An *ant*onym is the *opposite* of a word.
An *anti*septic works *against* infection.

To *contra*dict a person is to say the *opposite*.
A *counter*claim is an *opposite* or *opposing* claim.
A *counter*balance is an *opposite* force or weight.

Note: Quite often *ob–* means *against* as in *object, obsess, obstruct, opponent, obtrude*.

2. NON–, UN–, IN– . . . . not

A *non*resident does *not* reside where he happens to be living or working.
An *un*wanted visitor is one who is *not* wanted.
An *in*eligible person is one who is *not* eligible.

Other examples: *nonsense, nonunion, nonexistent, unrealized, undesirable, unattached, ungovernable, incautious, infrequent, indecisive, inconvenient, inattentive.*

Note 1: Sometimes *un–* carries the idea of reversing as in *untwist, untangle,* and *undress,* but this meaning is less common and seldom confusing.

Note 2: *In–* becomes *im–* before *m* and *p, il–* before *l, ir–* before *r: immovable, impossible, illogical, irreligious,* and so on. It often means *in* or *into* instead of *not*.

3. MIS– . . . . wrong(ly), incorrect(ly)

*Mis*behave — behave *wrongly.*
*Mis*calculate — calculate *incorrectly.*
*Mis*conduct — *wrong* conduct.

Prefixes of Parting and Separation

1. **AB–**
2. **DE–**   (down from, especially)
3. **DIS–**   (not, opposite) . . . . away from, down
4. **EX–, EC–**   (out)   from, out from, apart
5. **SE–**

To *ab*duct is to lead *away* or kidnap.
If you *ab*hor something, you shrink *away from* it.

*De*populate — take the inhabitants *from*
*De*press — push *down*
*De*scend — climb *down*

*Dis*miss — send *away*
*Dis*arm — take arms *away from*

*Ex*clude — shut *out from*
*Ex*communicate — cut *off from* (membership)
*Ef*fusion — a pouring *out*
*Ec*lipse — a going *out* of sight

Note: *Ex-* is reduced to *e* before *d, g, l, m, n, r, v,* and one or two other consonants. It becomes *ef* before *f* and sometimes *es-* or *ec-*. Compare *edict, educate, egress, elude, elect, emit, enunciate, erupt, evaporate.*

*Se*cede — go *apart*, separate
*Se*cure — without (*apart from*) care
*Se*duce — lead *apart* (from doing right)
*Se*gregate — gather *apart* or separately

ACTIVITIES

1. Make a list of 25 words using one of the prefixes in this unit. Consult the dictionary to get ideas and to check spellings.
2. Write the opposite of each of the following, using the correct prefix: *ability, certain, comfortable, continue, courage, definite, ease, easy, formal, graceful* (two forms), *happy, known, necessary, pleasant, reasonable, satisfactory, sense, understand, use, valid.*
3. What *in-* word means *harmless* or *guiltless?* What *dis-* word means an *argument? far off?*

FIRST PRACTICE SET

Can you supply for each blank the meaning of the italicized prefix?

1. To *mis*guide a person is to guide him __?__.
2. An *un*identified person is one __?__ identified.
3. A *non*descript person is one who is __?__ readily described.
4. An *anti*tank gun is one used __?__ tanks.
5. An *in*sufficient supply is __?__ enough.
6. To *ex*tract a tooth is to draw (*–tract*) it __?__.
7. To *se*clude is to shut (*–clude*) __?__.
8. An *ab*erration is a wandering (*–err–*) __?__.
9. To *de*duct a sum is to "lead" (*–duct*) or take it __?__ the original amount.
10. To *dis*pel the mist is to drive (*–pel*) it __?__.

SECOND PRACTICE SET

Can you think of a good word for each blank? It may be formed from the word in parentheses.

1. The performance was __?__ (not satisfactory).
2. The boy was very __?__ (not polite).
3. The reporter was __?__ (incorrectly informed).
4. The book contains __?__ (not American) ideas.
5. Most cars use __?__ (knock preventing) gasoline.
6. Traffic moves around the circle in a __?__ (opposite-to-the-hands-of-a-clock) direction.
7. Father and mother sometimes __?__ (opposite of agree).
8. Newspapers will sometimes __?__ (twist away from the truth) the actual facts.
9. Bad habits __?__ (draw down) from one's chances of success.
10. The king threatened to __?__ (drive out) all the Jews.

A DAY IN COURT

Useful Facts

Can you fill the blanks correctly from the list at the right?

1. Either __?__ or a __?__ will get you released from prison.
2. The law will __?__ you to get you into court and __?__ you before you leave if you are believed guilty.
3. A __?__, a __?__, a __?__, and a(n) __?__ could all be at different times a single person if that person had attended both a medical school and a law school.

● *How many of the verbs and nouns of this unit can you find in the illustration above?*

Verbs
1. arraign
2. attest
3. extradite
4. prosecute
5. refute
6. waive

Nouns
1. attorney
2. bail
3. coroner
4. deputy
5. felon
6. legacy
7. misdemeanor
8. parole
9. posse

A DAY IN COURT—STUDY GUIDE

1. ARRAIGN . . to call before a court, summon for trial

The youth was arraigned on a charge of reckless driving.
Arraignment followed his arrest.

2. ATTEST . . . . to testify, bear witness to

The father attests his son's innocence.
The attestations of other witnesses were heard.

**3. EXTRADITE . . to transfer a wanted person from an-
other state or authority**

Illinois will extradite a man wanted for forgery in Ohio.
Extradition papers were prepared in Columbus.

4. PROSECUTE . . . . . . to subject to trial at law

The state will prosecute the man for starting fires.
The prosecution had very little evidence.
Jim will prosecute (pursue) his studies faithfully.

5. REFUTE . . . . to disprove, bring contrary evidence

No one could refute the prosecutor's evidence.
The bus driver testified in refutation.

6. WAIVE . . . . to forego, give up (a right or claim)

A prisoner may waive the right of trial by jury.
She signed a waiver releasing the company from liability if
she was injured while visiting the plant.

---

1. ATTORNEY . . . . lawyer

The defense attorney began to question his client.

**2. BAIL . . money or security offered as a guarantee (of
appearance for trial if released)**

The suspect was released on $5,000 bail.
If the charge is murder, a prisoner is not bailable (that is,
is not eligible for bailment).

See *bailiff* and *bailiwick* if time permits.

---

3. CORONER . . . official (a doctor) who determines the cause of death

The coroner conducted an inquest and found that the man had been poisoned.

Who is the coroner in your locality? How is he chosen?

4. DEPUTY . . . . representative, agent

The sheriff's deputy was hurt fighting outlaws.

Several men were deputized (authorized as agents) to help village police quell a riot.

5. FELON . . . . criminal

The felon was shot as he tried to escape.

A felony is a fairly serious crime.

6. LEGACY . . . . . something inherited, a bequest

A legacy from his uncle put him through college.

It made him a legatee.

7. MISDEMEANOR . . . . a minor offense

A misdemeanor is much less serious than a felony.

Spitting in busses is usually a misdemeanor.

8. PAROLE . . . early, conditional release from prison

Seven of the prisoners are out on parole. They must avoid bad company and report regularly to the Parole Board.

9. POSSE . . a group deputized to hunt down a criminal or maintain order

The sheriff's posse found the murderer in a swamp.

Questions

1. How many of the following charges can you define: arson, bigamy, forgery, homicide, larceny, vagrancy? Can you add any to the list?
2. What word, spelled the same as *prosecute* except for the second and third letters, means *to harry*?

3. Change one letter in *refute* and get a little fame.
4. Where does *ai* appear in the base words?
5. Can you think of ten one-syllable words which end, like *parole,* in *–ole?*
6. What other word ends in the same four letters as *arraign?*
7. Can you find twelve three- and four-letter words contained in the base words without rearranging?

PRACTICE SET

Copy the italicized words and beside each write its meaning in the sentence:

1. We must *extradite* the man before we can *prosecute* him.
2. The *coroner* will *refute* the suicide theory.
3. A *felon* on *parole* received a *legacy.*
4. The suspect will *attest* to his statement in the presence of the *attorneys.*
5. The prisoner *waives* the right to get out on *bail.*
6. The marshal's *deputy* committed a *misdemeanor.*
7. The kidnaper was *arraigned* in the town where the *posse* found him.

AT LARGE

Can you fill the blanks, using each base word once? Fill first the blanks you are sure about.

The bandit was at large. He had jumped __?__. The sheriff and his __?__ organized a __?__ to search. The __?__ had crossed the Ohio line in his flight, but state __?__s in Indiana had agreed to __?__ him as soon as he could be captured and __?__ed in Indiana.

It turned out that the bandit was a convict on __?__ from a prison in Utah. Ohio, unwilling to __?__ its claims against him as the result of a __?__'s inquest, decided to __?__ him on suspicion of murder. Witnesses __?__ed to his resemblance to the wanted man, and his lawyer was unable to __?__ their evidence. The man had been arrested in the first place merely for a __?__ while trying to claim a --?-- from the old man who had been found dead.

VARIED ADJECTIVES

A Play

Can you fill the blanks sensibly?

Adjectives

1. Putting on a play is an __?__ undertaking.
2. A boy looks very __?__ in the part of a middle-aged businessman.
3. The director needs to be very __?__.
4. The boy who operates the lights should be very __?__ in handling the switches.
5. The furniture is usually provided __?__.
6. Each one who has a part must be very __?__ in learning his lines.

1. adept
2. arbitrary
3. arduous
4. assiduous
5. callow
6. deft
7. dulcet
8. edible
9. feasible
10. fervent
11. festive
12. flaccid
13. flagrant
14. garish
15. gratis

VARIED ADJECTIVES—STUDY GUIDE

1. ADEPT . . . . highly skillful

Uncle Joe is an adept fisherman.
He is also known for adeptness in arithmetic.

2. ARBITRARY . . . . . . positive and unreasoning

Her decisions seemed very arbitrary.
Arbitrariness often irritates people.

3. ARDUOUS . . . . . . trying, difficult, laborious

Shell racing is an arduous sport.
The story describes the arduousness of a lumberman's life.

4. ASSIDUOUS . . . . . diligent, patient, unremitting

As a salesman, he is very assiduous, but assiduousness is not
   enough.
She practices assiduously.

5. CALLOW . . . . immature, unformed

An eighteen-year-old boy is too callow for the presidency of
   the company.

6. DEFT . . skillful (especially with one's hands), adroit

With a few deft strokes, he drew a lifelike sketch of Aunt
   Maisie.

7. DULCET . . . . sweet, melodious

The dulcet tones of a cello could be heard.

8. EDIBLE . . . . fit to eat, suitable for food

Horsemeat is edible but not appetizing.
Food experts discussed the edibility of grass.

9. FEASIBLE . . practicable, capable of being carried out
readily

Use of roof tops for landing fields is feasible.
The feasibility of building a swimming pool depends on the
   cost.

10. FERVENT . . . . eager, glowing, ardent

The boy had a fervent desire to become a doctor.
The speaker argued with great fervor for world brotherhood.
A fervid appeal by radio failed.

11. FESTIVE . . . . joyous, sportive, gay

They went to the game in a festive mood.
May Day is a festal (festive) occasion.
The festivities began at noon.

12. FLACCID (FLACK-sid) . . . . . flabby, limp, soft

Unused muscles gradually become flaccid.

13. FLAGRANT . . . . glaring, notably bad

Playing in the street is a flagrant violation of safety rules.
The flagrancy of the deed amazed the populace.

14. GARISH . . . . gaudy, showy, extravagantly gay

Her clothes were a garish display of bad taste.
The garishness of the party surprised everyone.

15. GRATIS (GRAY-tis) . . . . free, gratuitous

The company will send the book gratis.
A gratuitous compliment is one given willingly; a gratuitous
insult is one not deserved or justified.

Compare *gratuity*, a fee or tip (because given freely); and *gratitude*.
The root is Latin *gratus*, agreeable, pleasing. It appears in *grateful* and *congratulate*. What does the Latin phrase *persona non
grata* mean?

Questions

1. Change the first letter of one word and get *restless;* of another and get *the territory of a pastor;* of another and get
torn; of a fourth and have *to make sacred* — or *yellowish* —
and other words, depending on which letter you use.

---

2. Change the middle letter of one word and get *to take as one's own.* Change it again and get *to make suitable.*

3. What three- and four-letter words can you find contained in the base words?

PRACTICE SET

Copy the italicized words and beside each write its meaning in the sentence:

1. He was as *flaccid* as mashed potatoes and as *callow* as a new-born calf.
2. A good secretary is *deft* with a pencil, *adept* at taking dictation, and *assiduous* in filing.
3. An *arbitrary* answer as to whether the plan is *feasible* will not satisfy us.
4. Can one be *fervent* and *festive* at the same time?
5. The pageant was a *garish* spectacle, full of *flagrant* historical errors.
6. Finding *edible* foliage was an *arduous* task.
7. The *dulcet* music of the mouth organ comes *gratis.*

"JUICY"

Can you fill the blanks appropriately, using each base word once?

We call him "Juicy" because he looks like a ripe grapefruit. His muscles are very __?__, but he is __?__ at playing checkers and very __?__ with tiddledy winks. He has a __?__, rather musical voice and is very __?__ and patient in collecting stamps. His mistakes in grammar are __?__, but by __?__ application he has managed to improve.

Juicy can be quite __?__ on holidays, and he will sing __?__ when asked. He thinks toads are __?__ for human beings and believes a trip to the moon will be __?__ in a few years. Most Christmas displays he considers __?__. He is really very __?__ in his judgments, and quite __?__ in his opinions. He is a __?__ admirer of a certain radio comedian.

WELDED WORDS

Many words which sometimes bother pupils who have not looked at them carefully are actually two words welded together without any change in either word. Study the following, which are found in most spelling books. Divide them in your mind, and notice the way each part contributes in most cases to the meaning of the combination. Use them in sentences.

elsewhere	horseback	salesman
evergreen	household	somewhat
extraordinary	inasmuch	sweetheart
farewell	invoice	thereby
forenoon	meantime	therefore
forever	necktie	throughout
friendship	nevertheless	tiresome
gentleman	outline	township
handsome	outrage	understanding
hardship	overcharge	underwear
hardware	overdue	warehouse
headquarters	overlook	whereas
hereafter	overnight	whereby
heretofore	peanut	wherein
herewith	postmaster	withdraw
highway	roommate	

MISCELLANEOUS

Most spelling books include the words grouped below. Review them — or *study* each group, as your teacher directs, by reading the words aloud, dividing into syllables, spelling aloud, or putting into sentences. Any which you miss should be added promptly, with proper mental ceremonies, to your Never Again list.

AGE words: *average, bandage, damage, foliage, manage, passage, percentage, postage, savage.*

ATE words: *adequate, candidate, climate, create, delegate, delicate, elaborate, estimate, fortunate, moderate, private, Senate, temperate.*

DOM words: *freedom, kingdom, seldom, wisdom.*

GRAB BAG: *alcohol, anxiety, bonus, buckle, camera, carbon, castle, cement, choice, choir, chorus, cistern, clause, comrade, concern(ing), concert, concrete, convince, cripple, dawn, decay, decide, delay, discount, district, divine, empire, Europe, faucet, feeble, female, folks, future, gasoline, glimpse, hawk, lemonade, liberty, license, madam, magic, material, measles, monthly, napkin, neglect, obtain, owing, paragraph, phrase, poultry, poverty, property, publish, puddle, pulse, raisin, recipe, record, rejoice, repair, retail, sacred, session, shelves, shove, shrewd, skeleton, sponge, squeeze, taxicab, tournament, vision, wound, youth.*

From this list, select pairs which have similar spelling, like *delay* and *decay*. List short words contained in longer ones, like *male* in *female*.

SENTENCES FOR PRACTICE

Write some or all of the following from dictation:

1. The postmaster said farewell to his necktie and underwear.
2. The average candidate promises freedom.
3. What is your estimate of the damage to the foliage?
4. A siege of measles reduced the youth almost to a skeleton.
5. Boys rejoice at the first glimpse of raisins or lemonade.
6. The choir gave a concert for crippled children.
7. The taxicab uses gasoline made from carbon.
8. The feature picture is seldom first on the program.
9. A cushion acts like a sponge when squeezed.
10. Her roommate spent the forenoon on phrases and clauses.

FAR AND NEAR

Explorations

What word from the list at the right goes in each blank?

The __?__ are about 8,000 miles apart, and the nearest __?__ are many light-years away. The __?__ of the highest mountain is 29,000 feet above sea level. __?__ consist of land but are found in the sea, and the function of an __?__ is to separate two oceans. A long journey is often called a(n) __?__.

● *How many of the nouns of this unit can you find in the illustration above?*

Nouns
1. antipodes
2. archipelago
3. cannibal
4. constellation
5. declivity
6. delta
7. hinterland
8. isthmus
9. oasis
10. odyssey
11. promontory
12. rivulet
13. summit
14. tributary
15. vista

1. ANTIPODES . . . . . opposite parts of the earth

The antipodes are farther apart than the Halls of Monte-zuma and the shores of Tripoli.

The two speakers represent the antipodes (opposite **ex-tremes**) of religious thought.

2. ARCHIPELAGO (*ar-ki-PELL-a-go*) . . a group of small islands (or body of water containing them)

The Solomon Islands form an archipelago in the South Pacific.

3. CANNIBAL . . . . beings which eat their own kind

Stories about cannibals give him bad dreams.

There are cannibals among animals as well as among men.

Taking parts of a wrecked plane to repair another plane is known as "cannibalizing."

4. CONSTELLATION . . . a group or pattern of stars

Orion, the Hunter, is a familiar constellation.

These six writers comprise a kind of literary constellation.

5. DECLIVITY . . . . . . a downward slope, descent

There is a declivity on the other side of town.

6. DELTA . . . flood-deposit land at the mouth of a river

A river delta is so called, probably, because it is triangle-shaped like the Greek letter delta ($\triangle$). Made up of soil deposited by the river, a delta is very productive but often flooded.

The Nile has a famous rice-producing delta.

7. HINTERLAND . . regions away from the coast; back country

Tourists are attracted more to the coast than to the hinter-land of Maine.

Note: Hinterland is thought of as not having large towns or cities. Why not, especially long ago?

8. ISTHMUS . . a narrow neck of land connecting two larger land areas

The isthmus is only two miles wide.
Look up the Isthmus of Corinth on a map.

9. OASIS . . . . a grassy or fertile area in the desert

The water on the oasis saved their lives.
An oasis in a dull, dry speech is a spot that is interesting or funny.

10. ODYSSEY . . . . . a long journey or wandering

The original *Odyssey* was the long travel story of Odysseus (also called Ulysses). Who wrote it?
The speaker described his African odyssey.

11. PROMONTORY . . headland, projecting cliff or rock

The promontory is visible far out at sea.
Gibraltar is a famous promontory.

12. RIVULET . . . . a small river or brook

A quiet rivulet crosses our farm.

13. SUMMIT . . . . highest point, apex

Several brave adventurers have tried to climb to the summit of Mt. Everest.
The pinnacle (high or highest point) of the temple was struck by lightning.

14. TRIBUTARY . . . . a river which flows into another

The Ohio River is a tributary of the Mississippi.
Palestine two thousand years ago was a tributary (tribute-paying "province") of the Roman Empire.
Compare *tribute, contribute, distribute.*

15. VISTA . . a view (broad or long, outdoors or in one's mind)

A vista of tree-covered mountains loomed up ahead.
In the vista of the years, he could see steady progress.

Questions

1. What is a peninsula? a strait? What are aborigines?
2. How many constellations can you name?
3. How many words of three letters or more can you find within the base words of this unit without rearranging letters?

PRACTICE SET

Copy the italicized words and beside each write its meaning:

1. The aborigines of the *archipelago* were *cannibals.*
2. The *vista* of sky and sea was cut by a coastline above which loomed the rugged *hinterland* behind it.
3. The *delta* formed by a *tributary* of the Amazon could be seen from the *promontory.*
4. Near the *summit* of the glacier was an ice-fed *rivulet.*
5. A desert *odyssey* moves from *oasis* to oasis.
6. The sea is beyond the *declivity* on the far side of the *isthmus.*
7. Viewed from one of the *constellations,* the earth's *antipodes* would seem close together.

A SUMMER ADVENTURE

Fill the blanks, using each base word once:

Our __?__ took us past a __?__ that looks like a huge goat's head from below and up to the __?__ of a mountain. The __?__ of Italian __?__ that opened up before us as we approached the __?__ leading back to sea level was awe inspiring. At length we reached a slender __?__, the __?__ of a large stream that waters the valley below, and followed the stream to the __?__ at its mouth near the sea. Later, on the other side of the earth, we crossed from one continent to the other by means of an __?__, which was only a hundred yards wide in spots, and set sail for an __?__ that lies about eighty miles to the westward. There are no longer any __?__s on any of the islands, each of which is like an __?__ in a wasteland of sea. It was fun thus to explore the very __?__, and we saw several __?__s which are never visible in the northern latitudes where we live.

FINAL TESTS ON REGULAR UNITS

Copy the italicized words (or prefixes) and beside each write its meaning in the sentence:

Unit 1

1. I *exhort* you not to *emit* such sounds.
2. The board will *rescind* its decision to *segregate* Negroes.
3. Did you *verify* the demand to *ransom* him?
4. The book *portrays* a man who likes to *wield* authority.
5. Did he *recoil* when you *immersed* his hand in tar?

Unit 2

1. The salesman is *affable* and at the same time *canny*.
2. She is *coy* and *fickle*.
3. A wise man is *prudent* and *diligent*.
4. *Impulsive* girls are sometimes *timorous* too.
5. Is the man *gullible* as well as *pliable?*

Unit 3

1. War makes one *callous* toward suffering and *despondent* about the future.
2. He raised the gun with *resolute* courage and took *deliberate* aim.
3. A *peevish* child makes a *surly* father.
4. She is *wistful* because she is *passive*.
5. She becomes *flippant* when she is *hysterical*.

Unit 5

1. The *orifice* is to use in inspecting the *pinion*.
2. The *rabble* stormed the *portals* of the prison.
3. Will a song *exorcise* the *qualms* which afflict you?
4. He was *confronted* by a *paucity* of volunteers.
5. Delilah *beguiled* Samson and *divested* him of his power.

Unit 7

1. A piece of *parchment* fell into the *moat*.
2. The *minstrels* rode to the *jousts*.
3. The *esquire* took pride in his *lineage*.
4. An *ancestor* is buried in the *crypt*.
5. Put on the *gauntlets* and pull your *visor* down.

Unit 8

1. Did you *imply* that the attendance will *diminish?*
2. He will *endorse* our brand if it leaves no *residue*.
3. A fighter with *stamina* may *emerge* unbeaten.
4. They are *imbued* with eagerness to heal the *rift*.
5. Promises of a *rebate encumber* the plan too much.

Unit 10

1. *Lingerie* is sometimes made of *satin*.
2. *Cravats* are an item of *haberdashery*.
3. *Serge* is usually a warmth-giving *textile*.
4. A *trousseau* contains a variety of *apparel*.
5. She wants a *suede* jacket and *oxfords*.

Unit 11

1. He ordered a *fricassee* with *lyonnaise* potatoes.
2. Would you prefer a *mousse* or an *éclair?*
3. The oil is *rancid* and the water *brackish*.
4. The *repast* included oysters *au gratin*.
5. *Julienne* and *demitasse* are both liquid.

Unit 12

1. Can the *damsel transmute* her emotion into poetry?
2. Why *speculate* about who will *supplant* you?
3. It *transpired* that the *compact* was illegal.
4. The council will *ratify* the plan to *reinstate* him.
5. An *apostle* of hate tried to *pervert* our good will.

Unit 14

1. Fear *congeals* one and makes him less *resilient*.
2. Flood waters *erode* the banks as they *gyrate* downstream.
3. *Bevel* the insulator before you *glaze* it.
4. Sponge rubber is *porous* and quite *durable*.
5. The new metal is *ductile,* and it will not *tarnish*.

Unit 15

1. They were quick to *avenge* and to *ravage*.
2. Why *blaspheme* about the *marauder?*
3. A *brigand* is not content to *pilfer* pennies.
4. To call him *dastard* is to *impugn* his courage.
5. After such *depredations,* he will hesitate to *encroach*.

Unit 17

1. Each *platoon* held an Indian as a *hostage*.
2. *Munitions* were stored too near the *barracks*.
3. *Infiltrate* their lines as their troops *deploy*.
4. Can you describe the *insignia* of the *infantry?*
5. The *artillery* units did not know about the *truce*.

Unit 18

1. The *boatswain* inspected the *binnacle*.
2. The *corvette* seized a cargo of *contraband*.
3. The *barge* was pumping out *bilge*.
4. Lower the *ensign* after they *debark*.
5. *Jettison* the cargo, but do not *scuttle* the ship.

Unit 20

1. He *exudes* enthusiasm as he mounts the *dais*.
2. An *influx* of funds gave the drive new *impetus*.
3. How would you *appraise* this *facsimile?*
4. I had an *inkling* he would *commute* the sentence.
5. Can we *eradicate* the feelings that *engender* hatred?

Unit 21

1. To *mis*apply a remark is to apply it __?__.
2. *Anti*-British feeling is directed __?__ the British.
3. A *counter*clockwise motion is __?__ to clockwise motion.
4. *Dis*cord is the __?__ of good feeling.
5. A *se*duction is a leading __?__ what is right.

Unit 22

1. The *attorney* could not *refute* the evidence.
2. The *deputy* wanted to *prosecute* us.
3. Several *felons* were to be *arraigned*.
4. The prisoner decided to *waive bail*.
5. Will he *attest* my claim to the *legacy?*

Unit 23

1. The settings are *garish* and the story *flagrant*.
2. It is not *feasible* to give out vacuum sweepers *gratis*.
3. He is *assiduous* in devotion but *callow* in understanding.
4. One should be *fervent* rather than *festive* during Lent.
5. Making model planes is *arduous* labor requiring one to be *deft*.

Unit 25

1. How is an *archipelago* like a *constellation?*
2. The *cannibals* gathered at the bottom of the *declivity*.
3. At the foot of the *promontory* is a *tributary*.
4. His *odyssey* took him into the *hinterland* of Burma.
5. A *rivulet* flows in near the *isthmus*.

DIVISION TEST (BASE WORDS ONLY)
REGULAR UNITS

Copy the italicized words (or prefixes) and beside each write its meaning in the sentence:

1. Do you *indulge* in *flippant* remarks?
2. He is remarkably *prudent* and very *deliberate*.
3. Should we *extol* a leader who is *ruthless*?
4. It is hard for a *haughty* person to be *contrite*.
5. How can one *exorcise* a *despondent* mood?
6. *Ancestor* worship began to *diminish* in China.
7. He was *imbued* with the spirit of *chivalry*.
8. The visitors *emerged* from the *crypt*.
9. It took *stamina* for him to *assert* his authority.
10. Why *speculate* about the cost of *lingerie*?
11. What can *supplant* *chenille* for bedspreads?
12. The *repast* was spread on a *damask* cloth.
13. The *éclair* was served with a *demitasse*.
14. The grease will *congeal* in the *caldron* when it cools.
15. No one in the *barracks* dared to *malinger*.
16. One *platoon* began to *ravage* the city.
17. *Acrid* fumes arose from the *artillery*.
18. Our *insignia* began to *tarnish*.
19. The *attorney* called his rival's remarks *bilge*.
20. The *coroner* had once been a *boatswain*.
21. The *ensign* was *arraigned* for murder.
22. To *mis*state the *gravity* of an error is to state it __?__.
23. To *counter*act the *influx* of cheap goods is to act __?__ it.
24. Widening the *isthmus* is not *feasible*.
25. The climb to the *summit* was *arduous*.

DIVISION TEST—SUPPLEMENTARY WORDS IN REGULAR UNITS

Copy the italicized words and beside each write its meaning in the sentence:

1. He approached the *precipitous* gorge *warily.*
2. Is she *disconsolate* or just *demure?*
3. He is often *petulant* and sometimes *splenetic.*
4. The *dowager* left a *gratuity* under her plate.
5. A man wearing a *biretta* read the words: "And why take ye thought for *raiment?*"
6. There is a display of *edible* fish on the *rostrum.*
7. Did he *vilify* the officers of the *battalion?*
8. The *coxswain* signed the *covenant.*
9. The leader of the *serfs* rode on a *stallion.*
10. Something was seen to *submerge* near the *jetsam.*

DIVISION TEST — WORD-BUILDING UNITS

Write for each blank the correct form of the key word(s) in parentheses. Spelling counts.

1. The new program will __?__ (drama) famous literary events.
2. The new gift shop requests your __?__ (patron).
3. Try to __?__ (visual) the effects of the __?__ (critic).
4. The bureau demands __?__ (verify) and __?__ (certain).
5. Savages tend to __?__ (deity) the sun and moon.
6. It is hard to __?__ (make domestic) a raccoon.
7. Does red __?__ (make vigorous) and __?__ (make furious) a bull?
8. Police will __?__ (make intense) their search.
9. He is __?__ (can't be endured) because he __?__ (vary) complains.
10. A small amount of error is considered __?__ (allow).
11. The teacher likes __?__ (persevere) and __?__ (persist).
12. Salesmen are sometimes very __?__ (insist).
13. I will permit no __?__ (interfere) in my affairs.
14. Try not to __?__ (calculate incorrectly) the distance.

15. At one time cholera would __?__ (take the population from) a city rapidly.
16. The police can __?__ (take arms from) a man quickly.
17. The church will __?__ (cut *off from* communication) him.
18. The new governor is violently __?__ (against Communists).
19. The new boy is __?__ (not eligible) for the team.
20. The game offers a __?__ (opposite attraction) to the movies.

DIVISION TEST—SPELLING

The sentences below contain more than fifty words that are covered in the special units of Part Two. Write some or all from dictation.

1. My friend grieves because he has so little leisure.
2. The thief is a fiend who will never yield.
3. Our neighbors had quite a siege of illness.
4. The receipt shows the weight of each tier.
5. The financier tried in vain to achieve his goal.
6. The librarian was deceived about the family.
7. The athletic banquet is usually held in December.
8. Lightning struck a dairy near the college.
9. The champion plans to become a physician and surgeon.
10. The secretary requested the privilege of testing the apparatus.
11. The pianist positively will not appear in a film.
12. Cleanliness is a weapon against diseases which threaten.
13. Who could foretell the need for ninety pairs of scissors?
14. The kindergarten has rhythm exercises on Wednesday.
15. A knowledge of psychology is a help in marriage.
16. The scientist had pneumonia while seeking vengeance.
17. Her efforts in the current canvass will complement his.
18. Nevertheless the candidate has extraordinary ability.
19. You were fortunate to come before the foliage fades.
20. Concrete evidence of alcohol is necessary hereafter.

WORD WEALTH JUNIOR

PART THREE

E PLURIBUS UNUM

"My ancestors did not come over on the Mayflower," declared Will Rogers. "They went out to meet it." Will Rogers was only part Indian, however, and even the Indians did not originate here. They came from Asia.

Where did *your* parents come from? If they were born here, where did their parents or ancestors come from? Probably Europe, but perhaps it was Asia or Africa. Wherever it was, they brought foreign ways with them — and foreign words. They learned most of the ways of the people who were already here, and the people who were already here took over some of theirs. The same thing happened with their words.

This process of collecting hundreds of thousands of the finest people from three continents has helped make the United States a nation that can do almost anything well. The same process in words has given us a language that is exceptionally expressive because it has a wealth of words for every need. No one knows how many there really are, but the largest dictionaries contain about half a million.

Most of these words came from England, but we have added thousands from other countries, discarded thousands we didn't like or didn't need, invented new ones by the hundred, and changed a great many of those we kept. *Colour* is *color* in America, for example; *honour* is *honor, tyres* are *tires,* and British "wireless" is radio to us.

But where did the British get this language we still call English, even though American is a more correct name for it on this side of the Atlantic? That is a long story because Great Britain, like the United States, is a blend of many elements including Roman, Danish, French, German, and Italian, as well as Scottish, Irish, and Welsh. All of them contributed words, words, words.

Mod. English	Old English	Mod. German
1. God	Gode	der Gott
		Words we get in English:
2. man	mann, monn	der Mann
		Words we get in English:
3. woman	wifmann	die Frau
		Words we get in English:
4. father	faeder	der Vater
		Words we get in English:
5. mother	modor	die Mutter
		Words we get in English:
6. son	sunu	der Sohn
		Words we get in English:
7. daughter	dohtor	die Tochter
		Words we get in English:
8. brother	brothor	der Bruder
		Words we get in English:
9. sister	sweostor	die Schwester
		Words we get in English:
10. friend	freond	der Freund
		Words we get in English:

EIGHT DIFFERENT LANGUAGES

Latin	French	Spanish	Italian	Greek
Deus Deity, deify	Dieu	Dios	Dio	θεός (theos) theology
vir, homo virile, homicide	homme	hombre	uomo	ἄνθρωπος (anthropos) anthropoid
femina mulier feminine	femme	mujer femenino (adj.)	donna femmina	γυνή (gune) Pron: *GOO-nay* gynecology
pater paternal	père	padre	padre	πατήρ, πατρός (pater, patros) patriarch, patriot
mater maternal	mère	madre	madre	μήτηρ, μητρός (meter, metros) metropolis
filius filial, affiliate	fils	hijo	figlio	υἱός (huios)
filia filial	fille	hija	figlia	θυγάτηρ (thygater)
frater fraternal	frère	hermano	fratello	ἀδελφός (adelphos) Philadelphia
soror sorority	sœur	hermana	sorella	ἀδελφή (adelphe)
amicus amicable, amity	ami	amigo	amico	φίλος (philos) philanthropist

Three sources stand out, however. Most of the words in our English-American hoard came from (1) Anglo-Saxon, (2) Latin, or (3) Greek. Anglo-Saxon or Old English was the language more than a thousand years ago of what is now England, the language the Angles and Saxons brought with them from the forests of Germany when they invaded the island and took possession, driving the Celtic people who already lived there into the hills of Wales and Scotland.

When the Norman French invaded England two or three hundred years later and subjugated the Anglo-Saxons (as pictured in *Ivanhoe*), they brought a language evolved largely from Latin. The Germanic speech of the Anglo-Saxons mixed gradually with the Latin-derived language of the invaders, and Greek words accumulated — hundreds of them — from the study of Greek and Latin. They have been accumulating ever since, and new words are created every year from Greek roots, especially scientific terms.

In Part Three you will find words grouped largely according to their origins. The next two units, for example, contain words from Anglo-Saxon. Other units consist entirely of words from Latin or Greek. A few units are devoted to words taken over almost unchanged from Latin-derived modern languages like French, Spanish, and Italian. There is a sampling from Germanic, Russian, and Hebrew sources in Unit 21, and Unit 22 presents words that came mostly from the Orient.

Out of many peoples we are building one nation. Out of many languages we are building one language. The chart on pages 196–197 shows you how some words have changed as they migrated from one language to another and how other words have disappeared.

Sources of English Words (Approximate)

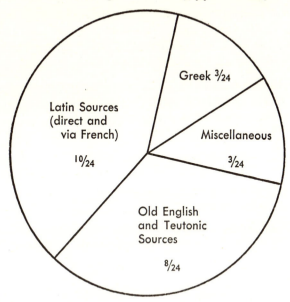

THE FOUR ELEMENTS

For many centuries before science got under way, men imagined that everything on earth was made from four elements: earth, air, fire, and water. Let's see what these four words were in the two languages from which English is principally derived:

	Anglo-Saxon (German)		*Latin*
1. earth	eorthe	(die Erde)	terra
	Modern words we get:		territory
2. air	lyft	(die Luft)	aer (same in Greek)
	Modern words we get:		aeroplane
3. fire	fyr	(das Feuer)	ignis, flamma
	Modern words we get:		ignite, flame
4. water	waeter	(das Wasser)	aqua
	Modern words we get:		aquatics

Questions

1. What given names do you find on the chart and what does each mean? Look up your own name in the dictionary. What language did it come from? What does it mean?
2. What light does the chart throw on the meaning of each of the following terms?

Philanthropist   Anthropoid apes
Christadelphian Church   A Russophile
Theocracy   Virility
Paternity   Maternity

3. How many foreign terms can you think of which include one of the words on the chart? Look up the pronunciation and meaning of each unless you know it already. Here are a few, half of them French:

Cherchez la femme   The Sierra Madre Mountains
Fratres in urbe   The Goddess Demeter
Mon Dieu!   The Jung Frau
"The Bonhomme Richard"   Frère Jacques
Dumas père and Dumas fils   Mater dolorosa

4. What is Sanskrit? How is it related to the English language?

OLD ENGLISH HEIRLOOMS

The words of this unit and the next all came from Old English, a language which took shape among the Angles, Saxons, and Jutes who settled in England more than a thousand years ago. They drove the people who were living there into what are now Wales and Scotland. From their words have come the everyday words that we use the most in conversation and letter writing. Most of the words in this very paragraph, in fact, came from Old English, including *loom* in *heirloom;* but *heir* came through France from the Romans.

Professor Quiz

How many questions can you answer?

1. Which word contains feathers?
2. Which one has to do with gardening?
3. Which one is lazy?
4. Which one hurts?
5. Which one attracts?
6. Which one is sad or gloomy?

Nouns

1. bleach
2. dole
3. fledgling
4. fortnight
5. hassock
6. husbandry
7. lodestone
8. mildew
9. pall
10. seer
11. sloth
12. smock
13. tithe
14. twinge
15. wiles

OLD ENGLISH HEIRLOOMS—STUDY GUIDE

1. BLEACH . . . . whiteness, chemical for producing whiteness

The bleach of her hair and the blank in her eyes are a blend of the blistering sky.

The bones bleach (whiten) on the desert.

See *blench* and *blanch*.

2. DOLE . . a distribution, payment, or grant, especially to needy persons

Many went on the dole when the factory closed.

Father hates to dole out money for broken windows.

Note: *Doleful* (sorrowful) comes from a *Latin* word.

3. FLEDGLING . . a beginner, person ready to start out

A fledgling soon becomes a full-fledged scout.

Literally, a fledgling is a bird with feathers enough for flight.

4. FORTNIGHT . . . . a two-week period

The carnival lasted a fortnight.

5. HASSOCK . . . a stuffed object used as a footstool

The baby likes to roll a hassock on the floor.

6. HUSBANDRY . . farming; wise care and management (of one's affairs generally)

He learned husbandry from his father.

By careful husbandry he built up quite a fortune.

Animal husbandry is a profitable occupation.

Husband originally meant householder or one who cared for livestock and land, making it prosperous and productive.

7. LODESTONE . . a kind of magnetic rock, something strongly attractive

In the legend, a ship sailed too close to a lodestone deposit.

The nails were drawn out, and the ship collapsed.

8. **MILDEW . . . a whitish growth somewhat like mold**

Mildew gathers on clothes left damp too long.
Hepzibah was "a mildewed [moldy] piece of aristocracy."

9. **PALL . . . a dark covering, something gloomy which overspreads**

The pallbearers (from the black cloth once spread over a coffin) wore gray gloves.
A pall of fog hung over the swamp.

10. **SEER . . . . a prophet, one who foresees**

The seer was nearly 80 when his prophecy came true.

11. **SLOTH (pronounced *slowth*) . . . laziness, indolence**

Sloth will bring a man from riches to rags.
A slothful person often dislikes slothfulness in others.

12. **SMOCK . . a washable outer garment to protect one's clothes**

Barbers and internes wear a kind of white smock.
She wears a smock while doing the chores.

13. **TITHE . . a tenth part, or small part, set aside for religious purposes**

Many church members give a tithe.
Jacob was a tither of early Bible times.

14. **TWINGE . . . . a sharp sensation, pang**

Rheumatism causes frequent twinges in damp weather.

15. **WILES . . . . . deceiving, beguiling ways or tricks**

He had learned to beware of his sister's wiles.
The word is usually used in the plural.

ANGLO–SAXON WORDS IN PART ONE

Old English words presented as base words in the regular units of Part One include: *quell* (page 8), *swerve* (page 9), *loathe* (page 12), *seethe* (page 12), *singe* (page 13), *sheathe* (page 13), *wane* (page 13), *writhe* (page 13), *drone* (page 18), *sheaf* (page 19), *stud* (page 19), *ghastly* (page 22), *lithe* (page 22), *sallow* (page 23), *stowaway* (page 33), *foster* (page 40), *mingle* (page 40), *shackle* (page 41), *fawn* (page 60), *foal* (page 60), *mongrel* (page 60), *swine* (page 61), *weasel* (page 61), *dwindle* (page 66), *stalk* (page 67), *hamper* (page 67), *smolder* (page 67), *swath(e)* (page 67), *ember* (page 70), *sinew* (page 71), *bight* (page 78), *doldrums* (page 78), *lee(ward)* (page 79), *tarpaulin* (page 79), *cove* (page 82), *dell* (page 82), *glade* (page 83), *gloaming* (page 83), *knoll* (page 83), *drivel* (page 89).

If time permits, find out which of the words studied in Unit 4, Unit 7, or Unit 12 of Part One are of Anglo-Saxon origin. Pages 207–208 contain a partial list of Anglo-Saxon derivatives in Part Two.

FIRST PRACTICE SET

Copy the italicized words and beside each write its meaning:

1. He was a *fledgling* pilot for a *fortnight*.
2. She sat on the *hassock,* talked about *bleaches,* discussed *husbandry,* admired *sloth,* and said a *tithe* was too much to give.
3. Her *wiles* stirred *twinges* of anger in him.
4. The *seer* wore a *smock* while he fixed his car.
5. News of the *dole* cast a *pall* over the audience.
6. There was *mildew* in the container for the *lodestone*.

SECOND PRACTICE SET

Which of the base words in this unit fits in each of the blanks best? Fill the ones you are sure about first.

1. A __?__ of jealousy.
2. A __?__ to sit on.
3. Foretold by a __?__.
4. A __?__ of darkness.
5. A __?__ for the unemployed.
6. A __?__ to wear at work.
7. A __?__ prize fighter.
8. The __?__ of a turtle.
9. Some church members give a __?__.
10. __?__s that draw him like a __?__.
11. The courses in __?__ lasted a __?__.
12. Chemists discuss __?__es.
13. __?__ collects on damp wallpaper.

MORE HEIRLOOMS

All of the words of this unit, like those in Unit 2, come from the language of the Angles, Saxons, and Jutes who settled in England before and during the Dark Ages. The majority thus came to us from Germany via England. You will find that many of them resemble modern German words in spelling, pronunciation, or both.

A Rough Trip

Can you fill each of the blanks appropriately with a word from the list at the right?

Air pockets and up-currents made the ride above the mountains very bumpy that day, but the stewardess by her __?__ manner did much to __?__ our anxiety and __?__ our courage. The view __?__ed us and made us __?__ for wings like a bird.

Adjectives
1. blithe
2. buxom
3. listless
4. stalwart
5. uncouth
6. winsome

Verbs
1. allay
2. atone
3. bolster
4. enthrall
5. forbear
6. spurn
7. sunder
8. winnow
9. yearn

1. **BLITHE** . . . . light-hearted, gay, cheerful
"Hail to thee, blithe spirit!" is addressed to a skylark.

2. **BUXOM** . . . . . pleasingly plump, robust, comely
She is a buxom country girl.
One can be comely (pleasing in appearance) without being
buxom.

3. **LISTLESS** . . . . spiritless, indifferent
Rainy weather makes one listless.
We lost the game because of our listlessness.

4. **STALWART** . . . . . strong and upstanding, brave
The stalwart defenders of the castle never wavered.
Their stalwartness gave them the victory.

5. **UNCOUTH** . . . . rough, rude, unrefined
Daniel Boone was somewhat uncouth.
Lincoln's uncouthness was one of his handicaps.

6. **WINSOME** . . . . pleasant, charming, captivating
Her winsome ways are most appealing.
His winsomeness won him many friends.

---

1. **ALLAY** . . . . . to put at rest, to quiet, to relieve
This news will allay her fears.

2. **ATONE** . . . . to make amends (for)
He tried to atone for his mistake.
Buying the car was an act of atonement.

Atone (from *at one*) means literally to put two persons at one with
each other who have been estranged in some way.

3. **BOLSTER** . . . . . . to support, sustain, reinforce
He whistled in the dark to bolster his courage.
A pillow is a kind of bolster.   (See dictionary.)

4. ENTHRALL . . . . . **to captivate, hold spellbound**

The lecturer knows how to enthrall an audience.

5. FORBEAR . . **to restrain oneself, hold back, be patient**

"Good friend, for Jesus' sake forbear
   To dig the dust enclosed here."
Forbearance toward one's enemies is a noble quality.

6. SPURN . . . . . **to reject or push aside scornfully**

Why did she spurn his offer of assistance?
Spurns did not discourage him.

7. SUNDER . . . . . . **to sever, cut apart, separate**

War sunders all normal ties with the enemy.
The tent was torn asunder by the wind.

8. WINNOW . . **to blow the chaff from (usually grain), sift**

Winnow the popcorn after shelling it.
Tests have a winnowing effect on a class.

9. YEARN . . . . . . **to long for, desire earnestly**

Uncle Herbert yearns for the good old days.
There was a yearning look in Mary's eyes.

Questions

1. What words can you get by dropping the first letter of words in this unit? the first two?
2. Change a letter of *bolster* and get *pistol sheath;* a letter of *winnow* and get *a small fish.*

ANGLO–SAXON WORDS IN PART TWO

Words of Old English derivation presented as base words in the regular units of Part Two include: *wield* (page 101), *fickle* (page 104), *ruthless* (page 105), *uncouth* (page 206), *wistful* (page 109), *beguile* (page 114), *anneal* (page 144), *truce* (page 155), *boatswain* (page 158), *wale* in *gunwale* (page 159), *callow* (page 176). Beyond this unit no more will be found except in the special units.

FIRST PRACTICE SET

Copy the italicized words and beside each write its meaning:

1. Nothing will *allay* his grief or *atone* for the crime.
2. You may want to *spurn* the offer, but please *forbear*.
3. The bride is *blithe* and *buxom*. She *yearns* for the groom.
4. The groom is *stalwart* and *winsome*.
5. The best man had to *bolster* his courage, but now nothing can *sunder* him from the bride.
6. The bride's brother is *uncouth* and somewhat *listless*.
7. *Winnowing* the beans is not an *enthralling* task.

SECOND PRACTICE SET

Using a different one of the base words of this unit for each blank, what is the best thing to do with each of the following? Fill first the blanks you are sure about and rearrange until each word fits reasonably well.

1. Angry words? __?__.
2. Good intentions? __?__ them. How? __?__ly.
3. Temptations? __?__ them in a __?__ manner.
4. A degrading friendship? __?__ it.
5. Lofty ambitions? __?__ to achieve them.
6. Serious mistakes? __?__ for them, if possible.
7. Unfounded suspicions? __?__ them. Be __?__.
8. An assortment of good and bad friends? __?__ them.
9. People you meet while selling brushes? Be __?__ and __?__ them. Even if they are __?__, they may have money, and they need the brushes.
10. Sickly, underfed girls? Good food and outdoor sports may make them __?__.

ABLE AND IBLE

Once there were two boys, Able and Ible. Able was stronger and older. They spent most of their time attaching themselves to words. Gradually they became great rivals, and each went to work to see how many words he could enroll. Able was more normal than Ible, however, and most of the words preferred him to Ible. Here are some of the familiar members of each tribe:

Able I	*Able* II	*Ible* I
agreeable	adorable	contemptible
available	advisable	convertible
commendable (page 114)	comparable (page 127)	discernible
considerable	desirable	perceptible
damnable	durable (page 145)	resistible
eatable	imaginable	(page 141)
enjoyable	irritable	
explainable	likable	
fashionable	miserable	*Ible* II
favorable	pleasurable	audible
habitable	receivable	credible
honorable	recognizable	divisible
payable (page 5)	removable	eligible
portable	retrievable (page 117)	forcible
preferable (page 142)	usable	intelligible
profitable	valuable	legible
remarkable		negligible
respectable	pliable (page 105)	permissible
suitable	reliable (page 141)	plausible
transferable (page 142)	variable (page 141)	possible
workable	veritable	sensible
		terrible
changeable	capable	visible
manageable	hospitable (page 127)	
noticeable	probable	
pronounceable		

ACTIVITIES

1. Can you discover how the words in Able I or Ible I differ from those in Able II or Ible II? If not, cover Able and Ible with a piece of paper in each column. Can you supply the missing letter(s) of a base verb or noun in Able II and Ible II if there is one?
2. How many words can you add to each column? (See pages 141–142.)
3. Why don't the four words at the end of Able I lose an *e* like most of the base words in Able II? See page 5 for a hint.
4. How do *regrettable* and *controllable* differ from most of their tribe?
5. Make a list of prefix opposites of Able and Ible words.
6. Write sentences containing Able and Ible words. Divide the class into pairs and dictate sentences to each other — or perhaps the teacher will ask one pupil to dictate to the entire class.

SENTENCES FOR PRACTICE

Write some or all of the following from dictation:

1. Writing should be legible, speech audible, hands visible.
2. She is likable, fashionable, and generally commendable.
3. Bills are payable, accounts receivable, insurance convertible.
4. Be sensible! The story is not plausible and the plan is not workable.
5. The weather is favorable, winds variable, golf desirable.
6. The idea is profitable, the boss favorable, and you eligible for promotion.
7. Rain made us miserable, the camp became uninhabitable, and departure was advisable.
8. The cloth is durable, its color agreeable, and its use permissible.
9. She is changeable. Her variability is quite noticeable.
10. Their name is unpronounceable, but they are hospitable.

LATIN WEAVINGS

Each of the base words in this unit may be traced to a word in Latin, the language of the Romans. Some came directly to English, with little change, some by way of French or Old French, with changes that give the word a French appearance.

Sister Sue

Can you fill the blanks appropriately, using words from the list at the right?

She likes to __?__ her cheeks and go "poof." She is not old enough to __?__ her face with lipstick, and she will not __?__ her eating no matter how much Mother __?__s with her. She seldom goes to bed of her own __?__. She displays a truly breath-taking __?__ when she starts climbing the pantry shelves. Father's __?__ will hardly suffice as she gets older. She is only three.

● *How many of the verbs and nouns of this unit can you find in the illustration above?*

Verbs

1. desecrate
2. dishevel
3. distend
4. edify
5. embellish
6. expedite
7. expostulate

Nouns

1. rudiment
2. simile
3. stipend
4. suffrage
5. temerity
6. tenure
7. vestige
8. volition

1. DESECRATE . . to violate the holiness or sacredness of, to profane

Soldiers desecrated the church by keeping their horses in it.
Trampling on the flag is an act of desecration.

Sacred comes from the same root. Compare *consecrate* (devote), *consecration*, *execrate* (curse), *execration*.

2. DISHEVEL . . . . . . to muss up, put in disorder

Do not dishevel my hair.
He had a dishevelled appearance.

Note: *Dishevel* comes from a Latin word by way of a French word for hair.

3. DISTEND . . . . to stretch, enlarge, swell

Overeating will distend one's abdomen.
Gas causes painful distention.

4. EDIFY . . . . . . to make (one) better, improve

Prejudices do not edify anyone.
Read books for edification as well as amusement.

5. EMBELLISH . . . . to decorate, adorn

Crayon marks embellish the back fence.
Father's signature has no embellishments.

6. EXPEDITE . . . . . to hasten, speed up, accelerate

How can we expedite the shipment?
A Government expediter was appointed.

7. EXPOSTULATE . . . to remonstrate, entreat a person (about his shortcomings)

"Did you expostulate with him about his tardiness?"
"Yes. Expostulation proved useless."

1. **RUDIMENT** . . . . **first step or principle**

A grade school gives only the rudiments of an education.
Rudimentary (very crude) drawings are found in the cave.

2. **SIMILE** . . . . . . **a comparison using *like* or *as***

"Proud as a peacock" is a too-familiar simile.
Similes are frequently found in poetry and prose.

3. **STIPEND** . . . . **wage, salary, pay**

His weekly stipend is $60.00.

4. **SUFFRAGE** . . . **the right to vote (in political matters)**

The campaign for women's suffrage was a long one.
Should suffrage be extended to the Indians?

5. **TEMERITY** . . . . **rashness, rash boldness**

Sally had the temerity to accost the President.

6. **TENURE** . . . . **(act or right of) holding; possession**

The Republican's tenure lasted twelve years.
The man has Civil Service tenure in his job.

7. **VESTIGE** . . . . **a trace, remnant**

Not a vestige of the food remains.

8. **VOLITION** . . . . . . **act of will, desire, or choice**

Robert went of his own volition.
For free men, volition takes the place of compulsion.

Questions

1. What is the root meaning of *stipend, rudiment, dishevel,* and *embellish?* Look up the others, if possible.
2. Change the first three letters of *temerity* and get *harshness.* Change the first two of *rudiment* and get *dregs;* the first two of *tenure* and get *fertilizer.*
3. Find ten or more four-letter words within the base words of this unit without rearranging letters.

4. Change the first letter of *volition* to three other letters and have the results of an explosion.
5. Change two separate letters of *dishevel* and get a verb *to cut off* or *separate*. It is found in Poe's "Annabel Lee."
6. Make a list or a collection of similes. Cross out those which you think or your teacher thinks are overworked or worn out. Try to think of fresh ones based on your own observations.

PRACTICE SET

Copy the italicized words and beside each write its meaning:

1. Why does universal *suffrage* tend to increase a man's *stipend* and also his *tenure* in his job?
2. Randolph does not know the *rudiments* of politeness, he lacks every *vestige* of good manners, and he never of his own *volition* says "thank you." His influence is not *edifying.* •
3. "Mad as a March hare" is a *simile* for *temerity.*
4. A *dishevelled* lady *desecrated* the flag by trying to *embellish* it with ornaments.
5. Why *expostulate?* There is no way to *expedite* the project. Its cost will be *distended* by politics and graft.

TOO MUCH AND TOO LITTLE

What is the result, in terms of the base verbs, of too much:

1. Food? It __?__s one.
2. Nonsense? Teachers __?__.
3. Delay? You __?__.
4. Slang? It does not __?__.
5. Rough house? It __?__s one.
6. Loud noise? It __?__s the church.
7. Of too plain an appearance? You try to __?__ it.

Which of the base nouns goes in each blank for too little?

1. Of the __?__s of refinement.
2. Of jobs that carry __?__.
3. A __?__ to support a family.
4. Of __?__ under a dictator.
5. Of __?__ in a mouse.
6. Of __?__s of self-respect.
7. Of __?__-appeal in "brown as a berry."
8. Of __?__ in America before 1776.

ROMANIFIC ADJECTIVES

All of the adjectives in this unit are derived directly or indirectly from Latin words.

Applications

Which word from the list at the right may best be applied to:

Adjectives

1. A shiny nose? __?__
2. A hobo? __?__
3. An insurance company? __?__
4. An ocean liner? __?__
5. A birthmark? __?__
6. Tooth brushing? A __?__ duty.

1. abstruse
2. colossal
3. congenital
4. conjugal
5. consecutive
6. diurnal
7. effulgent
8. eternal
9. eventual
10. imminent
11. insurgent
12. itinerant
13. momentous
14. mutual
15. palpable

ROMANIFIC ADJECTIVES—STUDY GUIDE

1. ABSTRUSE . . . hidden, hard to understand, obscure

Girls often find algebra very abstruse.

Its abstruseness discourages them.

2. COLOSSAL . . . . huge, immense

The national debt is colossal.

Have you read about the Colossus of Rhodes?

Compare *mammoth* (of Russian origin), *titanic* (of Greek), and *gigantic* (Latin derivation).

3. CONGENITAL . . . . existing or beginning at birth

The deformity on his hand is congenital.

Compare *hereditary*, which has quite a different meaning.

4. CONJUGAL . . pertaining to husband and wife or to marriage

The speaker talked about better conjugal relationships.

Compare *connubial, marital*.

5. CONSECUTIVE . . following one another (in numerical or logical order)

The order of the cards is consecutive.

Arrange the license plates consecutively.

6. DIURNAL . . . . (occurring) daily

Our diurnal routine continues unchanged.

Oversleeping is a diurnal occurrence for her.

7. EFFULGENT . . . . . shining, radiant, resplendent

The sky was effulgent with sunshine.

Imagine the effulgence of a knight in silver armor.

8. ETERNAL . . . . timeless, everlasting, never ending

Fame is not eternal.

"Eternal Life" was the topic that day.

What to wear is a girl's eternal problem.

9. EVENTUAL . . . . **final, ultimate**

What is the eventual solution of the unemployment problem?
Are you prepared for all eventualities (outcomes)?

10. IMMINENT . . . **about to happen, threatening, impending**

Death was imminent for 20,000 men.
We waited because of the imminence of the storm.

11. INSURGENT . . . . **rising in opposition, rebellious**

An insurgent group arose within the Democratic party.
Insurgents won control of the party in several states.

Surge (rise) words: *surge, upsurge, insurrection, resurgent, resurgence* (rising up again), *resurrection.*

12. ITINERANT (eye-*TIN*-er-ant) . . **traveling from place to place**

A company of itinerant actors came to town.
What will your itinerary (route of travel) be in Europe?

13. MOMENTOUS . . . **very important, of great consequence**

A political convention is a momentous affair.
The momentousness of the day must not be forgotten.

14. MUTUAL . . **common to, shared, benefiting each (party)**

The fondness between teacher and pupil was mutual.
The time proved mutually satisfactory.
Between citizens and their government a high degree of mutuality should exist.

Compare *reciprocal.*

15. PALPABLE . . **evident (to the senses), capable of being felt**

He showed palpable delight over winning.
The lady was palpably impressed.

See *palpitate* and *palpitation.*

Questions

1. Change the first two letters of *palpable* and get *blameworthy*.
2. Reduce *im* in *imminent* to a single letter and get *outstanding*.
3. How many four-letter words can you find in the basic list?
4. Change three letters of *effulgent* and get *easy-going* (page 100).
5. Look up the root meanings of the words, if possible, and list another word or two from each root.

PRACTICE SET

Copy the italicized words and beside each write its meaning:

1. An attack by the *insurgents* appeared *imminent*.
2. The Great Pyramid is *colossal* and rather *abstruse* mathematically.
3. He has *itinerant* habits and a *congenital* distaste for work.
4. Christmas is a *momentous* day with a *palpable* effect on everybody's *mutual* happiness.
5. Arranging the receipts in *consecutive* order is part of the *diurnal* round of duties.
6. They seem to have found the *effulgent* joy of *conjugal* bliss.
7. Is *eternal* joy the *eventual* lot of everyone?

OUR COW — EFFIE

Which of the base words of this unit fits best in each blank? Use each word once. Fill the blanks you are sure about first.

Chewing her cud with __?__ satisfaction, Effie seems __?__ to little Sue and rather __?__ or at least mysterious. When a storm is __?__, Effie grows restless, but is not at all __?__ or inclined to wander. With Sue she exchanges glances of __?__ curiosity. With __?__ or perhaps hereditary distaste for rapid motion, Effie stands in the calm water of an __?__ little stream, chewing her cud in __?__ monotony, never suspecting that the days follow each other in __?__ order and that __?__ events are happening in Washington. The years seem __?__ to her, and she has no ideas as to what her __?__ fate will be. She has no tendency to be __?__, and little does she realize that Sue's parents have __?__ problems.

GREEK GIFTS

Each of the base words in this unit may be traced back to the ancient Greek language. As a group, Greek-derived words are mostly technical terms pertaining to the theater, to geography, to philosophy, to religion, and to the sciences, especially medicine.

At Church

Can you fill the blanks correctly?

Base Words

The minister gave a __?__ of the life of Moses and the __?__ of the children of Israel from Egypt. The choir sang with __?__, but the director had a __?__ for waving his arms. The sermon was a __?__ about __?__ in American life because of race or color.

1. alabaster
2. canopy
3. ecstasy
4. elegy
5. exodus
6. genesis
7. homily
8. lyric
9. mania
10. mastication
11. moron
12. ostracism
13. phenomenon
14. phobia
15. synopsis

GREEK GIFTS—STUDY GUIDE

1. **ALABASTER** . . . . . . .a fine white (calcite) stone

   Ancient perfume bottles were made of alabaster.
   "Thine alabaster cities gleam, undimmed by human tears."

2. **CANOPY** . . . a tentlike (overhanging) covering or shelter

   The queen sat under a canopy.
   The sky is a canopy that covers us all.

3. **ECSTASY** . . . . wild delight, or other strong feeling

   The diamond filled her with ecstasy.
   Simmons was in an ecstasy of rage.
   Baseball makes men ecstatic.

4. **ELEGY** . . a poetic lament for someone who has died

   The poet offered to write an elegy.
   For whom is Gray's "Elegy" a lament?

5. **EXODUS** . . . a large-scale departure or migration

   The exodus from the burning building was orderly.
   What is the exodus in the Book of Exodus?

6. **GENESIS** . . . . the beginning

   The feud had its genesis in a minor disagreement.
   Why is the Book of Genesis so called?

7. **HOMILY** . . . a moralistic discourse, a sermon(ette)

   The meeting began with a brief homily on patience.

8. **LYRIC** . . . . a poem of strong feeling

   Wordsworth wrote many lyrics.
   The play has a lyric (musical or songlike) quality.
   She sang in a light, lyrical voice.

9. **MANIA** . . . . a craze or passion

   Aunt Sahara has a mania for antiques.
   A maniac is a madman, frenzied and disordered.

10. MASTICATION . . . process of chewing (thoroughly)
The importance of mastication was discussed.
Take time to masticate your food properly.

11. MORON . . . a stupid person, one of low intelligence
A moron is often very happy.
Practical jokes are a rather moronic pastime.

12. OSTRACISM . . . . exclusion, banishment
Orientals are often victims of social ostracism.
The people of the village tried to ostracize the stranger.
Review *oust* (page 8).

13. PHENOMENON . . . . (unusual) fact or occurrence
A new star is a scientific phenomenon.
The man's skill in organizing is phenomenal (extraordinary).
Note: The plural is *phenomena*.

14. PHOBIA . . . . . a deep-seated, unreasoning fear
She has a phobia about ants.
A Russophobe is a person who fears Russia.
What is *hydrophobia? xenophobia? claustrophobia?*

15. SYNOPSIS . . . . a summary, condensed statement
Could you give a synopsis of the play?
Matthew, Mark, and Luke are the "Synoptic Gospels."

OTHER GREEK GIFTS

Other Greek-derived words in English include: *acme* (page 46), *acrobat, acrostic, agony, antarctic, anthem, archipelago* (page 182), *arctic, basilisk* (page 61), *caper* (page 88), *cataract* (page 82), *catechism, chasm* (page 82), *comedy, delta* (page 182), *elastic, epidemic, epileptic, hysterical* (page 108), *isthmus* (page 183), *mimic* (page 88), *monarch, myriad* (page 115), *oasis* (page 183), *ocher, odyssey* (page 183), *organ(ic), parable* (page 28), *phantom* (page 29), *pharmacy, pigmy, spasm, sporadic, tragedy, treacle.* Can you explain the large number on pages 182–183?

Questions

1. How many words can you list ending in *–sis?*
2. Look up the root meanings of the words in this unit, if possible.
3. Change three letters of *ecstasy* and get something imaginary.
4. Make a list of manias or phobias, using a thesaurus or medical dictionary if you can obtain one.
5. What does *enthusiasm* mean literally?

PRACTICE SET

Copy the italicized words, and beside each write its meaning in the sentence:

1. Some have a *mania* for *mastication.*
2. He wrote an *elegy* for a scientist who studied atomic *phenomena.*
3. A *homily* is much different from a *lyric.*
4. The doctor will read a *synopsis* of his book on *phobias.*
5. There was an *exodus* of *morons,* all victims of *ostracism.*
6. With *ecstasy* he described the *genesis* of his housing plan.
7. The king sat on a throne of *alabaster* under a silken *canopy.*

NEEDS OR CAN BECOME

Which of the base words of this unit fits best in each blank?

1. Tough beefsteak needs __?__.
2. Rude persons should expect __?__.
3. Patriotism calls for a __?__ or a __?__.
4. World unity needs a __?__.
5. A busy man appreciates a __?__ of a long novel.
6. A __?__ needs intelligent guidance.
7. A victory by our team calls for __?__.
8. The builder of a war memorial needs __?__.
9. A Colonial bed needs a __?__ to look right.
10. Hate can become a __?__.
11. Nervousness about snakes can become a __?__.
12. The departure became a full-scale __?__.
13. A calf with three heads is a __?__.
14. A tribute to a dead hero can become a memorable __?__.

WISE AND LIES

If you insist that words with a *y* in them or an *–ly* at the end never bother you, you may be lying — or lying down on the job, at any rate. The Y-in-the-middle words are really quite simple if you mispronounce them a few times, divide them into syllables, and write them thoughtfully. Here are a few, all of Greek or partly Greek origin except *lying:*

analysis	cylinder	oyster	system
analyze	gymnasium	style	typewriter
crystal	lying	sympathy	typhoid
cycle			typical

How many can you add to the list?

The *–ly* words are far more numerous but curiously regular in their habits. In most cases you simply add *–ly* to an adjective — *without dropping anything* — and you get an adverb or occasionally another adjective. Try it on the following — in writing:

absolute, bare, definite, direct, extreme, fair, hurried, immediate, intense, large, like, live, mere, positive, proper, rapid, recent, regular, safe, scarce, separate, serious, sincere, slight, strict, undoubted, unfortunate

What could be easier? Be sure you can spell *all* of each word.

If the adjective that wants to be an adverb is a Y-at-the-end word, the *y* changes to *i*, and the result is just what you would expect, with a few exceptions like *shyly:*

dryly, hastily, ordinarily, readily, satisfactorily, shyly, tastily

You have only to make sure you can spell the rest of the word. What is the adjective in each case?

Able and Ible words (pages 209–210) are often rather long. Perhaps that is why they always drop the *e* and replace it with a *y: considerably, reasonably, regrettably, terribly.*

MISCELLANEOUS WORDS

Study, divide, and pronounce them — every syllable of each word — and use them in sentences, if time permits.

PH words: *atmosphere, camphor, hemisphere, nephew, orphan, pamphlet, photograph, sphere, stenographer, stratosphere, symphony, telegraph, triumph, typhoid* (mostly of Greek origin)

(T)URE words: *culture, enclosure, literature, legislature, mixture, moisture, pressure, signature, temperature, venture*

UAL (*you-AL*) words: *individual, manual, spiritual, usual*

UM words: *cucumber, gymnasium, maximum, medium, minimum, museum, premium, umpire, volume*

PURR words: *disturb, furnish, further* (more), *murder, murmur, purchase, purpose, suburb, surface, surplus, survey, turtle, urge*(*nt*)

GRAB BAG: *alfalfa, appendicitis, bacteria, balance, bracelet, cafeteria, campus, century, certificate, cigarette, community, complexion, compromise, diameter, dispatch, emergency, epidemic, faculty, gratitude, lieutenant, merchandise, millionaire, miscellaneous, pension, petition, philosophy, preliminary, republic*(*an*)*, revenge, sandwich, semester, speedometer, statistics, tendency, thermometer, trousers, welfare, wilderness, wither*

SENTENCES FOR PRACTICE

Write some or all of the following from dictation.

1. The temperature is usually high in the museum.
2. The governor's signature was on a surplus-purchase order.
3. Gymnasium work improves more than the surface of one's complexion.
4. The faculty epidemic created a real emergency.
5. The millionaire got the manual from a lieutenant.
6. Survey statistics place the minimum working age at 16.
7. One of the miscellaneous sandwiches contained cucumber.

LEARNING TO COUNT—IN LATIN AND GREEK

Each of the classical languages had a set of numbers which survives today as a set of prefixes. The object of this unit is to find out what they are and how they are used.

Number, Please

What number goes in each blank? The number prefix in each sentence is italicized.

1. A *centi*pede has __?__ feet.
2. A *tri*logy is a series of __?__ books or plays.
3. A *quinque*reme had __?__ banks of oars.
4. A *mill*ennium lasts __?__ years.
5. A *bi*ped has __?__ feet.
6. A *hepta*gon has __?__ sides.
7. A *decem*vir was one of __?__ men.
8. A *demi*god is a __?__ god.
9. An *octo*pus has __?__ tentacles.
10. A *penta*thlon is an athletic meet having __?__ events.

Number Prefixes

	Latin	*Greek*
1.	uni–	mono–
2.	du(o)–	bi–
3.	tri–	tri–
4.	quad(ri)–	tetra–
5.	quin(que)–	pent(a)–
6.	sex–	hex(a)–
7.	sept–	hept(a)–
8.	octo–	octa–
9.	non(a)–, nov–	ennea–
10.	dec(im)–	deca–
11.	cent(i)–	hect(o)–, hec(a)–
12.	mill(e)–, mill(i)–	kilo–
13.	semi–	hemi–, demi–

LEARNING TO COUNT—STUDY GUIDE

1. UNI– . . . . . MONO– . . . . one

A *uni*cycle has only *one* wheel.
The class studied *uni*cellular (*one*-celled) animals.
The count raised his *mono*cle (*single* eyeglass).
The *mono*logue (*one* person talking) continued.

Compare *unite, unify* (to make as *one*), monopoly (only *one* person selling), *monoplane* (*one*-winged plane).

2. DU(O)– . . . . BI– . . . . two

The car has *du*al (*two*) controls.
*Du*plicate (*two*fold) prizes were given.
*Bi*weekly (every-*two*-weeks) payments are expected.

Note: *di–* means *two* in words like *dicotyledon*, a plant having two seed leaves. Do not confuse with *dia–* (through, between, or across) in words like *dialect, diameter, diaper, diocese, dielectric.*

3. TRI– . . . . . TRI– . . . . three

*Tri*plets were born.
Type it in *tri*plicate (*three*fold).
It is a *tri*ennial (every-*three*-years) event.

4. QUAD(RI)– . . . TETRA– . . . . four

*Quadru*plets (*four* babies at one birth) are rare.
A *quadr*ant is one-*fourth* of a circle.
A *quadr*angle is a *four*-cornered court, usually in a college.
A *tetr*arch (*TEE-trark*) ruled one-*fourth* of a province.

5. QUIN(QUE)– . . PENT(A)– . . . . five

The Dionnes are called *QUIN*-tu-plets. (Note accent.)
Our basketball *quin*tet played well.
A *penta*style is a building with *five* columns in front.
*Pente*cost is the *fiftieth* day (after the Passover).

6. SEX– . . . . . HEX(A)– . . . . six

A *sex*tet is a group of *six* (singers, usually).
A *sex*agenarian is a person in his *sixties*.
A *hexa*gon is a *six*-sided figure.

---

7. SEPT– . . . . . **HEPT(A)–** . . . . **seven**

In Roman times *Sept*ember was the *seventh* month.
A *sept*uagenarian is a person in his *seventies*.
A *hept*agon has *seven* sides. It is *hept*angular.

8. OCTO– . . . . **OCTA–** . . . . **eight**

An *octo*roon is one-*eighth* Negro.
An *octa*ve is the *eight* tones of a musical scale.
*Octo*ber was once the *eighth* month.

9. NON(A)–, NOV– . . . . . **ENNEA–** . . . . **nine**

A *nona*gon is a *nine*-sided figure.
A *nona*genarian is in his *nineties*.
A *nov*ena is a Catholic act of worship lasting *nine* days.
An *ennea*d is a group of *nine* (gods, usually).

Note: *Nov(a)*– and *novo*– mean *new*, as in *novelty*.

10. DEC(IM)– . . . **DECA–** . . . . **ten**

A *dec*ade is a *ten*-year period.
The *Ten* Commandments are known as the *Deca*log.
To *decim*ate an army is to destroy every *tenth* man.

Compare *decimal, decasyllable, decemvir, decapod.*

11. CENT(I)– . . . **HECT(O)–, HEC(A)–** . . **one hundred**

A *centi*pede has *one hundred* legs.
A *cent*ury is *one hundred* years.
A *hecto*graph makes *one hundred* copies.
A *heca*tomb was the mass sacrifice of *one hundred* oxen.

12. MILL(E)–, MILL(I)– . . . **KILO–** . . . **one thousand**

A *milli*on is a *thousand* thousand.
A *milli*gram is *one-thousandth* of a gram.
A *kilo*gram is *one thousand* grams.

13. SEMI– . . . . . **HEMI–, DEMI–** . . . . . **half**

A *semi*annual event comes every *half* year.
A *hemi*sphere is *half* a sphere.
A *demi*god is *half* god and half man.

Questions

1. *Unilateral* means *one-sided.* Continue the series through four.
2. Continue the series beginning *baby, twins, triplets* through eight.
3. List the singer series — *solo, duet, trio* — through eight.
4. How many can you add to the series beginning *double, triple, quadruple?*

PRACTICE SET

What is the meaning of each italicized prefix?

1. An *octo*syllable is a word with __?__ syllables.
2. A *deca*pod has __?__ feet.
3. A *quadri*lateral has __?__ sides.
4. To *quin*tuple a figure, multiply it by __?__.
5. *Tri*une means __?__ in __?__.
6. A *sex*partite agreement involves __?__ parties.
7. A *bi*polar battery has __?__ poles.
8. A *hecto*graph is a duplicator that will make __?__ copies.
9. A *semi*annual event occurs every __?__ year.
10. A *mono*tonous voice stays on __?__ tone most of the time.
11. An *octa*vo is a book from sheets folded into __?__ leaves.
12. A *milli*volt is __?__ of a volt.
13. A *kilo*watt hour is __?__ watts for an hour.
14. A *sept*ennial event occurs every __?__ years.
15. A *demi*volt in horsemanship is a __?__ leap.
16. A *penta*hedron has __?__ sides, a *nona*gon __?__.
17. A *di*morphic substance has __?__ forms.
18. A *centi*grade thermometer has __?__ degrees or steps.
19. *Hept*archy is the rule of __?__ persons.
20. *Duodecimal* refers to __?__ plus __?__ or twelve as a basis.
21. *Tetra*meter has __?__ feet or measures per line.
22. A *hexa*gonal figure has __?__ angles.
23. *Tri*meter is a verse form having __?__ measures per line.
24. A *hemi*cycle is a __?__ circle.
25. A *mille*pede has, literally, __?__ feet.

FAMILIAR PREFIX PAIRS
(Greek and Latin)

Knowing the meanings of common prefixes and roots gives you a magic key that will unlock many unfamiliar or half-familiar words. You will remember new words more easily and read with more accurate understanding.

The prefix pairs (and a few roots) in this unit are not twins, but they have similar meanings. They are teamed up because it is easier to study them that way. Review pages 168–169.

Blanks

How many can you fill, using the correct prefix from the list at the right?

1. A __?__syllabic word has *many* syllables.
2. __?__lithic behavior is the kind one would expect from a man of the "new" Stone Age.
3. An __?__present person would seemingly be *everywhere* at once.
4. __?__locution is talking all *around* a subject — without getting anywhere.
5. The __?__cardium is a membrane *around* the heart.

Prefix Pairs

	Latin	*Greek*
1.	circum–	peri–
2.	con–, com–, co–	sym,– syn–
3.	lux–, luc(i)–	photo–
4.	magn(i)–	mega–
5.	multi–	poly–
6.	nov–	neo–
7.	omni–	pan(to)–
8.	prim–	proto–
9.	sui–	auto–
10.	super–, ultra–	hyper–
11.	sur–	epi–
12.	tele–	

FAMILIAR PREFIX PAIRS—STUDY GUIDE

1. CIRCUM– . . . **PERI–** . . . . **around**

Who was the first to *circum*navigate (sail *around*) the world?
The *peri*meter is the measure (*–meter*) *around* a body or figure.

Compare *peritonitis, pericardium, periscope, period.*

2. CON–, COM–, CO– . . **SYM–, SYN–** . . **together, with**

A *con*vention is a coming (*–vent–*) *together.*
*Com*pression is a pressing *together.*
*Co*operation is working *together.*
*Sym*pathy is feeling (*–pathy*) sad — or happy — *with* someone.
A *syn*thesis is a placing *together* of elements or ideas to make something new.

3. LUX–, LUC(I)– . . **PHOTO–** . . . . **light**

*Luci*fer is *light* bearer (*–fer*). Please e*luci*date (en*light*en).
A *photo*electric cell responds electrically to *light.*

4. MAGN(I)– . . . **MEGA–** . . **(very) large or great**

Why *magni*fy (make *large*) the dangers or discuss their *magni*tude (*large*ness)?
A *mega*phone produces a very *large* sound.

5. MULTI– . . . . **POLY–** . . . . **many**

A *multi*graph makes *many* copies.
A *poly*glot can speak or write *many* languages.

Compare *multilateral, multicellular, multipartite, polyphonic, polygamy, polytheism.*

6. NOV– . . . . **NEO–** . . . . **new**

A *nov*ice is one who is *new* at something.
A *nov*a is a star *new* at least in brightness.
*Ne*on was the *new* gas when discovered.

Compare *novel, novitiate, neolithic, neologism, neophyte.*

7. OMNI– . . . . PAN(TO)– . . . . all

An *omni*scient person is an *all*-knowing one.
*Pan*chromatic film responds to *all* colors.
A *panto*mime is *all* dumb show — no speaking.

8. PRIM– . . . . PROTO– . . . . first

A *prime* minister is the *first* minister in importance.
A *proto*type is a *first* or original model or pattern.
Compare *primary, primitive, primeval, primate, primer, protocol.*

9. SUI– . . . . . AUTO– . . . . self

An *auto*matic machine or *auto*maton is *self*-operating.
*Sui*cide is the killing or cutting off of one*self*.

10. SUPER–, ULTRA– . . HYPER– . . over, above, beyond (normal), excessive(ly)

*Super*sonic speeds are *beyond* the speed of sound.
An *ultra*modern person is *beyond* what is normally modern.
A *hyper*critical person is *excessively* critical.

11. SUR– . . . . . EPI– . . . . on, upon, to, above

A *sur*tax is a tax *upon* or *on top of* a tax.
The *epi*dermis is *upon* or *on top of* the dermis.
An *epi*taph is an inscription *upon* a tombstone.

12. TELE– . . . . far off, at a distance

*Tele*vision is seeing (*–vision*) *at a distance.*
A *tele*scope is another instrument for *far-off* seeing.

Question for Quiz Kids

What connection does each of the following words have with this unit, and what is its meaning?

cenotaph, fratricide, neophyte, novel(ty), omnibus, photosynthesis, polychrome, empathy, perisphere, panoply, coincidence, photogenic, epistle, episode, syntax, megacephalic, neo-silvol, novocain

PRACTICE SET

What is the meaning of each italicized prefix in the sentences which follow?

1. *Poly*technical training involves __?__ skills.
2. An *epi*cycle is a cycle __?__ a cycle.
3. An *auto*mobile is so called because it is __?__ moving.
4. *Hyper*acidity is __?__ acidity.
5. A *neo*logism (*nee-OLL-o-jizm*) is a __?__ word or phrase.
6. What does a *photo*meter measure? The intensity of __?__.
7. To *circum*vent a plot is to get (come) __?__ it or thwart it.
8. *Tele*type machines typewrite news __?__.
9. A *peri*scope is a device for looking __?__ something.
10. A *magn*animous person is __?__ of soul (*anima*).
11. An *omni*potent person is __?__ powerful (*potent*).
12. Stephen is called a *proto*martyr because he was the __?__ martyr.
13. A *sym*posium is a placing __?__ of ideas on a given subject.
14. To *sur*mount an obstacle is to go __?__ it.
15. The *super*intendent is __?__ the men in his department.
16. *Ultra*violet rays are __?__ the violet in wave length.
17. *Mega*lomania is an insane sense of one's own __?__ness.
18. An in*nov*ator starts something __?__.
19. A *prima* donna is the __?__ lady in an opera.
20. *Pan*-Americanism is the cooperation of __?__ the republics of North and South America.
21. A trans*luc*ent substance permits __?__ to pass through.
22. A *multi*millionaire has __?__ millions.
23. To *col*laborate is to work (labor) __?__.
24. A *con*federacy is a group of persons or states working __?__ in a league.
25. To be *sui* generis is to be in a class by __?__.

A LATIN BREAKDOWN

A Latin breakdown is not like a nervous breakdown. It is more like analyzing something in a chemical laboratory to find out what is in it. It would be a good idea to review Unit 21 in Part Two (pages 168–169), if time permits, before starting this unit.

Where?

Can you fill the blanks correctly? One in each sentence answers the question *where* in terms of the italicized prefix. The other, in Questions 3, 4, and 5, requires the meaning of the italicized root.

1. A *pro*motion is a moving __?__.
2. A *trans*oceanic flight is one __?__ the ocean.
3. A *suspic*ious person is always __?__ __?__ the surface of things.
4. What is a *prevision?* A __?__ __?__.
5. To *repel* an invader is to __?__ him __?__.

Prefixes

1. ad–
2. inter–
3. post–
4. pre–, ante–
5. pro–
6. re–
7. sub–
8. trans–

Roots

1. –cede–, –ceed–, –cess–, –grad–, –gress–
2. –cur(r)–, –curs–
3. –duc(t)–
4. –fer–, –lat(e)–, –port–, –portat–
5. –flect–, –flex–
6. –fus(e)–
7. –pel–, –puls–
8. –spec(t)–, –spic–, –vide–, –vis–

A LATIN BREAKDOWN—STUDY GUIDE

1. AD-- . . . . **to, toward**

Note: The *d* frequently changes to the first letter of the root to which it is joined. Sometimes the *d* is dropped before *s*, as in *aspect*.

To *ad*here to the original plan is to stick (*–here–*) *to* it. *Ad*hesive tape sticks *to* something.

To *ap*pease is to give peace *to* or pacify.

Compare *allocate, allot, allure, append, ascribe, addict, adjoining, astringent,* and others.

2. INTER– . . . . **between or among**

To *inter*cept a pass is to take (*–cept–*) or seize it *between* the passer and receiver.

*Inter*scholastic contests take place *between* schools.

Compare *interchange, intercede, intercommunicate, interfere* (strike between), *interlude, intermarriage, international, interpenetrate.*

3. POST– . . . . **after, behind**

What does it mean to *post*date a check?

The *post*erior end of a cow is *behind*.

Compare *postlude, postgraduate, postpone, postscript.*

4. PRE– . . . . . **ANTE–** . . **before, ahead of time, in front of**

A *pre*monition is a warning *before*hand.

Murder is *pre*meditated (planned-*ahead-of-time*) killing.

*Ante*meridian (A.M.) means occurring *before* noon.

Compare *prelude, preplan, prepay, preheat, pre-exist, anteroom, antechamber.*

5. PRO– . . . . **forward, favoring, before**

To *pro*mote a plan is to move or push it *forward*.

*Pro*crastination is *favoring* (putting off until) tomorrow.

Compare *pro-Russian, proclivity, propose* (place before).

---

6. RE– . . . . back(ward), again

To *re*act is to act *back*.

To *re*cognize is to know *again*.

When a condition *re*curs, it happens *again*.

Compare *reborn, readjust, reform, regain, refresh.*

7. SUB– . . . . under, beneath

A *sub*cellar is *under* a cellar, a *sub*agent works under an agent, and apartments are sometimes *sub*let.

Note: The *b* often changes to agree with the first letter of the root, as in *suffer, suffuse, succeed, succumb, suggest.*

8. TRANS– . . . . across

*Trans*verse lines cut *across* each other.

To *trans*cend is to climb *across* or beyond.

Compare *transport, transatlantic, transoceanic.*

---

1. –CEDE– . . . **–CEED–, –CESS–** . . . . go
–GRAD– . . . **–GRESS–** . . . . .go or walk

To pro*gress* or to pro*ceed* is to *go* forward.

An ag*gress*ive man is a *going*-toward (*ad*–) or pushing man.

An ante*ced*ent is the noun which *goes* before a noun or pronoun and thus identifies it.

A di*gress*ion is a *going* away from or a wandering.

Compare *ingress, egress, regression, recede, precede, proceed, exceed, secede.*

2. –CUR(R) . . . . . –CURS– . . . . . . run(ning)

*Curr*ent literally means *running*. So does *course*.

To in*cur* dislike means to *run* into it. A *courier* is a *runner*.

An ex*cur*sion is a *running* out from (the place where one lives).

Compare *concourse,* a running together; *recur,* to run back, that is, happen again.

---

3. −DUC(T)− . . . . lead

To ab*duct* is to *lead* away or kidnap a person.
What do *induce, induct, deduce, deduct, ductile* (page 145), *conduct, product, nonconductor, aqueduct, introduce,* and *duct* mean? How many other *−duct−* words can you list?

4. −FER− . . . . −LAT(E)− . . . .
−PORT− . . . −PORTAT− . . carry, bear, bring

To col*late* is to *bring* together books or data for critical study.
A sopori*fer*ous drug is sleep-*bringing.*
An odori*fer*ous article is odor-*carrying.*

Compare *confer, refer, defer, interfere, transfer, translate, superlative, relate,* and many others.

Report, export, import, purport, porter, and *support* are a few of the commonest from *−port−.*

Compare *portage,* a canoe *carry;* de*port*ment, one's *carriage, bearing* or *behavior.*

5. −FLECT− . . . . . −FLEX− . . . . bend

To de*flect* a blow is to *bend* it away from one.
An in*flex*ible person is an un*bend*ing one.

Compare *reflect, circumflex, reflex, inflect.*

6. −FUS(E)− . . . . pour

To inter*fuse* good feeling is to *pour* it *among* people.
A spring tonic will in*fuse* (*pour in*) new life.

Compare *suffuse,* pour under; *confuse,* pour together; *refuse,* pour back (literally).

7. −PEL− . . . . −PULS−. . . . . drive or push

Bad manners re*pel* (*drive* back) a person.
Jet pro*puls*ion (*driving* forward) attains terrific speed.

Compare *pulsate,* throb; *dispel,* drive away; *impulse,* a *pushing* (toward action).

8. –SPEC(T)– . . . . –SPIC– . . . . . . to look (at)
   –VIDE– . . . . . –VIS– . . . . .to see

A *suspicious* person is always *looking* (*–spic–*) or *peeking* under (*–sus–*) what appears on the surface.

Introspection is *looking within* oneself.

The *prospect* (*forward look*) appears good.

Compare *expect, inspect, respect, conspicuous,* and their kin; also, *spectator, spectacle, spectacular, specter* (ghost), *spectrum,* and *speculate.*

A *provident* person *looks forward* or *foresees* his needs.

A *visor* has to do with *seeing,* and a *vista* (page 183) is a *sight* or *view.*

PRACTICE SET

Write the word or words which belong in each blank:

1. A *post*humous book appears __?__ the author's death.
2. A *spec*ter is something startling to __?__, that is, a ghost.
3. *Pre*mature effort is expended __?__.
4. A *pro*-British policy is one __?__ the British.
5. One who *transgresses* the law literally __?__ __?__ it.
6. To *re*habilitate men is to make them useful __?__.
7. A *sub*marine sails __?__ the sea.
8. An *ad*junct is something joined __?__ an arrangement.
9. *Intercession* is the act of __?__ __?__.
10. The in*curs*ion of barbarians means their __?__ in.
11. To ex*pel* a man is to __?__ him out.
12. *Revision* means literally, __?__ a piece of work __?__.
13. To im*port* merchandise is to __?__ it into the country.
14. To in*duct* officers is to __?__ them into office.
15. Coni*fer*ous trees are cone-__?__ trees.
16. To *transfer* one's baggage to another train is to __?__ it __?__ to the other train.
17. When you in*flect* a verb you __?__ it into various forms.
18. An in*fus*ion of new life is a __?__ing in.
19. It *ante*dated the voyage of Columbus (occurred __?__ 1492).

LATINSTRUCTION

In the language of the ancient Romans, *–struct–* was a root which meant *build,* and it means the same today. To *instruct* is literally to *build in* facts, ideas, or attitudes. To *construct* is to *build together* a mass of materials. A *destructive* person is one who *un-builds.*

This unit is an activity in building up words from Latin prefixes and roots, many of which you have had in previous units or will encounter soon. You will discover that the process has more of a system to it than you realized. This discovery will help you spell words correctly, and you should study the meanings of words that are unfamiliar and use them in sentences.

Can you write the words that go in the blanks below?

Verb	*Noun*	*Adjective*
1. accede (ad + cede) — *comply*	_ _?_ _ or _ _?_ _	
2. _ _?_ _ — *plead, go between*	intercession	_ _?_ _
3. _ _?_ _ — *go back*	_ _?_ _	recessive
4. concede — *grant or yield*	_ _?_ _	_ _?_ _
5. _ _?_ _ — *withdraw*	_ _?_ _	secessive
6. _ _?_ _ — *go before*	precedence*	
1. proceed — *go forward*	_ _?_ _ or _ _?_ _	
2. _ _?_ _ — *go beyond*	excess	_ _?_ _
3. _ _?_ _ — *accomplish one's purpose*	_ _?_ _	successive
1. _ _?_ _ — *go forward*	progression	_ _?_ _
2. _ _?_ _ — *wander from topic*	_ _?_ _	digressive
3. transgress — *do wrong*	_ _?_ _	

What Washington noun belongs to the Gress Family? What noun that means *an outgoing?*

* Look up *precession,* an astronomical term, if possible.

FURTHER ACTIVITY

1. Can you build a set, like those at left, from each of the following groups of guide words? There are a few irregularities.

   compel, expulsion, propulsive, repulsive
   abduct (no adjective), *induct, deduction, conductive*
   produce, reduction, introductory
   recur, occurrence (adjective rare), *concurrent*
   respect (watch spelling), *inspector, prospective*
   reflect, inflection, deflective
   import, transporter, deportation
   report (careful!), *supporter, exportation*
   translate, dilation, relatable
   construct, destruction, instructive

2. Write the verb for each word in the groups below. Then change it to past tense. If the word is starred, write an adjective form beside the verb. Study the meaning of each word.

   SCEND, SCENT (climb): *ascent, descent*
   CLINE (lean or lie): *inclination, declension, reclining*
   SERT (join together): *assertion*, desertion, insertion*
   TORT (twist): *contortion, distortion, extortion, tortuous*
   STINGU, STINCT (prick): *distinction*, extinction**

3. Write the *–tion* noun form for each of the words below. If a word is starred, write its adjective beside the *–tion* form.

   institute*, constitute*, destitute
   exhibit, inhibit, prohibit*
   attend*, contend, distend (page 212), *extend*, intend, pretend** (watch spelling)
   repute, compute, dispute, impute

4. What are the verb and noun (*–tion, –sion, –ment*) to go with *admissible, advertiser, applicable*, attainable, connective, corporate, decisive, divisive, inquisitive, inventive*, permissive, preventive, professional*, promotional*, submissive.* Can you give a person noun for each starred word?

5. Write the noun (*–ion*) for *confuse, convene, decide, define, detest, direct, elect, except, profuse, receive.* Write the verb for *advice, despicable, detection, detention, erection, exhaustion, intervention, protestant, provision, recollection, retention, revision, selection, supervision.* Change each verb to past tense.
6. Write the following words in a column and supply the verb and *–tion* noun for each: *composer, disposable, impostor, opposite, proposer, suppositional.* Change the verbs to past tense.

WORD–BUILDING EXERCISE

Write for each blank the correct form of the word in parentheses:

1. His fondness for candy is __?__ (excess).
2. The man was convicted on charges of __?__ (extort).
3. The cost of materials is __?__ (prohibit).
4. Do you have a __?__ (retain well) memory?
5. The case against her is entirely __?__ (suppose).
6. Criticism should be partly __?__ (construct).
7. The new rule is not __?__ (apply) to this case.
8. Is __?__ (inquisitive) a sign of intelligence?
9. Political leaders expect __?__ (oppose).
10. An eclipse is a rather uncommon __?__ (occur).

CHALLENGE SET

Copy the italicized words, and beside each write its meaning in the sentence:

1. He *contends* that *importation* of cotton is not necessary.
2. The doctors *concur* in stating that malaria is *recurrent*.
3. We will *accede* to the demand for *deportation* of Communists.
4. Her eyes *dilated* when she saw the *repulsive* creature.
5. He will *intercede* for the *transgressors*.
6. Watch the clouds *recede* under the *compulsion* of the wind.
7. *Deduct* the time spent on *digressions*.
8. A *reflector* helps shut out *excessive* sunlight.
9. The leaders will *confer* regarding tax *deductions*.
10. The musicians will *secede* unless granted *precedence*.

FIFTEEN LATIN ROOTS

If you set them out in your word garden and water them carefully, they will produce a useful and varied harvest for you.

Information, Please

1. The an*nunci*ation to Mary was a __?__ to her that she would have a son.

2. To re*vert* to a bad habit is to __?__ back to it again.

3. To e*ject* a person is to __?__ him __?__.

4. A con*fid*ant is someone you __?__ very much.

5. A *fact*otum is a __?__-it-all.

● *How many words derived from the list of roots in this unit can you find in the illustration?*

Roots

1. –clude–, –clus–
2. –dic(t)(a)–
3. –fact–, –fect–, –fic(t)–
4. –fid(e)–
5. –flu(en)–, –flux–
6. –fract–
7. –ject–
8. –mit(t)–, –miss–
9. –nounc(e)–, –nunci–
10. –pli(c)–, –plex–
11. –serv–
12. –sist–
13. –solv–, –solut–
14. –ven(i)–, –vent–
15. –vert–, –vers–

1. –CLUDE– . . . **–CLUS–** . . . . shut

include, inclusion — *shut(ting)* in
exclude, exclusion — *shut(ting)* out
seclude, seclusion — *shut(ting)* apart

2. –DIC(T)(A)– . . . . say, command

A *dicta*tor is one who has "the say." — He *commands*.
The king issued an *edict* (*command*).
A *dicta*phone is a mechanical ear that records *dicta*tion.
Compare *indicate, addict, dictate, dictatorial.*

3. –FACT– . . **–FECT–** . . **–FIC(T)–** . . make or do

A clothing *fact*ory is a place that *makes* clothes.
Literally, to manu*fact*ure is to *make* by hand (*manu–*).
*Fict*ion is *make*-believe. Af*fect*ation is a "making" toward
   (*ad–*) what one is not.

4. –FID(E)– . . . . faith, trust

*fid*elity — *faith*fulness, loyalty
in*fid*el — one having no *trust* (in God)
per*fid*y — breach of *faith*, disloyalty

5. –FLU(EN)– . . . **–FLUX–** . . . . . . flow(ing)

con*flu*ence — *flowing* together (of two rivers or lives)
ef*flu*ence — an out*flowing*; af*flu*ence — a *flowing* toward
super*flu*ous — *flowing* above or beyond what is needed

6. –FRACT– . . . . break, bend

A *fract*ured (*broken*) leg resulted.
In*fract*ion (*breaking*) of the rules will be punished.
Compare *fraction, refract, diffract.*

7. –JECT– . . . . cast or hurl

A pro*ject*ile is an object *hurled* forward or forth.
Ab*ject* means *cast* down or down*cast*.
Compare *interject(ion), project(ion), inject(ion), deject(ion), ob-
   ject(ion), subject(ion).*

---

8. **–MIT(T)–** . . . . . **–MISS–** . . . . send, sen⸱

emit — *send* forth (emission, emissive)

dismiss — *send* away (dismissal)

transmit — *send* across (transmission, transmitter)

Compare mission (a *sending*), missionary (one *sent*), commission (a *sending* or group *sent*), committee.

9. **–NOUNC(E)–** . . **–NUNCI–** . . . . declare

Denouncing graft is *declaring* it down (de–).

An annunciator *declares* a call and tells where it came from.

Compare announce, pronounce, enunciate, nuncio.

10. **–PLI(C)–** . . . . . **–PLEX–** . . . . fold

To implicate one in a crime is literally to *fold* him into it.

A complicated situation has many *folds*.

Quadruplex operation is four*fold* operation.

Compare duplicate, triplicate, quadruplicate, multiplication, multiplex, application.

11. **–SERV–** . . . . keep, save

Why preserve this any longer?

Did he reserve (*keep* back) the tickets for you?

Compare conserve, reservation, preservation.

12. **–SIST–** . . . . (to make to) stand

Will you assist (*stand* to, help) me?

She insists (*makes a stand*) that I was there.

Compare consist, desist, exist, persist, resist, subsist; also insistence⸱ extant.

13. **–SOLV–** . . . . . **–SOLUT–** . . ⸲ . . . . loosen

solve — "*loosen*" a problem

dissolve — "*loosen*" a solid substance

absolve — "*loosen*" a person from (guilt)

Compare solution, soluble, solvent.

---

14. –VEN(I)– . . . –VENT– . . . . come, coming

A conven**ti**on (*coming* together) takes place soon.

Will the government inter**vene** (*come* between) in the dispute?

Compare *convene, intervention, prevent(ion), invent(ion)*.

15. –VERT– . . . . –VERS– . . . . turn

avert	aversion	averse
convert	conversion	converse
divert	diversion	diverse

*Vert*igo is a *turning* or *whirling* called dizziness.

PROJECTION

Set up a tabulation like the ones on page 238 for each of the following groups of guide words:

1. *include, exclusion, conclusive, exclusiveness*
2. *reject, objector, injection.* (Include the most common adjective forms.)
3. *infect, defective, perfection*
4. *transmit, remitter, commission*
5. *pronounce, announcer, denunciation*
6. *implicate, explication, complicate, duplication*
7. *preserve, conserver, reservation*
8. *insist, resist, assistant, subsistence, consistent, persistence.* (Be careful. This is partly a review of Ence and Ance on pages 141–142.)
9. *absolve, resolvable, solve, dissolution*
10. *invert, reverse, conversion, diverse*

PRACTICE SET

How many of the blanks can you fill correctly?

1. To con*fide* in a person is to __?__ that person with one's secrets. The expression "bona *fide*" means "in good __?__."
2. What word means to *keep together* that which is left? __?__

3. To sub*sist* on apples and graham wafers is, literally, to __?__ with them beneath, that is, to live on them.
4. To re*mit* a sum of money is to __?__ it back in return for something received.
5. It is impolite to contra*dict* (__?__ the opposite).
6. A con*jec*ture is a __?__ at the truth.
7. Pro*nounce* means to __?__ a word correctly.
8. Ap*plic*ation of a rule means to __?__ it to fit the situation.
9. A break in a bone is called a __?__ure.
10. A *flui*d is so called because it __?__.
11. Arti*facts* are objects __?__ by men of the earliest times.
12. This does not pre*clude* (__?__ out) the possibility of murder.
13. When the Elks __?__ (come together) there will be a celebration.
14. Will the wolf-dog __?__ (turn back again) to his wolflike ways?
15. The in*flux* (__?__ in) of new people made the housing problem very __?__ (much folded together).

WORD — ROOT HUNT

Can you write a word for:

1. One who is *sent?* __?__
2. A sum of money *sent* with an order? __?__
3. The *flowing-in* effect of one person on another? __?__
4. *Make-believe* writing? __?__
5. A year-*turning,* such as a birthday? __?__
6. A court term (from *–fid*) for a sworn statement? __?__
7. A verb meaning *to make something come about,* and its adjective? __?__, __?__
8. The *breaking* of a rule? __?__
9. A word meaning *to loosen away,* as sugar? __?__
10. A *toss* or *cast* about what really happened? con__?__

Spelling counts.

FIFTEEN MORE—MOSTLY LATIN

Root Meanings

Can you supply for each gap an appropriate word formed from one of the roots in the list at the right?

1. In a voice scarcely __?__ she begged the clerk to __?__ the error.

2. The __?__ reason for requesting an __?__ (fair) adjustment was fear of the con__?__.

3. __?__ requirements make medicine a difficult __?__ to enter.

Roots

1. –aud(i)–, –audit–
2. –domin–
3. –equ(i)–, –par(i)–
4. –jur(e)–, –juri(s)–
5. –merge–, –mers–
6. –micro–
7. –mort–
8. –pend–, –pense–
9. –rect–, –ortho–
10. –sequ–, –secut–
11. –string–, –strict–
12. –tain–, –ten(t)–
13. –tort–
14. –voc–, –vocat–
15. –volve–, –volu(t)–

FIFTEEN MORE—STUDY GUIDE

1. –AUD(I)– . . . –AUDIT– . . . . hear, listen to

An *audi*ence is a group of *hearers* or *listeners*.

An *audi*torium is a place for *hearing* programs. An *audi*tion is a *hearing*.

Note: *Phon*(e) means *sound* as in *telephone, phonetics, antiphonal, dictaphone* (page 242), *euphony, megaphone* (page 230), *cacophony*.

2. –DOMIN– . . . . rule, ruling

A *domin*ant trait is a *ruling* trait.

To *domin*ate is to *rule*.

Compare *domination, dominion, domineer, Anno Domini.*

3. –EQU(I)– . . . –PAR(I)– . . . . . equal(ly)

The two hills are *equi*distant from the village.

*Equ*animity is *equal*ness, *evenness,* or *calmness* of mind (*–anim–*).

An *equ*able climate is an *equal* or *even* climate.

The two teams seem almost on a *pari*ty (equal terms) in performance.

Compare *equilateral, equation, equipoise, equilibrium, par, disparity, disparage.*

4. –JUR(E)– . . . . . –JURI(S)– . . . right, law, justice

An in*jury* is literally something not according to the *law*.

*Juris*prudence is the study of *law* or *justice*.

Compare *conjure, perjure, adjure* (embodying the *I-swear* idea). *Jurisdiction* is the *right* to say what shall be done.

5. –MERGE– . . . –MERS– . . . . dip

sub*merge, dip* under — submersion

im*merse, dip* into — immersion

6. –MICRO– . . . . very small, tiny

*Micro*be means *small* life.

A *micro*meter measures *very small* distances.

A *micro*phone handles *very small* sounds.

7. –MORT– . . . . **death**

A *mort*al wound is a *deadly* one. The *mort*ality rate is the *death* rate. What is a post *mortem?*

Look up *mortify, mortification.*

8. –PEND– . . . . **–PENSE–** . . . . **hang or weigh**

To ex*pend* money is literally to *weigh* it out.

An inde*pend*ent person is one not (*in–*) *hanging* (*–pend–*) down from (*de–*) anything. What is an ap*pend*age?

9. –RECT– . . . . **–ORTHO–** . . . . **(make) right, correct**

*rect*ify — make *right* (an error)

*ortho*dox — *right* teaching(s)

*rect*itude — up*right*ness

*ortho*gonal — having *right* angles

Compare *orthopedics, orthodontic.*

10. –SEQU– . . . . **–SECUT–** . . . . . . **follow**

A *sequ*ence is a *series* or *following.*

Con*sequ*ences are what *follow* one's actions.

Compare *consecutive* (page 216), *sequel, execute, persecute, inconsequential.*

11. –STRING– . . . **–STRICT–** . . . **draw together, tighten**

To re*strict* one's privileges is to *draw* back or *tighten* them.

*String*ent laws are *tight* laws. An a*string*ent *contracts* bodily tissues.

Note: –TRACT– means *draw* in a slightly different sense: *attract* (draw toward), *contract* (draw together) the opening, *extract* (draw out) the poison, *retract* (draw back or withdraw) a statement.

12. –TAIN– . . . . **–TEN(T)–** . . . . . . **hold**

A re*ten*tive memory *holds* facts well.

A bulldog has great *ten*acity or *holding* power.

Compare *detain, retain, tenable, tenets, detention.*

---

13. –TORT– . . . . **twist, wrest**

Ex*tort*ion is *wresting* money or information from someone.
To con*tort* one's face is to *twist* it out of shape.

14. –VOC– . . . . –VOCAT– . . . . **call**

One's *voca*tion is his *calling* or occupation.
A con*voca*tion is a *calling* together or assembly.

Compare *revoke* (call back or cancel), *provoke, invoke.*

15. –VOLVE– . . . –VOLU(T)– . . . . . . **roll**

In*volu*tions are *rollings* in or folds.
A re*volu*tion is a *rolling* over — or back — in human affairs.

Compare *revolve, involve, evolve, evolution, volume, voluble.*

Questions

1. Can you expand each of the following groups of guide words into a set like the ones on page 238? (These are rather hard.)

   erect, direction, corrective
   execute, persecution, prosecutor
   detract, subtraction, protractor
   invoke, revocation, provocative (use dictionary for adjectives)
   involve, revolution, evolutionary

2. Can you think of the opposite form of some of the following? *attainable, audible, consecutive, consequential, dependent, distorted, equitable, expensive, involved, mortal, orthodox, provocative, revocable, tenable.* If you can think of a fairly familiar noun form for ten of the words, you are eligible for the degree of M.W.B. (Master Word Builder).

PRACTICE SET

Can you fill all of the blanks correctly without looking back once?

1. What does *emerge* mean literally?   To __?__ __?__.
2. *Equi*poise involves __?__ weights.
3. "La *Morte* d'Arthur" means "The __?__ of Arthur."
4. An *audi*tor in a course is, literally, a __?__er (and not a doer).
5. A *pend*ulum is a weight that __?__s.
6. A *ten*able belief is one which a person can __?__.
7. He struck without pro*vocat*ion (literally a __?__ forth).
8. A *strict*ure of the intestine is a __?__ing together.
9. A task which de*volves* literally __?__s down upon one.
10. The *seque*l to an event is the incident which __?__s.
11. *Micro*chemistry is the chemistry of __?__ quantities.
12. An *orthophonic* speaker produces the __?__ __?__s.
13. A *jury* determines the __?__ of a case.
14. *Domin*ation is the process of __?__.
15. *Pari*ty is a condition of __?__ity.
16. A *recti*fier makes current flow in the __?__ direction.
17. To pro*tract* a discussion is to __?__ it forth to great length.
18. Dis*tort*ion of the truth is __?__ it.

ROOTSOME PAIRS

This unit stars fifteen Latin-Greek pairs which are often seen in print. Those to the left are of Latin origin, while the ones in the right-hand column are Greek.

Can You?

Do you "know your way around"? Not unless you can answer the following questions:

1. What is a *pod*iatrist? (A __?__ doctor)

2. What is a *bene*factor? (A __?__ doer)

3. What is the *astra*dome on a modern train? (Place from which you can see __?__)

4. What is *manu*al labor? (__?__ labor)

5. Eo*hipp*us was a kind of __?__.

6. A *chrono*graph measures and records __?__.

7. *Psycho*therapy is __?__ cure.

Rootsome Pairs

	Latin	*Greek*
1.	–ami(c)–	–phil–
2.	–aqua– –aque–	–hydro–
3.	–bene–	–eu–
4.	–civi(s)– –urb(s)–	–polit– –poli(s)–
5.	–equ(es)–	–hipp(o)–
6.	–hal(e)–	–spir(e)–
7.	–man(u)–	–chiro–
8.	–ment–	–psych(o)–
9.	–nat(e)– –nasc–	–gen(e)–
10.	–nomen– –nomin–	–onym–
11.	–ped–	–p(o)us– –pod–
12.	–scribe– –script–	–graph– –gram–
13.	–stell(a)–	–astra(a)–
14.	–temp(o)–	–chron(o)–
15.	–vita–	–bio–

ROOTSOME PAIRS—STUDY GUIDE

1. **—AMI(C)—** . . . **—PHIL—** . . . friend(ship), love(r)

The *phil*anthropist (*friend* of mankind) is very *ami*able.
*Ami*cable relations exist with England.
An Anglo*phile* loves or is *friendly* to the British.

2. **—AQUA—, —AQUE—** . . . **—HYDRO—** . . . water

*Aqua*planing is great fun. What is an *aque*duct?
*Hydro*dynamics is a branch of engineering.

3. **—BENE—** . . . . **—EU—** . . . . well

What is a *bene*factor? What does *Bene*dict mean, literally?
*Eu*phonious music is *well* sounding or harmonious.

Compare *benefit, benediction, eugenics, eulogy.*

4. **—CIVI(S)—** . . . **—POLIT—** . . . . . . citizen
—URB(S)— . . . **—POLI(S)—** . . . . . . city

Civic pride is a *citizen's* pride, and *politics* is the expression
of *citizen*ship.
A metro*polis* is literally a "mother" *city,* and sub*urb*an areas
are "under" the *city* in a sense.

5. **—EQU(ES)—** . . . **—HIPP(O)—** . . . . . . horse

An *eques*trian statue is one of a person on *horse*back.
An *equ*ine manner is *horse*like.
A *hippo*potamus, literally, is a river *horse.*

6. **—HAL(E)—** . . . **—SPIR(E)—** . . . . . breath(e)

To in*hale* is to *breathe* in; ex*hale,* to *breathe* out.
An a*spir*ant *breathes* or *strives* toward something.

Compare *inhalation, respiration, spirit, inspirit, dispirited.*

7. **—MAN(U)—** . . . **—CHIRO—** . . . . . (by) hand

*Man*icure is care (*—cure—*) of the *hands.*
A *chiro*practor is one who treats by use of the *hands.*

Compare *maneuver, manifold, manipulate, manufacture* (page 242),
chirography (handwriting).

---

252   **WORD WEALTH JUNIOR**   Unit 15

8. –MENT– . . . . –PSYCH(O)– . . . . . mind

A de*ment*ed person is out of (down from) his *mind*.
*Psycho*logy is the study of the *mind*.

Compare *mental, dementia* (madness), *Psyche, psychoanalyze.*

9. –NAT(E)–, –NASC– . . –GEN(E)– . . born, (giving) birth, producing

A *nat*ive of Philadelphia was *born* there.
*Nasc*ent energy is fresh, *new-born* energy.
Eu*gen*ics is the science of providing well-*born* children.

Compare *nativity, natal, innate, progeny, genesis, congenital.*

10. –NOMEN–, –NOMIN– . . . –ONYM– . . . name

To *nomin*ate a person is to *name* him for an office.
An ant*onym* is an opposite word or *name*.

Compare *cognomen, denomination, synonym, homonym, eponym.*

11. –PED– . . . . . –P(O)US–, –POD– . . . . foot

A *ped*estrian is one who travels by *foot*.
To im*ped*e one's progress is to put his *foot* against it.
What is a chiro*pod*ist? an octo*pus*? ortho*ped*ics?

Compare *pedal, pedestal, impediment, podiatrist.*

12. –SCRIBE–, –SCRIPT– . . –GRAPH–, –GRAM– . . write, writing

To sub*scribe* to a magazine is to under*write* it.
A *script* is in *writing*, and a *graph* is a kind of *writing*.

Compare *inscribe, prescribe, conscript(ion), phonograph, telegram.*

13. –STELL(A)– . . . –ASTR(A)– . . . . . . star

He played a *stell*ar game of basketball.
*Astr*onomy is the study of the *stars*.

Compare *Stella, constellation* (page 182), *astrology, astral, disaster.*

14. –TEMP(O)– . . . –CHRON(O)– . . . . . time

That which is *tempo*rary exists for a *time* only.
The *chrono*logical order of events is the *time* order.

Compare *tempo, temporize, chronicle, chronology, synchronous.*

---

15. –VITA– . . . . –BIO– . . . . life

Literally, a *vital* issue is one involving *life* itself.
*Bio*chemistry is the chemistry of plant and animal *life*.
Note: *Vivi–* alive, appears in *vivify* (to make alive), *vivid*.

Questions

1. Complete the following triplets: *aspire, respiration, inhalator; subscribe, description, prescriber.*
2. Can you write a noun form of *lucid, elucidate, magnify, magnificent, nominate, impede, amiable,* and *beneficent?*

PRACTICE SET

Can you fill *all* of the blanks without looking back?

1. *Ami*ty or __?__ship should prevail in *Phil*adelphia, the city of brotherly __?__.
2. To ex*pire* is to __?__ one's last. Ex*hal*ations are out__?__.
3. A *hippo*drome was once a __?__ racecourse devoted to *equine* (__?__) achievements.
4. An *aqua*marine (color of ￼a __?__) *hydro*plane (landing on __?__) would be hard to see.
5. A *bene*volent (__?__-wishing) lady discussed the post*natal* (after __?__) care of a child.
6. A *eu*logy (a speaking __?__) was in*scribed* ("__?__" on) the statue.
7. A *chrono*meter measures __?__, a *pedo*meter the distance traveled by __?__.
8. The *tempo* of the music is the __?__ rate at which it is played.
9. *Civil* as well as *polit*ical rights are those of a __?__.
10. Those in the *psycho*pathic ward are suffering (*path*) from disorders of the __?__. They are __?__al cases.
11. The cog*nomen* Swift became the family __?__.
12. *Man*euver means __?__ work, literally.
13. *Astral* light comes from the __?__.
14. To de*vital*ize a food is to take out its __?__-giving properties.
15. *Bio*physics is the physics of plant and animal __?__.

DOUBLE TROUBLE?

Read carefully the word list below, exaggerating the pronunciation of shy vowels and syllables. Then sort the words into clubs or sets such as these:

I The Prefix Set — in which the double letter is traceable to a prefix. Use the dictionary if in doubt.

II The Stiff Set — words ending in a double *f*.

III The Sally Set — most of them end in *ally* — because *–ly* was added to a word that already ended in *al*.

IV Verb Forms — They end in *–ing, –ed,* or *–en.* In making these forms, a final consonant of the simple verb is doubled *if it has a short vowel in front of it.* Thus, *hop* takes *hopping* and *hopped* for its other forms, but *hope* takes *hoping* and *hoped.* (See page 43.) *Begin* takes *beginning* for its *–ing* form, *get* has *getting,* and *rot* has *rotting* and *rotten,* but *become* has *becoming.*

V The Middle Set — Some have a double chin, some a large bosom, some a big stomach, and some have swollen ankles to make them memorable. Often they are short. They expect to be studied and humored.

VI The Double-Double Set — these include many of the real heavyweights of spelling, such as *embarrass.* Each contains *two* doubled letters.

If a word fits in two different sets, by all means list it twice. Here are the words:

accident, accidentally, accommodate, accompany, accompanying, accent, accordance, according, accomplish, accounts, accurate, accuse, accustom, addressed, affair, afford, allotment, ammunition, anniversary, annual, annually, apparatus, apparent, appeal, appe-

tite, approach, appropriate, approximately, assess, assume, attack,
attempt, attention, attitude, balloon, battalion, beginning, bliz-
zard, bookkeeping, cannon, career, cartoon, challenge, chauffeur,
collapse, comment, commission, commit, committed, committee,
corrupt, cunning, degree(s), disappoint, disapprove, dissatisfied,
dropped, embarrass, engineer, especially, essay, exceptionally, for-
gotten, gossip, gradually, hopped, immense, incidentally, mastiff,
misspell, molasses, necessity, occasion, occasionally, occupy, oc-
cur, occurred, opportunity, opposite, parallel, personally, pioneer,
plaintiff, pontiff, possess, recommend, sheriff, staff, stopped, strug-
gle, stubborn, success, summon, surrender, surround, syllable, tar-
iff, tennis, territory, tobacco, traffic, tunnel, unnecessary, vessel,
volunteer, warrant, wholly.

SENTENCES FOR PRACTICE

Write some or all of the following from dictation.

1. Gossips occasionally possess accurate information.
2. The chauffeur avoided an accident by running over the mastiff.
3. The sheriff appointed a committee to study traffic.
4. The danger does not warrant our possessing ammunition.
5. A commission will assess it and make recommendations.
6. The balloon gradually ascended to a height of approximately 16,000 feet.
7. By dividing words into syllables, you avoid the embarrassment of misspelling them.
8. A volunteer can usually manage the apparatus.
9. Family allotments made much bookkeeping necessary.
10. The battalion stubbornly refused to surrender.
11. The collapse of the tunnel occurred during a blizzard.
12. The tariff on tobacco seems wholly unwarranted.
13. The plaintiff occasionally challenged our statements.
14. The anniversary speech was an appeal for peace.
15. The editor disapproved of the cartoon about pioneers.

PARLEZ–VOUS FRANÇAIS?
(Do you speak French?)

All the words in this unit came from French and in most cases retain their French pronunciation. Some of the words are now used in English, like *boudoir*. Others such as *guerre* are used in familiar phrases like *croix de guerre* but have never become naturalized citizens of the American language. Some have accent marks in French which they have gradually lost in English usage.

Theater Project

Can you fill the blanks appropriately with words from the list at the right?

The actors formed a __?__ and began to build up a __?__ of plays they could present. Each selected the __?__ he thought he could play best. At first they had no actresses and the men were awkward in scenes such as a __?__-à-__?__ between ladies in a __?__. In May each year they held a __?__ for their wives and lady friends.

A Famous French Proverb:
"Cherchez la femme."
("Look for the woman.")

Base Words

1. amour
2. boudoir
3. corps
4. coup
5. denouement
6. enfant
7. fait
8. fete
9. guerre
10. jour
11. pièce
12. repertoire
13. reveille
14. role
15. tête

PARLEZ–VOUS FRANÇAIS?—STUDY GUIDE

1. **AMOUR (ah-MOOR)** . . . . . love, a love affair

   The amours of Henry VIII make quite a story.

   Compare *amorist, paramour, amorous, enamored.*

2. **BOUDOIR (BOO-dwar)** . . . lady's private room or bedroom

   She emerged from the boudoir in her negligee (*neg-li-ZHAY*) or dressing gown.

3. **CORPS (kore)** . . organized body or group, especially military

   He wanted to join the Marine Corps.

   A corps of volunteer relief workers was organized.

4. **COUP (koo)** . . . . a blow or stroke

   A coup d'état (*day-TAH*) is a military or political "stroke" that overthrows or upsets a government.

   A coup de grâce is a "blow of mercy" ending a man's suffering when he has been wounded by a firing squad.

   Compare *coup d'œil* (a glance), *coup de soleil* (sunstroke), *coup de maître* (master stroke), *coup de main* (unexpected attack).

5. **DENOUEMENT (day-NOO-mahng*)** . . the outcome or "untying" of a plot or situation

   The denouement brought the execution of the spy.

6. **ENFANT (AHNg-FAHNg*)** . . . . . . child, infant

   An enfant terrible (*teh-REE-bl'*) says shocking things.

7. **FAIT (fet)** . . . . an act or deed

   She was confronted by a fait accompli (an act already carried out beyond recall) when she tried to aid her sister.

---

* This is an attempt to represent the French nasal as in *bon.* Pronounce the syllable as though the g were part of it but not sounded. In other words, the *n* is pronounced the way you pronounce the *n* in *long* when you have a severe head cold.

8. FETE (*fayt*) . . . outdoor party, festival, social affair

The ladies held a lawn fete.

The much-feted (much-entertained) explorer is now in Texas.

9. GUERRE (*gare*) . . . . **war**

"C'est la guerre" (It's the war) was a common explanation for wartime inconveniences and dislocations.

Compare *guerrilla*, from the same root as *guerre*, via Spanish.

10. JOUR (*zhoor*) . . . . **day**

A plat du jour in a restaurant is the special plate or meal that day.

Compare *journal, adjourn, journey* from same root (Lat. *diurnus*, daily).

11. PIÈCE (*pee-ESS* or *p'yes*) . . . article, item, short play

The pièce de résistance (*duh ray-zees-TAHNS*) at a dinner is the main item or dish. If it happens to be tough beefsteak, the expression is singularly appropriate.

12. REPERTOIRE (*reh-per-TWAR*) . . list of plays or parts one can give

The company of actors has a repertoire of 21 plays.

The violinist played every number in his repertoire.

13. REVEILLE (*REV-eh-lee*) . . . . morning call to get up

Reveille is sounded by a bugle.

"Till Reveille" was a popular song during World War II.

14. ROLE (*roll*) . . a part one plays or function one assumes

Her role in the play is that of a chambermaid.

The once-rich heiress began her new role as a working girl.

15. TÊTE (*tet*) . . . . **head**

They sat tête-à-tête (face to face).

A tête-à-tête is a private, heads-together conversation.

Questions

1. Which words contain *ou?* Can you think of other French-borrowed words containing *ou*, pronounced *oo?*
2. Can you find out what *toujours l'amour* means? *amour propre? en avant? derrière? chacun à son goût?* What is a *ruse de guerre?*

FIRST PRACTICE SET

Practice reading the following sentences, with the teacher's help. Copy the italicized words or phrases and beside each write its meaning in the sentence:

1. The movie actor's *amours* had a tragic *denouement.*
2. A brilliant sales *coup* saved the company from failure.
3. How would you like the *role* of bugler for *reveille?*
4. He was awarded the *croix* (*crwah,* cross) *de guerre* for bravery.
5. The *soupe du jour* was cold and the *pièce de résistance* tough.
6. The two held a *tête-à-tête* in the lady's *boudoir.*
7. The delay of the drum *corps* produced a *fait accompli.*
8. She exhausted her *repertoire* of songs at the village *fete.*
9. The little boy became an *enfant gâté* (*GAH-tay* — spoiled).

SECOND PRACTICE SET

Which of the base words goes in each blank? Use each once — where it fits best.

1. __?__ is a __?__ that comes at dawn in every army __?__.
2. The little play is a __?__ which has its setting in a lady's __?__. We added it to our __?__ recently when we gave it at a May Day __?__.
3. The __?__ of a heart-broken father is harder to handle at the __?__ of the story than that of the son whose reckless __?__s have caused all the trouble.
4. A woman's secrets are usually transmitted __?__.
5. The word *tou__?__s* means *all the days, every day,* or *always.*
6. The croix de __?__ is a war decoration.
7. Is an __?__ gâté a __?__ accompli or can (s)he be unspoiled?

ENCORE

Problèmes

Les Mots (*The Words*)

1. Who are the elite?
2. What are belles-lettres?
3. What is a première?
4. How soon is *tout de suite?*
5. What is an hors d'oeuvre?
6. Who are the nouveaux riches?
7. Which girl in the class is the most petite?

1. beau, belle
2. bien
3. bon, bonne
4. elite
5. entre
6. gauche
7. hors
8. jeune
9. née
10. nouveau
11. passé
12. petit, petite
13. premier, première
14. sans
15. tout, toute

French motto: "Tout bien ou rien."
("[Do] everything well or not at all.")

ENCORE—STUDY GUIDE

1. BEAU (*bo* — masc.), **BELLE** (*bel* — fem.) . . . **beautiful**

"Le beau pays de la France" is the beautiful country of France.

She was the belle (beautiful one) of the ball.

Note: *Belles-lettres* (*bell LET-thr'*) is literature in the artistic sense.

2. BIEN (*bee-EN∮**) . . . . **well (as adverb)**

"Eh bien" is like our "Oh well . . ."

Bienvenue means *welcome*.

3. BON (*bohn∮** — masc.), **BONNE** (*bun* — fem.) . . **good**

"Bon jour!" means "Good day!" or "Good morning!"

Bonne foi is *good faith*.

Compare *bon mot, bon soir, bonhommie.*

4. ELITE (*aye-LEET*) . . . . **select, superior**

All of the socially elite were at the party.

5. ENTRE (*AHN∮-thr'**) . . . . **between**

Entr'acte is the intermission *between the acts* of a play.

Entre nous is *between ourselves* — strictly confidential.

6. GAUCHE (*gohsh*) . . . . . **left, awkward, clumsy**

His social behavior is gauche.

It was sheer gaucherie (awkwardness, bungling) to get into an argument with his hostess that way.

7. HORS (*orr*) . . . . **outside, without**

To be hors de combat is to be out of the fight, disabled, or no longer in the running.

The hors d'oeuvre at a banquet is an appetizer or relish enjoyed at the beginning *without* effort or work (*oeuvre*).

8. JEUNE (*zhyun*) . . . . **young**

Une jeune fille is a young girl.

Jeunesse dorée (*doe-RAY*) means *fashionable youth*.

* See note on page 258.

9. **NÉ(E)** (*nay*) . . . . . . .born (*né* is masc., *née* fem.)

Mrs. Frank Perry (née Mae Wilkins) was killed in a crash. (Mentioning her "born" or maiden name helps old friends identify her.)

10. **NOUVEAU** (*noo-VO*) . . . . new

The "noveaux riches" are the newly rich, who sometimes make a gaudy display of their wealth.

11. **PASSÉ** (*pah-SAY*) . . . . . out of date, out-moded

Short skirts are sometimes passé, sometimes in style.

12. **PETIT** (*peh-TEE* or *PEH-ti*), **PETITE** (*peh-TEET*) . . little, small, tiny, insignificant

She is playful and petite.
Petit (*PEH-ti*) larceny is a small or petty theft.

13. **PREMIER** (*PREE-mi-er*), **PREMIÈRE** (*preh-MYAIR*) . . first

A premier is the first minister of a state.
The première (first showing) will be in Salt Lake City.

14. **SANS** (*sahng**) . . . . lacking, without

Sans foi (fwah) means *without faith* or *faithless.*
To be *sans peur* (purr) is to be *fearless.*

15. **TOUT** (*too* — masc.), **TOUTE** (*toot* — fem.) . . all, everybody, everything

Tout le monde means *all the world* (*monde*).
Tout de suite (pronounced *sweet*) means *at once, immediately.*

Questions

Look up as many of the following as you can, learn to pronounce them, and use them in sentences:

billet-doux, blasé, cliché, clientele, crepe de Chine, en route, ensemble, exposé, faux pas, idée fixe, noblesse oblige, noir, outré, papier-mâché, résumé, rouge, sobriquet, volte-face.

* See note on page 258.

PRACTICE SET

Copy the italicized words or phrases and beside each write its meaning in the sentence:

1. The *"Bon*homme Richard" was the __?__man (*homme*) Richard.
2. The *Elite* Guard was presumably composed of __?__ persons.
3. *"Tout bien* ou rien" means "__?__ __?__ or not at all."
4. *"Entre* nous" is __?__ ourselves.
5. A *petit* jury is a __?__ jury as compared with a grand jury.
6. The British *première* (__?__) was held in Stratford.
7. Madame Beauchamps, *née* (__?__) Susan Turtleby, is now very much *passée* (__?__).
8. No longer a *belle,* she is *hors de combat* as regards amours.
9. He is rather *gauche* in handling the *nouveaux* riches.
10. *"Sans* culottes" (__?__ breeches) was a term used by French aristocrats to describe citizen leaders of the French Revolution, who wore long trousers instead of knee breeches.
11. Madame Beauchamps, though still *petite,* is no longer *une jeune fille.*
12. *"Tout* comprendre, c'est *tout* pardonner" is a French proverb meaning "To understand __?__ is to forgive __?__."

A DATE

Which of the base words of this unit belongs in each blank?

1. At the door he said, "__?__ soir!" [*Soir* (evening) is masc.]
2. "Shall we dance?" he asked. "Très __?__ [very well]," she replied.
3. She was young (__?__), beautiful (__?__), and small (__?__).
4. At forty-three he was really __?__ and rather __?__ because he weighed 211 pounds.
5. She was a cute __?__ d'oeuvre, but he was __?__ de combat.
6. His father had been __?__ of Monaco and her mother belonged among the __?__, for she was an Arbleberry, __?__ Teresa Wentworth. Neither belonged to the __?__ riches.
7. __?__ nous and in __?__ honnêteté (*honesty,* fem.), it was for her an affair __?__ l'amour.

IN ITALIAN

The Latin-born language of Italy has contributed many words to English usage, most of them without changes in spelling. The great majority of these importations belong to a single subject. Can you tell — or discover — what it is?

Presto

Can you find in the list at the right a word to answer each of the following questions?

1. Which one would you hide in?
2. Which is enthusiastic?
3. Which one is always swelling?
4. Which pertains to plucked strings?
5. Which is the most solemn?
6. Which is the fastest?
7. Which one is likely to prove fatal?

● *How many of the words of this unit can you find in the illustration above?*

Musical Modes

1. adagio
2. allegro
3. andante
4. crescendo
5. largo
6. pianissimo
7. pizzicato
8. presto

Music and Drama

1. grotto
2. gusto
3. impresario
4. intermezzo
5. libretto
6. stiletto
7. torso

1. **ADAGIO** (*ah-DAH-jo*) . . . . . slow and graceful

   The adagio movement is very restful.

   She played an adagio (composition in adagio rhythm).

2. **ALLEGRO** (*ah-LAY-gro*) . . . . brisk, lively

   Play the allegro part a little faster.

   Milton's "L'Allegro" is an active or lively man, who likes to go places and do things.

   Allegretto time is a trifle slower than allegro.

3. **ANDANTE** (*ahn-DAHN-tay*) . . . . moderately slow

   The andante section was written first.

   Tschaikowsky's "Andante Cantabile" has a flowing quality that is especially delightful.

4. **CRESCENDO** (*kreh-SHEN-doe*) . . . (with) increasing volume

   The crescendo measures come after the pause.

   The crescendo (increasing volume) of production rose to new heights after the war.

5. **LARGO** (*LAR-go*) . . . . . . very slow and stately

   Do you know the "Largo" from Dvořák's *New World Symphony?*

   Larghetto is faster than largo but not so fast as andante.

6. **PIANISSIMO** (*pee-ah-NISS-ih-mo*) . . very, very softly

   The part representing the lover's reply should be played pianissimo.

   Note: *Pianissimo* is the superlative of *piano,* soft. *Forte (FOR-tay)* means loud and *fortissimo,* very, very loud. The pianoforte got its name from the fact that it has a wide range of loudness.

7. **PIZZICATO** (*pit-seh-KAH-toe*) . . twanged or plucked

   The pizzicato effect portrays their startled looks.

   Staccato is used to describe quick, disconnected barks — by a piano, a dog, or a machine gun.

8. PRESTO . . . . quickly, rapidly

It takes nimble fingers to play well a passage marked presto
— or prestissimo (very, very rapidly).

---

1. GROTTO . . . . a cave or imitation of one

The boys hid in a grotto on the hillside.
The friars lived in a grotto near Naples.

2. GUSTO . . . . great zest or relish

Uncle Joshua eats lobster with great gusto.
The word *gusto* in Italian means *taste*.

3. IMPRESARIO (*im-preh-SAH-ri-o*) . . manager or director of a theatrical enterprise

The impresario weighs a sixth of a ton.

4. INTERMEZZO (*MET-so*) . . short, sparkling piece (between acts of a major work)

The violinist played an intermezzo entr'acte.

5. LIBRETTO (*lih-BRET-toe*) . . text or book(let) (giving the
words of an opera)

We bought a copy of the libretto beforehand.

6. STILETTO . . a kind of dagger (slender and pointed)

The murderer used a stiletto.
Stiletto may be traced to the same Latin word as *stylus* and
style.

7. TORSO . . trunk of human body (minus arms, legs, and
head)

Police found the torso stuffed in a trunk.

Questions

1. How many of these Italian importations do you know?

arpeggio	casa	concerto	scherzo
bambino	casino	oratorio	toccata
barcarole	canto	prima donna	
cantata	cantabile	sonata	

2. Can you name three Italian composers and a work by each?
3. Do *motto, mulatto, maestro,* and *inferno* come from Italian? What does *sotto voce* mean? *viva voce?*

FIRST PRACTICE SET

Copy the italicized words and beside each write its meaning.

1. The *adagio* section is harder than the *andante* part.
2. A *crescendo* of wails went up from the *grotto*.
3. The *impresario* announced this show with *gusto*.
4. According to the *libretto*, the theme is played *pizzicato*.
5. Children like the *presto* and *allegro* sections best.
6. The *largo* movement comes last and begins *pianissimo*.
7. The *torso* showed wounds from a *stiletto*.
8. The *intermezzo* was unusually brief.

SECOND PRACTICE SET

Can you answer each question appropriately?

1. What musical pace would you recommend for:
    A barn dance?   (Two possibilities)
    A wedding procession?   (Two possibilities)
    A stately funeral?
2. How would a love song be played as to loudness?   A song requiring plucked strings?   Music to represent a rising storm?
3. What would each of the following be looking for, most likely?
    The police?   A fleeing bandit?
    An operagoer?   A would-be murderer?
4. How would you describe a circus adventure? with _ _ ? _ _.
5. Who presents the show?   What comes between acts?

SPANISH CONTRIBUTIONS

Like France and Italy, the Iberian peninsula (Spain and Portugal) has its modern stake in our language. It is easier to find words for a unit on Spanish words than it is for German words because the German words which came directly (rather than via Anglo-Saxon) are largely technical and scholarly words which a junior high school student does not need to know.

What is the nature of the Spanish element in English? The words in this unit will give you an answer to that question.

A Cowboy

How many questions can you answer sensibly, each with a single word from the list at the right?

1. Where does he live?
2. What does he ride on?
3. Where could you see him perform?
4. Where are the cows and horses kept?
5. When does he rest?
6. When does he have the most fun?

Base Words

1. adios
2. bolero
3. bravado
4. caballero
5. calaboose
6. corral
7. cuspidor
8. desperado
9. fiesta
10. mesa
11. patio
12. pinto
13. rodeo
14. siesta
15. toreador

SPANISH CONTRIBUTIONS—STUDY GUIDE

1. **ADIOS** (*ah-DYOSE*) . . . . . . **good-by, farewell**
   The Spaniards say *adios,* the French say *adieu(x)* (from the Latin *ad Deum* — "to God" or "God be with you").

   The German word is *auf Wiedersehen* (*ouf VEE-der-zay-en*), *till we meet again,* similar to the French *au revoir* (*o re-VWAR*).

2. **BOLERO** (*bo-LARE-o*) . . **a short, loose jacket, usually open-fronted; a kind of gay Spanish dance**
   She was wearing a red bolero.
   The bolero was very popular at one time.

3. **BRAVADO** (*bra-VAH-do*) . . **boastful or defiant show of courage**
   The boy's defiance was sheer bravado.

4. **CABALLERO** (*kah-bahl-YAY-ro*) . . **Spanish gentleman or cavalier**
   There once was a gay caballero.

5. **CALABOOSE** . . . . **prison, jail**
   The caballero found himself in the calaboose.

   Note: *Calaboose* is still listed as *colloquial* (local) in the dictionaries. Is it really needed in English?
   Hoosegow, another jail word probably of Spanish origin, is listed as slang. How do you explain its popularity?

6. **CORRAL** (*ko-RAL*) . . . **large enclosure for livestock**
   The cowboys drove the herd into the corral.
   It took several hours to corral all of the animals.

7. **CUSPIDOR** . . . . **a spittoon**
   The cuspidor plays an important role in Western scenes.

   Note: The word is really Portuguese and thus still Iberian if not Spanish. It comes from the Latin *conspuere,* meaning *to spit.*

8. **DESPERADO** (*RAY* or *RAH*) . . **a desperate lawbreaker**
   Jesse James was a famous desperado. Can you name others?

9. FIESTA (*fee-ESS-ta*) . . . holiday, saint's day, festival

"For it was fiesta, and we were so gay,
South of the border, down Mexico way."

10. MESA (*MAY-sah*) . . . . . small, elevated tableland

A mesa is usually rock, with steep, clifflike sides.
Mesa Verde in Colorado is the green or verdant mesa.

11. PATIO (*PAH-tih-oh*) . . . . a courtyard

The serenaders gathered in the patio.
Certain types of modern homes have a patio.

12. PINTO . . . . a varicolored horse or pony

The boys were riding their pintos.
A dogie (*DOE-gee*) is a cowboy term for a motherless calf.

13. RODEO (*RO-dee-oh*) . . horse and cattle-roping show

A rodeo is like a medieval tournament with cowboys instead
of knights showing their skills. It represents a roundup,
with "broncobusting," pony roping, and similar contests.

14. SIESTA (*see-ESS-ta*) . . . . . rest period at midday

The rain brought an unexpected siesta.
The siesta custom prevails widely in hot climates.

15. TOREADOR (*TOR-ee-ah-dor*) . . a bullfighter, usually
mounted

"Toreador, make ready!" The toreador was injured fatally.

Other bullfight words: *picadores*, horsemen who prod the bull; *banderilleros*, footmen who distract the bull; the *matador*, who kills the bull.

Questions

1. What conclusions have you reached about the kind of words we have garnered from Spanish?
2. How many of the following Spanish or Spanish-derived words do you know? Can you add to the list?

cabana, esplanada, hacienda, humidor, mañana, palaver, peca-
dillo, pimento, pueblo, señor, señorita, sierra, sombrero, tamale,
tango, stampede.

PRACTICE SET

Copy the italicized words and beside each write its meaning:

1. *"Adios!"* the *desperado* shouted with *bravado* as he went to the *calaboose.*
2. Wearing a *bolero,* she stayed on the *mesa* during the *siesta.*
3. The *pinto* looked like a little *fiesta.*
4. A *patio* is not large enough for a *rodeo.*
5. The *caballero* had no use for a *cuspidor.*
6. The *toreador* rode over to the *corral.*

A MODERN _____?_____

Can you fill each blank sensibly, using each base word once? Fill first the blanks you are sure about. Rearrange the words if necessary.

1. He lives on a __?__.
2. He wears a __?__.
3. He was a __?__ in many bullfights.
4. He enjoys a __?__ after the midday meal.
5. Because of his wealth he fears every __?__ who is not already in the __?__.
6. He does not use a __?__ because his aim is poor.
7. Lounging in his __?__, he tells stories with great __?__.
8. He looks forward each year to the spring __?__.
9. He rides on a __?__.
10. He owns a large __?__.
11. He sponsors a __?__.
12. His last word is always, "__?__!"

What Happened to Him?

Can you finish the story about the gay Spanish gentleman? Make it serious or humorous — but not too long.

NORTHWARD AND EASTWARD

German words in the English language, naturalized and not naturalized, are much more numerous than this book seems to indicate. The great majority, however, came by way of Old English to form hundreds of everyday words like *man, wagon, here.* The rest are largely scientific or technical phrases.

Our Scandinavian word heritage came, like the German, largely by way of Old English — when bands of marauding Danes were making life miserable or at best *uncertain* for Anglo-Saxon settlements along the coasts of what is now England.

Interrogation

Can you answer the following questions from the lists of words at the right and below?

1. Which one is a story?
2. Which are damp or wet?
3. Which one is a teakettle?
4. Which gives approval?
5. Which is young and handsome?
6. Which one is almost insane?

German
1. fräulein
2. panzer
3. stuka

Dutch
1. bruin
2. maelstrom
3. trek

Scandinavian
1. berserk
2. saga
3. swain
4. thwart

Hebrew	*Russian*
1. kosher	1. samovar
2. seraph	2. tundra
3. shibboleth	3. ukase

NORTHWARD AND EASTWARD—
STUDY GUIDE

GERMAN

1. **FRÄULEIN** (*FROI-line*) . . . **unmarried girl, a miss**

   My sister corresponds with a German fräulein. Fräulein Schmidt is her name. Her mother is Frau (Mrs.) Schmidt. A *hausfrau* is a housewife.

2. **PANZER** . . . . **armor, armored**

   German panzer divisions invaded Poland in September, 1939.

3. **STUKA** (*STOO-ka*) . . . . **dive bomber**

   The world was terrified by German *stuka* planes when they first appeared.

   Note: The word *stuka* was originally an abbreviation for a particular type of plane used for dive bombing.

DUTCH

1. **BRUIN** (*BROO-in*) . . . . **a bear**

   The three little bruins lived in the forest.

2. **MAELSTROM** . . . . **whirlpool**

   Have you read Poe's "Descent into the Maelstrom"? Originally the word denoted one particular whirlpool off the coast of Norway.

   Review *vortex* (page 125).

3. **TREK** . . . . . **a journey (originally by oxcart)**

   The long trek over the prairie began in April.
   The trekkers returned from an all-day hike.

   Roster, a roll or list, and *morass* (page 83), are also of Dutch origin.

1. BERSERK . . . . . . frenzied, crazed, violent

College students sometimes go berserk after a big game.
The man went berserk after his wife died.

2. SAGA (*SAH-gah*) . . a heroic (Norse) legend or tale

Many sea sagas were brought to America by the Norse-
men.
The Forsyte Saga is the tale of a modern family.

3. SWAIN . . . . a country youth (in love)

"Who is Sylvia that all our swains commend her?"
Compare *coxswain* and *boatswain* (page 158).

4. THWART . . . . . . to prevent, frustrate, defeat

Is there no way to thwart the villain?

Waive (page 172), *rift* (page 125), *slaughter,* and *bark* are a
few of the other Scandinavian words that have come into
English.

---

1. SAMOVAR . . . . . urn for making tea in Russia

A samovar is tall and stately, like the urns our grand-
parents used to employ.

2. TUNDRA . . . . icy, treeless Arctic plains

Will the polar tundras ever be inhabited?
What kind of person is like a tundra?

3. UKASE (*you-CASE*) . . . . . an official decree

The Tennis Association gave its ukase in the form of a
new rule.

---

1. **KOSHER** *(KO-shur)* . . . sanctioned or clean (according to Jewish law)

The market sells only kosher meat.

It isn't kosher (*correct,* in colloquial use) to eat with dirty hands.

2. **SERAPH** . . . . heavenly being, angel

The cherubim (angelic beings, beautiful children) and the seraphim (plural, higher angelic order) are familiar figures in Hebrew and Christian literature.

He has a cherubic (babylike and beautiful) face, and she has a seraphic (angelic) smile.

3. **SHIBBOLETH** . . . . . . a password, test word

Good manners are a shibboleth in polite society.

Note: A person's life once depended on his ability to pronounce *shibboleth* correctly. Read the story, if possible. It is in the Bible, Judges 12:1–6.

Question

What is the meaning and origin of *alleluia, Boanerges, sapphire, balalaika, Zeitgeist, leitmotiv, monsoon, stipple, veldt, yacht, shekel?*

PRACTICE SET

Copy the italicized words and beside each write its meaning in the sentence:

1. The *fräulein* went *berserk* when she saw the American *panzer* units.
2. Have you read the *saga* of a *swain* who fell in love with a *seraph?*
3. The Jewish scouts took only *kosher* food on their long *trek.*
4. How could a *bruin* have been drowned in a *maelstrom?*
5. There was no way to *thwart* Father's *ukase.*
6. The *samovar* was lost somewhere on the *tundra.*
7. No *shibboleth* could prevent the attack by *stukas.*

WHERE FIND?

In terms of the base words of this unit, where would you be most likely to find:

1. Driftwood? In a __?__.
2. Speed? In a __?__.
3. Dust and noise? In a moving __?__ division.
4. Ice? In a __?__.
5. A bit of heaven? In a __?__.
6. Liquid refreshment? In a __?__.
7. A love affair? Between a __?__ and a __?__.
8. The newest rules or interpretations? In an official __?__.
9. Insanity? A person gone __?__.
10. Meat properly killed? In a __?__ market.
11. A good story? In a __?__.
12. Fur? On a __?__.
13. An ox cart? On a __?__.
14. Safety *after* a battle? In a __?__.
15. What would you do about a practical joke? __?__ it.

A FEW FROM THE ORIENT

Several units could be built from Oriental borrowings, but a sampling will suffice. These include one Eskimo and three Amerindian (American Indian) words. Can you suggest a reason for grouping them with words from Asia?

Asiatic Tour

Can you fill the blanks, using words from the lists at the right and below?

The most important city we visited was __?__. The most important person we saw was a __?__, and the most mysterious was a __?__. We saw a __?__ moving across the desert, and bought souvenirs at a __?__. We crossed Bering Strait in a __?__ and had quite a __?__ with customs officials before we got into Alaska.

Japan and China
1. hara-kiri
2. jujitsu
3. kowtow
4. kumquat

Persia
1. bazaar
2. caravan

India
1. juggernaut
2. nabob
3. swami

Eskimo
1. kayak

Amerindian
1. powwow
2. sachem
3. tepee

Arabia
1. mecca
2. salaam

S I N O · J A P A N E S E

1. HARA–KIRI (*HA-rah-KIH-ri*) . . suicide by slitting the abdomen

Hara-kiri was practiced by proud samurai (nobles) to escape disgrace.

2. JUJITSU (*joo-JIT-soo*) . . Japanese wrestling tricks putting mere weight at a disadvantage

Jujitsu is based on brains, skill, and knowledge.

"Judo" was a wartime term for simple jujitsu tactics which were taught in the armed services.

3. KOWTOW (rhymes with *powwow*) . . to show slavish deference to

A Chinese kowtow consisted of kneeling and touching one's forehead to the ground.

To kowtow is to bow down rather slavishly.

Review *grovel* (page 124). Compare *obsequious, abject* (page 242).

4. KUMQUAT . . . small orangelike (Chinese citrus) fruit or tree

Kumquats are used in preserves and candy.

Sometimes they are called cumquats.

Other Japanese terms: *banzai, kimono, jinrikisha, mikado, tycoon.* Other Chinese: *sampan, nankeen, typhoon.*

P E R S I A N

1. BAZAAR . . . . a market place, a fair

She bought the Persian rug in a bazaar near Damascus.

The ladies are planning a church bazaar.

Note: Do not confuse *bazaar* with *bizarre*, strange, queer.

2. CARAVAN . . . . a company or procession (of travelers)

The caravan moved slowly eastward across the desert.

A caravan of covered wagons crossed the Mississippi.

---

1. JUGGERNAUT . . . . any object of blind, self-destroying devotion

The Juggernaut was a huge car carrying the idol of the Hindu god Krishna in yearly processions. The story is that worshipers once in abject devotion threw themselves under the wheels and were killed.

In what sense was the Nazi machine a juggernaut?

2. NABOB . . . . a native ruler; a wealthy person

The dentist is quite a nabob in local politics.

The word *nabob* is not used in an entirely respectful manner.

3. SWAMI (*SWAH-mi*) . . . a Hindu mystic or seer

The bachelor consulted a swami.

The word originally meant lord or teacher and was a term of respect.

Compare *pundit,* a wise or learned man, and *mahatma.* Both are Hindu, the latter being derived from Sanskrit.

Other Hindu words: *fakir* (*FAY-ker*), *yoga, yogi, maharajah.* The word *bungalow* came from Bengal.

---

1. MECCA . . . . a goal much sought after

Mecca is the holy city of the Moslems; hence its meaning as a "goal" for pilgrims.

2. SALAAM (*sah-LAHM*) . . . . . a very low bow

The salaam is a very ceremonious greeting but less abject than a kowtow.

Note: Do not confuse *salaam* with *salami* (Italian), a kind of sausage meat.

Other Arab-obtained words: *caliph, simoon, amber, saffron.*

A M E R I N D I A N

1. POWWOW . . . . a festive ceremony, talkfest

The Elks held a big powwow last night.
A Scout powwow is in progress.

2. SACHEM (*SAY-chem — ch* as in *chair*) . . Indian big chief

The sachem favored friendship with the British.
What did the sachem say?

3. TEPEE (*TEE-pee*) . . . . Indian tent

Most Indians on the Great Plains lived in tepees.
Compare *wigwam, totem* (emblem).

E S K I M O

1. KAYAK (*KI-ack*) . . a small, light, canoelike boat

The Eskimos covered their kayaks with sealskins.
Many boys own a canvas-covered kayak.

Miscellaneous: From Australia came *boomerang;* from Egypt, *ebony;* from Africa *voodoo* and *hoodoo.*

ACTIVITIES

Read, if time permits, a few chapters in a book on word origins.

PRACTICE SET

Copy the italicized words, and beside each write its meaning in the sentence:

1. A Japanese lord committed *hara-kiri* rather than *kowtow* to the British.
2. A *swami* pretended to call up the spirit of a *sachem*.
3. The Indians held their *powwow* in a *tepee*.
4. A *kayak* is no place for a *salaam*.
5. The *caravan* carried goods to be sold in Persian *bazaars*.
6. Hollywood is the *mecca* of movie worshipers. Is it sometimes their *juggernaut?*
7. The Indian *nabob* chewed *kumquats* while taking lessons in *jujitsu*.

AMERICANS ABROAD

Which of the base words of this unit goes in each blank?

Europe is quite a __?__ for American __?__s. They travel in Cook __?__s, hold frequent __?__s in American hotels, and do many a __?__, so to speak, before famous paintings and statues.

One American I know goes abroad every summer. He likes to munch candy, to buy souvenirs at Parisian __?__s and to consult __?__s about his future, but he refuses to __?__ to native customs. His knowledge of __?__ is quite a protection. On a trip to the Orient he saw a Japanese commit __?__. He thinks Napoleon's army was a good example of a __?__. He likes to eat __?__s.

His boy Franklin has made a hobby of Algonquin lore. He has a __?__ in the back yard and likes to pretend he is a __?__. Last summer he bought a __?__ to take to camp.

AT THE HOSPITAL

All of the words in this unit are Latin-derived except *hemorrhage,* which is Greek. They are mostly within the 20,000 words most commonly used, according to Thorndike.

The Operation

Can you fill the blanks correctly with words from the list at the right?

A nurse made sure that the patient's blood would __?__ properly and that he would not die of a __?__. After the anesthetic, the surgeon made the __?__, removed the man's appendix, and closed the wound with __?__s. The operation had been delayed too long, however, and the man __?__ed.

● *How many of the words of this unit can you find in the illustration above?*

Nouns

1. abrasion
2. contusion
3. hemorrhage
4. incision
5. lesion
6. suture
7. tincture

Verbs

1. amputate
2. cauterize
3. coagulate
4. fumigate
5. lacerate
6. pollute
7. putrefy
8. succumb

1. **ABRASION . . surface or skin injury, a wearing away**

   Floor burns are a form of abrasion.

   Sandpaper is an abrasive which wears away a surface.

2. **CONTUSION . . . . bruise type of injury**

   A contusion does not break the skin but is an injury underneath, as from a blow.

   A concussion is an injured condition (of the brain, for example) caused by a heavy blow.

3. **HEMORRHAGE . . . . . . (extensive) bleeding**

   The accident caused internal hemorrhages.

   Bleeding from a pinprick is not a hemorrhage.

   Other *hemo–* (*blood*) words: *hemophilia, hemorrhoid, hemostatic* (serving to stop the flow of blood). See *styptic*.

4. **INCISION . . cut or gash (especially when made by a surgeon)**

   The surgeon made an incision two inches long.

   Incisive remarks are very penetrating.

   An incisor is a tooth for cutting or biting.

5. **LESION . . . any hurt, injury, or change in an organ from disease**

   The doctor studied the results of brain lesions.

   A hernia (rupture) is a kind of abdominal lesion.

6. **SUTURE . . . . surgical stitches or stitching**

   The sutures were removed after a few days.

   Suturing requires uncanny skill at times.

7. **TINCTURE . . . . alcohol solution**

   What is tincture of iodine? Iodine dissolved in alcohol.

   The more basic meaning of *tincture* is *a slight trace* or (as a verb) to *color* or *tinge something slightly*. For example: The new party seems to be tinctured with Communism.

1. **AMPUTATE . . . . to cut off (as a leg or arm)**
   The surgeon had to amputate the man's leg at the knee.
   The amputation was performed by a Dr. Smeed.
   A surgeon excises (cuts out, removes) a tumor. He severs
     (cuts) a nerve in some cases.

2. **CAUTERIZE . . . . to sear or burn**
   It is sometimes necessary to cauterize a wound.
   The surgeon used cautery to stop bleeding.

3. **COAGULATE . . . . to thicken or harden**
   Blood coagulates when exposed to the air.
   The white of an egg coagulates when it is cooked.

4. **FUMIGATE . . . to destroy germs with a gas or vapor**
   Doctors decided to fumigate the entire house.
   Fumigation is often used to destroy vermin (page 61).

5. **LACERATE . . . . . to tear, mangle, cut severely**
   One hand was severely lacerated in the accident.
   Lacerations are more serious than abrasions.

6. **POLLUTE . . . to render impure or unclean, to defile**
   Sewage pollutes a water supply.
   Good drainage prevented pollution of the well.
   Evil thoughts pollute the mind.

7. **PUTREFY . . . . to rot, decompose, decay**
   Dead fish putrefy rapidly.
   The doctor, examining the injury, found putrefaction.
   The odor of putrid meat pervades the shed.

8. **SUCCUMB . . . . to yield, give up (one's life)**
   She did not succumb to the salesman's technique.
   His uncle finally succumbed to Bright's disease.

Questions

1. Divide *hemorrhage* into syllables and look up its derivation. What other words in this unit have a double letter? Why?
2. Change one letter of *lacerate* and get *to soften into pulp.*
3. List ten of the *–cide–, –cise–, –cision–* words if you can. Make sure they all come from the Latin verb meaning *cut.*
4. Change one letter of *lesion* and get *thousands;* one letter of *contusion* and get *disorder.*
5. Make a list of operations ending in *–ectomy* and *–tomy.*

PRACTICE SET

Copy the italicized words and beside each write its meaning:

1. The nurse will treat *abrasions* but not *contusions.*
2. The *incision* was closed with *sutures.*
3. A *hemorrhage* disclosed the nature of the abdominal *lesion.*
4. The *tincture* dried up and the benzoin *coagulated.*
5. The injured hand will *putrefy* if we do not *amputate* it.
6. The doctor decided to *cauterize* the *lacerated* part.
7. Rats may *pollute* the house if you do not *fumigate,* and you will all *succumb* to the disease.

MEDICAL REPORT

Can you fill each blank correctly? Use each base word only once. Rearrange if necessary to make all fit properly.

The man had been hit by a car. There were __?__s where the bumper struck him. The __?__s on his arms where they scraped the pavement were treated with __?__ of iodine. A __?__d finger had to be __?__d because it was so badly mangled. A deep cut on one leg, which looked like a surgeon's __?__, was __?__d to stop bleeding, disinfected so it would not __?__, and closed with __?__s. There was a slight __?__ which the doctor could not stop, and the man almost __?__ed because his blood would not __?__, but no internal __?__s could be found. A few weeks later when the milk supply became __?__ed the man became ill and died. His house was __?__ to prevent the spread of the disease.

AL—SE

He's a very simple fellow, this Al — and quite a pal. He makes an adjective out of every noun to which he attaches himself, and he seldom plays tricks. With *–ly* he becomes an ally. You have met him before. Subtract him mentally from each of the following words, and what do you get?

> *additional, colonial, conditional, controversial, experimental, global, incidental, jovial, monumental, proportional, topical, typical, supplemental*

Now add him as an ally and what do you have in each case?

Al also makes nouns out of verbs:

> *approval, arrival, burial, denial, refusal, renewal*

Write each verb and then change it to past tense.

The following words have a Latin-born way of changing the last letter of the verb to *se* in forming a noun or adjective. Can you fill all the blanks correctly?

Verb	Noun	Adjective
1. __?__	__?__	defensive
2. offend	__?__	__?__
3. __?__	response	__?__

Add lines for *expanse* and *expend*. *Extend, persuasive, pretense,* and *revert* (no adj.) belong to this group but are slightly irregular. Can you do them too?

MISCELLANEOUS — WILL THESE STOP YOU?

1. Change *deliver, discover, embroider, machine, milliner, perfume,* and *scene* to nouns. What word meaning *wretchedness* has the same ending? What word for a place where paintings are displayed?

2. Write the adjective for each of the four points of the compass.
3. Can you supply a noun correctly spelled for *divide* (sum to be distributed), *edit, launder,* and *remain?* a noun for *academic, capacious, efficient* and *metric?* an adjective for *supremacy* and *sufficiency?*
4. Can you write a noun and verb to go with *dramatic, energetic,* and *complaining?*
5. Write the noun for *confess, discuss, express,* and *profess.* What is the adjective from each?

WHAT ARE THE HARDEST TO SPELL?

The words below are among the hardest there are to spell correctly. Can you handle them all? If not, study them carefully. What words would you add to the list from your Never-Again collection?

accommodate	disappoint	misspell	toboggan
athletic(s)	embarrass	picnicking	tragedy
bouquet	grammar	rhythm	
congratulate	miscellaneous	separate	

Write the *–tion* form of three, a *–ment* form of two others, an adjective form for four or five. Which have *–ly* forms? Opposites?

SENTENCES FOR PRACTICE

Write some or all of the following from dictation:

1. Experimental devices are expensive to make.
2. Is it an offense to discuss controversial topics?
3. As an accommodation, she let the athletes have separate rooms.
4. Picnicking near the old toboggan slide is fun.
5. His misspelled words are a tragedy and his grammar disappointing.

ON BECOMING A NAME

"I am become a name." — Tennyson's *Ulysses*

A surprising number of our words are living memorials to the *name* of a person who did something unusual or acquired a reputation which has lasted for fifty years — or five thousand.

Methuselah and Lazarus have never become common nouns spelled with a small letter, but the words in the list at the right below have been so widely used as *words* that they have almost ceased to be *names*. There is an appealing story back of each one.

A "Screwball"

Can you fill each blank sensibly with one of the words from the list at the right?

1. What did he wear?
2. What does he carry?
3. What is his occupation?
4. How does he walk? He __?__s.
5. What does he deserve?

Nouns

1. czar
2. guillotine
3. havelock
4. hooligan
5. limerick
6. martinet
7. mausoleum
8. nimrod
9. shillelagh
10. solon
11. spoonerism

Verbs

1. boycott
2. lynch
3. meander
4. mercerize

ON BECOMING A NAME—STUDY GUIDE

1. CZAR . . . . king, ruler, dictator
(*From Caesar, via Russia. It was the emperor's title.*)

Who is the czar of the motion picture industry?

2. GUILLOTINE (GILL-o-teen) . . a beheading machine
(*From the "inventor", Dr. J. I. Guillotin, a Frenchman,
1738–1814*)

The guillotine claimed hundreds of victims, including its "inventor", during the French Revolution. It is used in France today.

3. HAVELOCK . . hat covering which protects the neck
(*From the name of an English general, Sir Henry Havelock*)

The WAVES wear their havelocks when it rains.
Sir Henry used his as a protection from the sun.

4. HOOLIGAN . . . . . . a shiftless person or ruffian
(*From a Hooligan family which lived in London*)

Only hooligans would harass a widow that way.
Hooliganism is often a problem for police at Halloween.

A *vandal* (from the Vandals who sacked Rome in A.D. 455) is one who defaces or destroys anything — especially what is sacred or beautiful.

5. LIMERICK . . . . a kind of nonsense poem
(*From a town in Ireland*)

A limerick has five lines, with rhythm and rhyme as in the following:

> "There was a young lady from Niger,
> Who smiled as she rode on a tiger.
>   They came back from the ride
>   With the lady inside,
> And the smile on the face of the tiger."

---

6. **MARTINET . . . a strict drillmaster or disciplinarian**
(*From the name of a French army officer*)

The sergeant is more of a martinet than the major.

7. **MAUSOLEUM (*maw-so-LEE-um*) . . a splendid tomb or sepulchre**
(*From Mausolus. His tomb was one of the Seven Wonders of the World.*)

Les Invalides (where Napoleon is buried) is a kind of mausoleum.

8. **NIMROD . . . . . . a hunter, one fond of hunting**
(*From Nimrod, a mighty hunter and ruler. See Genesis 10:8–10.*)

Hundreds of nimrods will be out the day the season opens.

9. **SHILLELAGH, SHILLALAH (*shil-LAY-lee*) . . a cudgel or club**
(*From a town in Ireland famous for its oaks*)

Men found it wise to carry a shillelagh at night.

10. **SOLON . . . . wise man, legislator**
(*From Solon, a wise Athenian lawgiver, 639?–559 B.C.*)

"Local Solons Kill Tax," the headline read.
Why is *solon* often used in headlines?

11. **SPOONERISM . . a transposing of sounds by mistake**
(*From a famous Oxford don, Rev. William A. Spooner, who was always doing it*)

Example: "The boy rode on a well-boiled icicle."
Usually it is initial sounds that are transposed, especially consonants.

1. BOYCOTT . . . to refuse to patronize, purchase, or use
   (*From a Capt. Boycott in Ireland who was thus treated in 1880*)

   The union urged everyone to boycott the new hotel.
   The boycott was extended to all the hotels in Ridgeville.

2. LYNCH . . . . . to execute a person without a trial
   (*Charles Lynch, 1736–96, was a planter in Virginia who as justice of the peace took into his own hands the punishment of disorderly persons.*)

   A mob gathered to lynch the Negro.
   Lynchings were once fairly common in the South and West.

3. MEANDER . . . . to wander aimlessly or listlessly
   (*From a river in Greece, famous for its windings*)

   The dog meandered across the fields.
   Cows meander across the meadows.

4. MERCERIZE . . . . . to treat cotton with an alkali
   (*From John Mercer, 1791–1866, who invented the process*)

   Mercerizing cotton makes it stronger and glossier.

Questions

1. What is a Jeremiah? a Paul Bunyan? a Johnny Appleseed? a Don Quixote or quixotic person? a Judas? an Odysseus? a Daniel Boone?
2. Bring in a few limericks if you can — or write one, using such a line as: "There was a young genius named Gene [or Jean]."
3. Why not make a collection of "I-am-become-a-name" words and their meanings? It could include the following:

dunce	nicotine (Jean Nicot)	maverick
quisling	shrapnel	macadam
pants	doily	
derrick	braille	

How many of them do you know? The class might take one apiece and look them up.

PRACTICE SET

Copy the italicized words and beside each write its meaning in the sentence:

1. A *hooligan* wanted to *lynch* the *czar* of gangland.
2. The French aristocrats tried to *boycott* the *guillotine.*
3. The *limerick* contained a *spoonerism.*
4. Unskillful *nimrods meander* through the woods.
5. A distinguished *solon* deserves a *mausoleum.*
6. The *martinet* was fond of swinging a *shillelagh.*
7. Is the *havelock* made of *mercerized* cotton?

MIKE

Can you fill each blank correctly, using each base word once? Some rearrangement may be necessary before each word fits.

As a boy the __?__ of the musician's union had been quite a __?__, the terror of his neighborhood. In the army he became a __?__, with the best drilled platoon in the regiment. He was fond of __?__s and other humorous poems, and he liked to swing a __?__ when he went walking. He was something of a __?__ too in hunting season, and he liked to wear __?__d sport shirts.

While in the South, he watched some planters __?__ a Negro. He urged his friends to __?__ recorded concerts. Fond of reading about the French Revolution, he kept a model of a __?__ on the mantel. When in New York, he liked to __?__ through Harlem. Later, as a __?__ in Congress, he proposed a __?__ for John L. Lewis. He was a very good speaker except for occasional slips called __?__s. He introduced the idea of having women pickets wear __?__s when it rains.

FINAL TESTS ON REGULAR UNITS

Copy the italicized words, prefixes, or roots and beside each write its meaning in the sentence:

Unit 2

1. It will *bleach* in the sun or gather *mildew* in the cellar.
2. Can he give a *tithe* without a *twinge?*
3. The *seer* despises *sloth.*
4. The *hassock* lasted only a *fortnight.*
5. He is a *fledgling* at animal *husbandry.*

Unit 3

1. He *yearns* for a chance to *atone.*
2. She is a *blithe* and *winsome* wife.
3. Fun will *allay* your griefs and *winnow* your cares.
4. He is *stalwart* enough to *spurn* a bribe.
5. Money alone will not *bolster* a *listless* campaign.

Unit 5

1. She *expostulates* with him for fighting woman's *suffrage.*
2. Of his own *volition* he will *expedite* the work.
3. The *simile* was about the regularity of one's *stipend.*
4. Only a *vestige* of the *tenure* law remained.
5. Any attempt to *embellish* the tomb will *desecrate* it.

Unit 6

1. The doctors' discussion of *congenital* defects was *abstruse.*
2. *Conjugal* problems often seem *colossal.*
3. *Effulgent* faces watched the *itinerant* minstrel.
4. The *eventual* solution had *momentous* results.
5. Our happiness was *palpable* and *mutual.*

Unit 7

1. The trees formed a *canopy* for the *elegy* he recited.
2. News of the *exodus* interrupted his *homily*.
3. The *phobia* had its *genesis* in a mishap during childhood.
4. The *moron* has a *mania* for fried chicken.
5. The *phenomenon* has to do with *mastication*.

Unit 9

1. A *mille*pede had a race with a *centi*pede.
2. An *octo*pus seized one of the *quin*tuplets.
3. Draw a *penta*gon inside the *nona*gon.
4. The *tri*umvirs ruled most of a *hemi*sphere.
5. The *sex*tet sings on a *bi*-weekly schedule.

Unit 10

1. Her *circum*locutions would drive one to *sui*cide.
2. The title of the story is "*Luci*fer's *Auto*graph."
3. The *magni*tude of *tele*vision plans is enormous.
4. A *neo*phyte teacher discussed *multi*cellular life.
5. He is *ultra*sensitive and seems *omni*scient.

Unit 11

1. Did she *intercede* for you? (two parts)
2. She is intro*spect*ive and rather dis*curs*ive.
3. The man is im*puls*ive and rather ef*fus*ive.
4. There was a *pre*lude (playing) and a *post*lude.
5. The di*gress*ion was *ap*pended to his speech.

Unit 13

1. There was no way to a*vert* inter*vent*ion.
2. His in*flu*ence is inex*plic*able.
3. The e*dict* ex*clud*ed foreigners.
4. Do you per*sist* in de*nounc*ing us?
5. His dis*miss*al made him very de*ject*ed.

Unit 14

1. Ap*pend* a note about *equi*lateral triangles.
2. *Micro*organisms had *mort*al effects.
3. Police ex*tract*ed a confession from the man guilty of ex*tort*ion.
4. The con*sequ*ences were discussed in the con*voca*tion.
5. *Recti*tude in*volve*s courage.

Unit 15

1. *Urb*an life is not always *bene*ficial.
2. Knowledge of pre*nat*al influences is no im*ped*iment.
3. Many a*spir*ants seem de*ment*ed.
4. *Aqua*planing does not require a *pedi*cure.
5. Dis*aster* overtook the Franco*phile*.

Unit 17

1. Her *role* was that of an *enfant* terrible.
2. The *corps* executed a skillful *coup*.
3. In her *boudoir* they discussed the *fete*.
4. His *repertoire* of jokes lasted until *reveille*.
5. *La guerre* interrupted his *amours*.

Unit 18

1. The *elite* of thirty years ago are now *passé*.
2. "*Bon* jour!" was his greeting *sans* peur (fear).
3. "*Bien* entendu!" was the *jeune* fille's greeting.
4. The lady *premier* is *petite*.
5. She has *beaux* yeux (eyes) but *gauche* manners.

Unit 19

1. *Allegro* music is youthful, *adagio* suggests adults.
2. The *crescendo* goes from *pianissimo* to fortissimo.
3. Part of the *intermezzo* is played *pizzicato*.
4. The *torso* was found in a *grotto*.
5. The *libretto* does not mention a *stiletto*.

Unit 20

1. A *toreador* visited the *corral*.
2. She visited the Indians on the *mesa* during *fiesta*.
3. The *caballero* faced the *desperado* bravely.
4. The *bolero* was left in the *patio*.
5. They entered the *rodeo* with great *bravado*.

Unit 21

1. He had a long *trek* across the *tundra*.
2. Have you heard the *saga* of the *samovar*?
3. We tried in vain to *thwart* the *stuka* attack.
4. Without the principal's *ukase* he will go *berserk*.
5. The *fräulein* dreamed about a *maelstrom*.

Unit 22

1. The *nabob* was eating a *kumquat*.
2. The *swami* committed *hara-kiri*.
3. The *powwow* was held in a *tepee*.
4. The *caravan* brought products for the *bazaar*.
5. The *sachem* will not *kowtow* to anyone.

Unit 23

1. His injuries include *abrasions* and *lacerations*.
2. The straw will *putrefy* and *pollute* the water supply.
3. He will *succumb* if he has another *hemorrhage*.
4. Remove the *sutures* when the *incision* heals.
5. A *contusion* is a kind of *lesion*.

Unit 25

1. *Hooligans* sometimes carry *shillelaghs*.
2. Who will build a *mausoleum* for a *martinet*?
3. Do *solons* like *limericks*?
4. The deer decided to *boycott* the *nimrods*.
5. The lumber *czar* is fond of *spoonerisms*.

DIVISION TEST (BASE WORDS ONLY)
REGULAR UNITS

Copy the italicized words, prefixes, or roots and beside each write its meaning in the sentence:

1. The *seer* demanded that I *atone* for the injury.
2. The *simile* about *lodestones* was a good one.
3. Not a *vestige* of the *smock* was left.
4. Her *wiles* seem to *enthrall* him.
5. It was fun to watch their *mutual ecstasy*.
6. The *eventual exodus* began in the spring.
7. Have you a *phobia* for *centi*pedes?
8. Does the *Deca*log *circum*scribe your actions?
9. Her *mono*gram is formed inside a *polygon*.
10. An extro*vert* is not intro*spect*ive.
11. The *confluence* of the two rivers is nearby. (Two parts)
12. A blush *suffused* her cheeks. (Two parts)
13. A *coup* im*pend*s.
14. A re*tent*ive mind is an asset in most *vocat*ions.
15. She plays the *role* of a *psycho*therapist (healer).
16. His uncle is a *chiropodist* (specialist). (Two parts)
17. There is a *grotto* near the top of the *mesa*.
18. As a *toreador*, he is definitely *passé*.
19. He seems *gauche* in the *andante* part.
20. The *swami*'s *bravado* fooled everyone.
21. The *impresario* sat in the *patio*.
22. The *bazaar* does not sell *kosher* meat.
23. The *panzer* division overtook a *caravan*.
24. The *guillotine* produces a severe *hemorrhage*.
25. The *hooligan* watched the white of an egg *coagulate*.

DIVISION TEST—SUPPLEMENTARY WORDS IN REGULAR UNITS

Copy the italicized words and beside each write its meaning in the sentence:

1. It was a *titanic* task to which the nation *consecrated* itself.
2. He *blenched* and his heart began to *palpitate*.
3. The *tycoon's marital* affairs got tangled up.
4. A *bambino* is more helpless than a *dogie*.
5. The *matador* was suffering from a *hernia*.
6. Each of his *progeny* has a touch of *claustrophobia*.
7. Play it *fortissimo* and *staccato*.
8. The *cherub* is *comely* to look at and very mischievous.
9. He made a *sotto voce* comment as they entered the *casino*.
10. If the relationship were *reciprocal*, he would not *sever* it.

DIVISION TEST — WORD-BUILDING UNITS

Can you write for each blank a prefix or word with the meaning indicated?

1. He rode a __?__ (one-wheel affair) wearing a __?__ (single eyeglass).
2. The __?__ (piece with one speaking) is about __?__ (four children born together).
3. The __?__ (man with many millions) is __?__ (excessively critical).
4. He was __?__ (poured together) and __?__ (downcast).
5. Try to avoid a __?__ (happening again) of the trouble.
6. Will you __?__ (keep back) four tickets for me?
7. Do not __?__ (go out of, beyond) the speed limit.
8. Radioactivity is __?__ (can't be destroyed).
9. They made the __?__ (climb down) quite rapidly.
10. The __?__ (wandering from topic) lasted ten minutes.
11. Modern trains are __?__ (driven forward) by electricity.
12. Should fraternities __?__ (shut out) Negroes?
13. The __?__ (inequality) in their ages is considerable.

---

14. He cannot escape the __?__ (things which follow together).
15. He is a __?__ (lover of mankind) and a __?__ (well-doer).
16. The __?__ (water leader or main) was broken.
17. Nothing can __?__ (put foot against) us now.
18. She wants to study __?__ (chemistry of life).
19. Cooking __?__ (takes the life from) some foods.
20. A __?__ is four-sided.

DIVISION TEST—SPELLING

The sentences below contain more than fifty words that are covered in the special units of Part Three. Write some or all from dictation.

1. Unfortunately the legislature proved unmanageable.
2. She is somewhat irritable but otherwise likable.
3. His statistics seem scarcely credible.
4. The lieutenant had an emergency operation for appendicitis.
5. The compromise is positively contemptible.
6. They entered the cafeteria separately.
7. A course in literature is desirable.
8. He left a sandwich in the gymnasium.
9. The orphan smiled with sincere gratitude.
10. The cylinder was lying near the typewriter.
11. The chauffeur was embarrassed by the gossip.
12. The sheriff used ammunition unnecessarily.
13. An engineer must be especially accurate.
14. The plaintiff may collapse if you approach her.
15. One syllable was accidentally omitted.
16. Is she accommodating enough to lend her toboggan?
17. The balloon ascended parallel to the chimney.
18. The committee announced its disapproval.
19. I congratulate you on your sense of rhythm.
20. The denial was gradually forgotten.

LIST OF WORDS

LIST OF WORDS

This list contains only the base words, prefixes, or roots in the regular units. The number following each entry gives the page on which the word may be found.

If all of the supplementary words in the regular units and all of the words presented or covered in the word-building and spelling-emphasis units were included, this section would contain several thousand items, and its bulk would be out of proportion to the rest of the book.

–astr(a)–, 253
atone (*a-TONE*), 206
attest (*a-TEST*), 172
attorney (*at-TURN-ee*), 172
–aud(i)–, –audit–, 247
au gratin (*oh-GRAHT'n*), 134
auto–, 231
avalanche (*AV-ah-lanch*), 82
avenge (*a-VENJ*), 148
avow (*a-VOW*), 56

baffle (*BAF-ful*), 66
bail, 172
ballad (*BAL-lad*), 28
banish (*BAN-ish*), 40
banter (*BAN-ter*), 88
barge (*barj*), 158
barnacle (*BAR-nah-kul*), 158
barracks (*BARE-racks*), 154
baste (rhymes with *paste*), 144
baton (*ba-TAHN*), 46
bazaar (*bah-ZAR*), 279
beau (*bo*), belle (*bel*), 262
beguile (*be-GILE*), 114
–bene–, 252
berserk (*BURR-serk*), 275
bevel (*BEV-el*), 144
bi–, 226
bien (*bee-ENg*), 262
bight (*bite*), 78
bilge (*bilj*), 158
binnacle (*BIN-nah-cul*), 158
–bio–, 254
blaspheme (*blass-FEEM*), 148
bleach, 202
blithe, 206
bludgeon (*BLUDJ-un*), 70

boatswain (*BO-s'n*), 158
boisterous (*BOY-ster-us*), 104
bolero (*bo-LARE-o*), 270
bolster (*BOLE-ster*), 206
bon (*bohng*), bonne (*bun*), 262
boudoir (*BOO-dwar*), 258
boulder (*BOLE-der*), 82
boycott (*BOY-cot*), 292
brackish, 135
bravado (*brah-VAH-do*), 270
breach, 18
brigand (*BRIG-and*), 149
bruin (*BROO-in*), 274
buccaneer (*BUCK-can-eer*), 32
buffoon (buh-FOON), 88
buoy (*BOO-ey*), 78
burlesque (*bur-LESK*), 88
burnish, 40
buxom (*BUCK-sum*), 206

caballero (*kah-bahl-YAY-ro*), 270
calaboose (*CAL-a-boos*), 270
caldron (*CALL-dron*), 138
callous (*CAL-us*), 108
callow (*CAL-lo*), 176
cannibal (*CAN-ni-bal*), 182
canny, 104
canopy (*CAN-oh-pi*), 220
canteen, 154
caper (*KAY-per*), 88
capsize (*cap-SIZE*), 40
caravan (*CARE-ah-van*), 279
casual (*CAZ-you-al*), 108
cataract (*CAT-ah-ract*), 82
cauterize (*CAW-ter-ize*), 285
cavalry (*CAV-al-ri*), 154

cede (*seed*), 12
–cede–, –ceed–, –cess–, 235
cent(i)–, 227
chafe (*chayf*), 12
chalice (*CHAL-iss*), 28
changeling (*CHANGE-ling*), 28
chapeau (*shah-PO*), 130
chasm (*cazm*), 82
chaste (*chayst*), 22
chasten (*CHASE-en*), 66
chenille (*sheh-NEEL*), 131
cherish (*CHAIR-ish*), 40
–chiro–, 252
chivalry (*SHIV-al-ri*), 120
–chron(o)–, 253
circum–, 230
–civi(s)–, 252
clamor (*clammer*), 66
–clude–, –clus–, 242
coagulate (*co-AG-you-late*), 285
colossal (*co-LAHS-sal*), 216
commend, 114
commute (*com-MUTE*), 164
compact (*COM-pact*), 138
comprise (*com-PRIZE*), 164
con–, com–, co–, 230
confront (*con-FRUNT*), 114
congeal (*con-JEEL*), 144
congenital (*con-JEN-i-tal*), 216
congest (*con-JEST*), 56
conjugal (*con-JEW-gal*), 216
conscript (*con-SCRIPT*), 155
consecutive (*con-SEC-you-tiv*), 216

constellation (*con-stel-LAY-shun*), 182
contra–, counter–, 168
contraband (*CON-trah-band*), 158
contrite (*CON-trite*), 108
contusion (*con-TOO-zhun*), 284
convoy (*con-VOY*, as verb), 159
coroner (*CORE-un-er*), 173
corps (*core*), 258
corral (*ko-RAL*), 270
corvette (*core-VET*), 158
coup (*koo*), 258
courier (*KOOR-ie-er*), 138
cove (rhymes with *rove*), 82
covert (*KUV-ert*), 50
cower (*COW-er*), 66
coy, 104
cravat (*krah-VAT*), 130
crescendo (*kreh-SHEN-doe*), 266
crest, 18
cringe (*krinj*), 12
crypt (*kript*), 120
cull (rhymes with *dull*), 8
culprit (*CUL-prit*), 46
cult, 70
–cur(r)–, –curs–, 235
cuspidor (*CUSS-pi-dor*), 270
czar (*zahr*), 290

dais (*DAY-iss*), 165
damask (*DAM-ask*), 131
damsel (*DAM-zel*), 138
dastard (*DAS-tard*), 149

de–, 169
debark, 159
deca–, dec(im)–, 227
declivity (*dee-CLIV-i-ti*), 182
defile (*dee-FILE*), 70
deft (rhymes with *left*), 176
delectable (*dee-LEC-tah-bul*), 135
deliberate (*dee-LIB-er-it*), 108
dell, 82
delta (*DELL-tah*), 182
demented (*dee-MEN-ted*), 108
demi–, 227
demitasse (*DEM-ih-tass*), 134
denouement (*day-NOO-mahng*), 258
deploy (*dee-PLOI*), 155
depredation (*deh-pre-DAY-shun*), 149
deputy (*DEH-pew-ti*), 173
desecrate (*DEH-see-crate*), 212
desperado (*deh-speh-RAY-doe* or *RAH-doe*), 270
despondent (*de-SPON-dent*), 108
–dic(t)(a)–, 242
diligent (*DIL-i-gent*), 104
diminish (*dih-MIN-ish*), 124
dis–, 169
dishevel (*dih-SHEV-el*), 212
distend (*dis-TEND*), 212
distort (*dis-TORT*), 56
diurnal (*die-ER-nal*), 216
divest (*die-VEST*), 114
doff (*o* as in *hot*), 8
doldrums (*DOLL-drums*), 78
dole, 202

–domin–, 247
dormant (*DOR-mant*), 22
dowry, 120
drivel (*DRIV-el*), 89
drone (rhymes with *phone*), 18
–duc(t)–, 236
ductile (*DUCK-til*), 145
dulcet (*DULL-set*), 176
du(o)–, 226
durable (*DEW-rah-bul*), 145
dwindle, 66

éclair (*aye-CLARE*), 134
ecstasy (*EK-stah-si*), 220
edible (*ED-i-bul*), 176
edict (*EE-dict*), 46
edifice (*ED-i-fiss*), 138
edify (*ED-i-fy*), 212
effulgent (*ef-FUHL-jent*), 216
elegy (*EL-e-ji*), 220
elite (*aye-LEET*), 262
embellish (*em-BELL-ish*), 212
ember (*EM-ber*), 70
emerge (*ee-MERJ*), 124
emit (*ee-MIT*), 100
encroach (*en-CROACH*), 148
encumber (*en-CUM-ber*), 124
endorse (*en-DORSS*), 124
enfant (*AHNg-FAHNg*), 258
engender (*en-JEN-der*), 164
ennea–, 227
ensign (*EN-s'n*), 159
enthrall (*en-THRAWL*), 207
entre (*AHNg-thr'*), 262
entreat (*en-TREET*), 56
epi–, 231
–equ(es)–, 252

—equ(i)—, 247
eradicate (*ee-RAD-i-cate*), 164
erode (*ee-RODE*), 144
esquire (*ESS-kwire*), 120
eternal (*ee-TER-nal*), 216
—eu—, 252
evade (*ee-VADE*), 56
eventual (*ee-VEN-tyou-al*), 217
ex—, ec—, 169
exempt (*eg-ZEMPT*), 57
exhort (*eg-ZORT*), 100
exodus (*EX-uh-dus*), 220
exorcise (*EX-or-size*), 114
expedite (*EX-pee-dite*), 212
exploit (*EX-ploit*), 57
expostulate (*ex-POSS-tyou-late*), 212
extinct (*ex-TINCT*), 22
extol (*ex-TAHL*), 100
extradite (*EX-trah-dite*), 172
exude (*ex-ZEWD*), 164

facet (*FAS-set*), 46
facsimile (*fac-SIM-i-lee*), 165
—fact—, —fect—, —fic(t)—, 242
fait (*fet*), 258
fantasy (*FAN-tah-si*), 28
farce (*farss*), 89
fawn, 60
feasible (*FEE-zi-bul*), 176
felon (*FEL-un*), 173
—fer—, —lat(e)—, 236
fervent (*FUR-vent*), 177
festive (*FESS-tiv*), 177
fete (*fayt*), 259
fetid (*FET-id*), 50

fickle, 104
—fid(e)—, 242
fiesta (*fee-ESS-ta*), 271
firmament, 82
flaccid (*FLACK-sid*), 177
flagrant (*FLAY-grant*), 177
—flect—, —flex—, 236
fledgling (*FLEJ-ling*), 202
flippant (*FLIP-pant*), 108
floral (*FLO-ral*), 50
flotsam (*FLOT* rhymes with *plot*), 78
—flu(en)—, —flux—, 242
foal (rhymes with *coal*), 60
foliage (*FO-li-ij*), 83
forbear (*for-BEAR*), 207
fortnight, 202
foster (*o* as in *cloth*), 40
—fract—, 242
fragile (*FRAJ-il*), 50
fräulein (*FROI-line*), 274
friar (rhymes with *liar*), 32
fricassee (*fric-ah-SEE*), 134
frigate (*FRIH-git*), 78
frivolity (*frih-VOL-i-ti*), 89
fumigate (*FEW-mi-gate*), 285
—fus(e)—, 236
fuse, 144

gainsay, 124
galleon (*GAL-lee-un*), 78
gambol (*GAM-bul*), 88
gamut (*GAM-ut*), 165
garble, 67
garish (*gare* pron. like *care*), 177
garner, 40

gauche (*gohsh,* rhymes with *kosh* in *kosher*), 262
gauntlet (*GAUNT-let*), 120
–gen(e)–, 253
genesis (*JEN-e-sis*), 220
ghastly (*GAST-ly*), 22
ghoul (*gool*), 28
gibe (*jibe*), 18
glade, 83
glaze, 144
gloaming (*GLOME-ing*), 83
gnome (*nohm*), 28
grace, 70
–grad–, –gress–, 235
–graph–, –gram–, 253
gratis (*GRAY-tis*), 177
gravity (*GRA-vi-ti*), 165
grotto (*GROT-toe*), 267
grovel (*GRAH-vel*), 124
guerre (*gare,* rhymes with *care*), 259
guillotine (*GILL-o-teen*), 290
guise (*guys*), 18
gullible (*GULL-i-bul*), 104
gunwale (*GUN'l*), 159
gusto (*GUS-toe*), 267
gyrate (*JI-rate*), 144

haberdashery, 130
–hal(e)–, 252
hamper, 67
hara-kiri (*HA-rah-KIH-ri*), 279
hassock, 202
haughty (*HAW-ti*), 104
havelock (*HAVE-lock*), 290
hec(a)–, hec(to)–, 227

hemi–, 227
hemorrhage (*HEM-er-ij*), 284
hept(a)–, 227
hex(a)–, 226
hinterland (*HIN-ter-land*), 182
–hipp(o)–, 252
hoax (rhymes with *coax*), 89
homily (*HOM-i-li*), 220
hooligan, 290
horde, 18
hors (*orr*), 262
hostage (*HOS-tij*), 154
hovel (*HUV'l*), 165
huckster, 32
husbandry (*HUZ-ban-dri*), 202
–hydro–, 252
hyper–, 231
hysterical (*hiss-TARE-i-cal*), 108

ignite (*ig-NITE*), 57
imbibe (*im-BIBE*), 40
imbue (*im-BEW*), 124
immerse (*im-MERSE*), 100
imminent (*IM-mi-nent*), 217
impetus (*IM-peh-tus*), 165
imply (rhymes with *reply*), 124
impresario (*im-preh-SAH-ri-o*), 267
impugn (*im-PEWN*), 148
impulsive (*im-PUHL-sive*), 105
in–, 168
incision (*in-SIZZ-yun*), 284
incite (*in-SITE*), 57
indorse (*in-DORSS*), 124

indulge (*in-DULJ*), 100
infamy (*IN-fah-mi*), 149
infantry (*IN-fan-tri*), 154
infiltrate (*in-FILL-trate*), 155
influx (*IN-flux*), 165
inkling (*INK-ling*), 165
insignia (*in-SIG-ni-a*), 154
insurgent (*in-SUR-gent*), 217
intact (*in-TACT*), 22
inter–, 234
intermezzo (*in-ter-MET-so*),
 267
intern (in-*TERN*), 100
invoke, 100
irate (*eye-RATE*), 109
isthmus (*ISS-mus*), 183
itinerant (*eye-TIN-er-ant*),
 217

–ject–, 242
jest, 88
jettison (*JET-ti-son*), 159
jeune (*zhyun*), 262
jibe, 18
jour (*zhoor*), 259
joust (*just* or *jowst*), 120
juggernaut (*JUG-ger-nawt*),
 280
jujitsu (*joo-JIT-soo*), 279
julienne (*joo-lih-ENN*), 134
–jur(e)–, –juri(s)–, 247

kayak (*KI-ack*), 281
keel, 78
kilo–, 227
knoll (rhymes with *toll*), 83
kosher (*KO-shur*), 276

kowtow (rhymes with *pow-
 wow*), 279
kumquat (*KUM-quat*, rhymes
 with *squat*), 279

lacerate (*LAA-sir-ate*), 285
lapse, 18
larboard (*LAR-bord*), 79
larceny (*LAR-seh-ni*), 149
largo (*LAR-go*), 266
–lat(e)–, 236
lavish (rhymes with *ravish*),
 50
lee, 79
legacy (*LEH-gah-si*), 173
lesion (*LEE-zhyun*), 284
libretto (*lih-BRET-toe*), 267
limerick (*LIH-meh-rick*), 290
lineage (*LIN-ee-ij*), 121
lingerie (*LAHN-zhuh-ree*),
 130
listless, 206
lithe (rhymes with *writhe* and
 scythe), 22
loathe (*th* as in *though*), 12
lodestone (*LODE-stone*), 202
luster, 46
lux–, luc(i)–, 230
lynch (rhymes with *pinch*),
 292
lyonnaise (*lie-uh-NAZE*), 134
lyric (*LIH-rick*), 220

maelstrom (*MAIL-strum*), 274
magi (*MAY-jie*), 32
magn(i)–, 230
malinger (*mah-LING-er*), 148

omni–, 231
–onym–, 253
option (*OP-shun*), 47
orifice (*OR-ih-fis*), 115
–ortho–, 248
ostracism (*OS-tra-sizm*), 221
oust (*owst*), 8
ovation (*oh-VAY-shun*), 115
oxford(s) (*OX-ferds*), 130

pagan (*PAY-gan*), 47
pall (*pawl*), 203
palpable (*PAL-pah-bul*), 217
pan(to)–, 231
panzer (*PAN-zer*), 274
parable (*PARE-ah-bul*), 28
parchment (*PARCH-ment*),
  121
–par(i)–, 247
parody (*PARE-uh-di*), 89
parole (*pah-ROLL*), 173
passé (*pa-SAY*), 263
passive (*PASS-sive*), 109
patio (*PAH-tih-oh*), 271
paucity (*PAW-sih-ti*), 115
pauper (*PAW-per*), 32
–ped–, 253
peevish (*PEE-vish*), 109
–pel–, –puls–, 236
–pend–, –pense–, 248
pent(a)–, 226
peri–, 230
pervert (as verb, *per-VERT*),
  138
petit (*peh-TEE* or *PEH-ti*),
  petite (*peh-TEET*), 263
phantom (*FAN-tum*), 29

phenomenon (*fee-NOM-e-
  non*), 221
–phil–, 252
phobia (*FOE-bih-uh*), 221
photo–, 230
pianissimo (*pee-ah-NISS-ih-
  mo*), 266
pièce (*pee-ESS* or *p'yes*), 259
pilfer (*PIL-fer*), 148
pilgrim (*PIL-grim*), 32
pinion (*PIN-yun*), 115
pinto (*PIN-toe*), 271
pixie, 29
pizzicato (*pit-seh-KAH-toe*),
  266
platoon (*pla-TOON*), 154
pliable (*PLY-a-bul*), 105
–pli(c)–, –plex–, 243
plumage (*PLOOM-ij*), 60
–pod–, –p(o)us–, 253
–poli(s)–, –polit–, 252
pollute (*poh-LOOT*), 285
poly–, 230
porous (*POR-us*), 145
portal (*POR-tal*), 115
–port(at)–, 236
portray (*por-TRAY*), 101
posse (*POSS-ee*), 173
post–, 234
potable (*PO-tah-bul*), 135
–p(o)us–, –pod–, 253
powwow, 281
pre–, 234
premier (*PREE-mi-er*), première (*preh-MYAIR*), 263
presto (*PRESS-toe*), 267
prim–, 231

prior (*PRY-or*), 50
pro–, 234
profile (*PRO-file*), 47
promontory (*PROM-un-toe-ri*), 183
prone (rhymes with *stone*), 23
prosecute (*PRAH-see-cute*), 172
proto–, 231
prowess (*PROW-ess*), 70
prudent (*PROO-dent*), 105
–psych(o)–, 253
putrefy (*PEWT-reh-fie*), 285

quad(ri)–, 226
quagmire (*quag* rhymes with *rag*), 70
qualm (*cwahm*), 115
quell, 8
quin(que)–, 226

rabble, 115
rampant (*RAM-pant*), 51
rampart (*RAM-part*), 70
rancid (*RAN-sid*), 135
ransom (*RAN-sum*), 101
ratify (*RAT-i-fie*), 139
ravage (rhymes with *savage*), 148
raze (rhymes with *gaze*), 8
re–, 235
rebate (*REE-bate*), 125
recoil (*ree-COIL*), 101
–rect–, 248
refute (*ree-FEWT*), 172
regent (*REE-jent*), 29

reinstate (*ree-in-STATE*), **139**
relish (*REL-ish*), 41
repast (*ree-PAST*), 135
repertoire (*reh-per-TWAR*), 259
rescind (*ree-SIND*), 101
residue (*REH-zi-dew*), 125
resilient (*ree-ZIL-i-ent*), 145
resolute (*REZ-oh-loot*), 109
reveille (*REV-eh-lee*), 259
revere (*ree-VEER*), 57
ricochet (*rik-o-SHAY*), 155
rift, 125
rigor (*RIH-ger*), 47
rivulet (*RIV-you-let*), 183
rodent (*ROH-dent*), 60
rodeo (*RO-dee-oh*), 271
role (*roll*), 259
rudiment (*ROO-dih-ment*), 213
rustic (*RUS-tick*), 51
ruthless (*ROOTH-less*), 105

sachem (*SAY-chem*), 281
saga (*SAH-gah*), 275
salaam (*sah-LAHM*), 280
saline (*SAY-line*), 135
sallow (rhymes with *tallow*), 23
samovar (*SAM-oh-var*), 275
sans (*sahng*), 263
satin, 131
saunter (*SAWN-ter*), 41
sauté (*so-TAY*), 135
scathe (rhymes with *bathe*), 12
scimitar (*SIM-ih-tar*), 121
scion (*SIGH-un*), 71

–scribe–, –script–, 253
scuttle, 159
se–, 169
secrete (*see-CREET*), 12
seep, 8
seer, 203
seethe (rhymes with *teethe*), 12
segregate (*SEG-reh-gate*), 101
semi–, 227
sept–, 227
–sequ–, –secut–, 248
seraph (*SAIR-af*), 276
serge (rhymes with *verge*), 131
–serv–, 243
sex–, 226
shackle, 41
sheaf (rhymes with *leaf*), 19
sheathe (rhymes with *breathe*), 13
shibboleth (*SHIB-bo-leth*), 276
shillelagh (*shil-LAY-lee*), 291
siesta (*see-ESS-tah*), 271
simian (*SIM-i-an*), 60
simile (*SIM-i-le*), 213
sinew (*SIH-new*), 71
singe (rhymes with *cringe*), 13
–sist–, 243
sloth (*slowth*), 203
smock (rhymes with *rock*), 203
smolder (rhymes with *bolder*), 67
sojourn (*SO-jurn*), 67
solon (*SOLE-un*), 291
–solv–, –solut–, 243
somber (*SAHM-ber*), 51
sorcerer (*SOR-ser-er*), 29
sparse (rhymes with *farce*), 23

–spec(t)–, –spic–, 237
speculate (*SPEC-you-late*), 139
–spir(e)–, 252
spoonerism (*SPOON-er-izm*), 291
spouse (rhymes with *louse*), 125
spume (rhymes with *fume*), 79
spurn (rhymes with *burn*), 207
stalk (rhymes with *chalk*), 67
stalwart (*STALL-wart*), 206
stamina (*STAM-ih-nah*), 125
stealthy (rhymes with *healthy*), 109
steed, 121
–stell(a)–, 253
stiletto (*stil-LET-toe*), 267
stipend (*STY-pend*), 213
stolid (rhymes with *solid*), 105
stowaway, 33
–string–, –strict–, 248
stripling, 33
stud (rhymes with *cud*), 19
stuka (*STOO-ka*), 274
sub–, 235
succumb (*suc-CUM*), 285
suede (*swayd*), 131
suffrage (*SUF-frij*), 213
sui–, 231
summit (*SUM-mit*), 183
sunder, 207
super–, 231
supplant (*sup-PLANT*), 139
sur–, 231
surly (rhymes with *burly*), 109
suture (*SOO-ture*), 284

swain (rhymes with *twain*), 275

swami (*SWAH-mi*), 280

swathe (*swayth, th* as in *thine*), 67

swerve (rhymes with *nerve*), 9

swine, 61

sym–, syn–, 230

synopsis (*sin-OP-sis*), 221

–tain–, –tent–, 248

talon (rhymes with *gallon*), 61

tarnish (rhymes with *varnish*), 145

tarpaulin (*tar-PAW-lin*), 79

tele–, 231

temerity (*teh-MARE-i-ti*), 213

–temp(o)–, 253

tenure (*TEN-your*), 213

tepee (*TEE-pee*), 281

tepid (*TEH-pid*), 51

termite (*TER-mite*), 61

terse (rhymes with *verse*), 23

tête (*tet*), 259

tetra–, 226

textile (*TEX-till*), 131

thwart (rhymes with *wart*), 275

timorous (*TIM-or-us*), 105

tincture (*TINK-ture*), 284

tinge (rhymes with *hinge*), 13

tithe (rhymes with *writhe, scythe*), 203

toreador (*TOR-ee-ah-dor*), 271

torso (*TOR-so*), 267

–tort–, 249

tout (*too*), toute (*toot*), 263

trance (rhymes with *prance*), 125

trans–, 235

transmute (*trans-MEWT*), 139

transpire (*tran-SPIRE*), 139

trek, 274

tri–, 226

tributary (*TRIB-you-teh-ri*), 183

trousseau (*true-SO*), 131

truce, 155

truss, 19

tundra (*TUN-drah*), 275

turbid (*TUR-bid*), 51

turpitude (*TURP-ih-tude*), 149

turret, 71

twinge (rhymes with *singe*), 203

ukase (*you-CASE*), 275

ultra–, 231

un–, 168

uncouth (*un-COOTH*), 206

undulate (*UN-dew-late*), 139

uni–, 226

–urb(s)–, 252

urchin (*ER-chin*), 33

vagabond (*VAG-ah-bond*), 33

valise (*vah-LEES*), 131

vassal (*VAS-sal*), 121

–ven(i)–, –vent–, 244

verify (*VARE-ih-fie*), 101

vermin (*VER-min*), 61

–vert–, –vers–, 244

vestige (*VEST-ij*), 213

–vide–, –vis–, 237

vie (rhymes with *die*), 9
vigil (*VIJ-il*), 71
viper, 61
viscous (*VIS-cus*), 145
visor (*VIE-zer*), 121
vista (*VIS-tah*), 183
–vita–, 254
–voc(at)–, 249
void, 23
volition (*vo-LISH-un*), 213
--volve–, –volu(t)–, 249
vortex (*VOR-tex*), 125

waft (*wahft*), 9
waif (*wayf*), 33
waive (*wave*), 172

wane (rhymes with *cane*), 13
warrant (*WAHR-rant*), 41
wayward, 105
weasel (*WEE-zel*), 61
wield (rhymes with *shield*), 101
wiles (rhymes with *miles*), 203
wince (rhymes with *since*), 9
winnow (*WIN-no*), 207
winsome (*WIN-sum*), 206
wisp, 19
wistful, 109
writhe (rhymes with *tithe*), 13

yearn (*yern*), 207
yeoman (*YO-man*), 29